MILITARY WARS AND RESCUE TECHNIQUES

MILITARY WARS AND RESCUE TECHNIQUES

A.K. Dixit

CYBER TECH PUBLICATIONS
4264/3, Ansari Road, Daryaganj, New Delhi-110002 (India)
Ph.: 011-23244078, 011-43559448 Fax: 011-23280028
E-Mail: cyberpublicationsdelhi@yahoo.com
Website: www.cybertechpublications.com

MILITARY WARS AND RESCUE TECHNIQUES

A.K. Dixit

First Edition 2010

Published by :

G.S. Rawat for **Cyber Tech Publications**
4264/3, Ansari Road, Daryaganj, New Delhi-110002 (India)
Ph.: 011-23244078, 011-43559448 Fax: 011-23280028
E-Mail: cyberpublicationsdelhi@yahoo.com
Website: www.cybertechpublications.com

Printed at: Asian Offset Printers, Delhi-53

Preface

Military wars without a reasonable prospect of success is unjustifiable, especially when it is done in the name of humanity. Couched in the debate on the responsibility to protect civilians from violence and drawing on traditional 'just war' principles, the central premise of the present book is that humanitarian military intervention can be justified as a policy option only if decision makers can be reasonably sure that intervention will do more good than harm.

This book argues that the central factors determining whether a humanitarian war succeeds are the objectives of the intervention and the military strategy employed by the intervening states. Four types of humanitarian military intervention are offered: helping to deliver emergency aid, protecting aid operations, saving the victims of violence and defeating the perpetrators of violence. The focus on strategy within these four types allows an exploration of the political and military dimensions of humanitarian intervention and highlights the advantages and disadvantages of each of the four types.

Humanitarian military intervention is controversial. Scepticism is always in order about the need to use military force because the consequences can be so dire. Yet it has become equally controversial not to intervene when a government subjects its citizens to massive violation of their basic human rights.

—Author

CONTENTS

1

Introduction

The Cold War dominated the world in the decades following World War II. On one side was the "West", dominated by the capitalist United States of America and acting mainly through the North Atlantic Treaty Organization (NATO), while on the other side was the "East", dominated by the communist United Soviet Socialists Republic (Soviet Union or USSR). The two sides were opposed ideologically, both in government styles and financial systems, and geographically. Nearly all events that occurred in the world during this time, such as the Vietnam War and the war in Afghanistan, became an exercise of will between the two super powers, the US and the USSR. The threat of a total nuclear war that will end life on Earth hung over the world during this era, even though neither side wanted to use their large nuclear arsenals.

The Soviet Union, after losing nearly 20 million people during World War II, was determined that it would never again be invaded and built the world's largest military at the time. While it did rely on numbers over technology, they still built some of the most advanced war machines in the world, and many were as good, if not better, than those of the more technologically advanced western countries. Realizing that they could never realistically match the Soviet Union in military size for any great period of time, NATO decided to use nuclear weapons as a deterrent for war. Most NATO countries built and maintained a large stockpile of nuclear arms, which were significantly cheaper to maintain then a large standing army. This caused the Soviet Union to respond by building its own large stockpile of nuclear weapons, but their numbers of lower than NATO's.

During the 1980's, the Soviet Union suffered a demoralizing setback when their military failed to defeat rebel factions in Afghanistan and increased military spending was tearing the country's economy to shreds. NATO and the United States did not realize the extent of collapse in the Soviet Union until in 1989 they allowed the reunification of Germany, which had been split into two countries following World War II, one side controlled by NATO, the other by the Soviet Union. Soon after, the entire Soviet Union collapsed leaving many former republics independent for the first time ever and a much weaker Russian Republic.

The now democratic Russia was suffering from economic collapse and many western countries were too used to viewing the Russians as enemies to offer any help. This forced the Russians, and many of the independent Republics to sell many of their weapons to third world countries, such as China, the Middle East, and many countries in Africa. Some of the weapons sold were even rumored to be nuclear warheads, which would garner a huge price on the black market.

In contrast, this was an impressive time for the western countries: they had easily won a war in the Middle East against Iraq and advances in space technology allowed the concept of a space station become a reality. Since Russia had one of the world's largest space agencies and the world's only existing space station, they were reluctantly included in the US dominated international space agency. As computers became widespread, information became more accessible to those that opposed the world's current notion of peace. With the Cold War over, and with many countries looking forward to a time of real pace, many powerful countries forgot that most of the world had been dominated by only a few countries and that with the collapse of colonialism, imperialism, and the end of the Cold War many of these countries were truly free for the first time ever. These countries, particularly China, India, Iran, and several countries in Africa, did not appreciate that the world had decided that there would be no more wars, no more taking from other countries what you wanted, which is exactly what the current Super Powers had done to achieve their power.

Tensions would rise continuously throughout the early half of the 1990's, as many countries fought the "world powers" both in the United Nations General Assembly, and in world markets to achieve what they believed was their fair share. Support ebbed and waned for international cooperation throughout the world and many countries felt cheated by the United States, as the US would treat them as partners with one hand and as enemies with the other.

New alliances were formed throughout the world, such as a growing bond between Islamic countries in the Middle East, between former enemies in Africa, and between China and India, but the United States viewed these alliances as strategic threats that it could not counter with traditional methods. A new world order was being built around the United States claiming the world had moved past imperialism and other countries finally moving into positions where they could execute their own imperialist goals. The International Space Station, named Freedom Station, was the focal point for the anger that had grown among the countries of the world.

Freedom Station: Excuse or Justification?

Freedom Station had cost over 100 billion American dollars to construct and had taken over three years to finish. When it was completed on February 16, 1996, the members of the International Space Agency cheered and looked forward to using the station for research into survival in space and industrial applications of space. Almost overnight, NASA had risen in importance in the American public's eyes and its popularity skyrocketed, but this was nearly overshadowed by criticisms from several countries that complained that they would not be given a fair portion of the station's facilities. China led the criticisms against the International Space Agency, when it had announced that Freedom Station's crew would be made up of Americans and Russians. While some countries, mainly other NATO members, would be given access to the station's laboratories through remote control, countries such as China, which had contributed several billion dollars to the project, would be refused access to the station during the first few years of the project. China also claimed that the United States had stated that the Chinese would be considered invaders if they tried to dock with the station without permission. China, India, and several other countries withdrew from the International Space Agency.

Tensions rose between the countries of the world, but nothing could stop the momentum that the Freedom Station incident had caused, all the world needed was an excuse to start a war. The excuse soon presented itself through a simple accident. The Russian complement of Freedom Station had already arrived at the station and was waiting for the American complement, when a routine diagnostic caused a mysteriously explosion that destroyed the Chinese module of the station. The Chinese were furious; they had spent billions of dollars and years of research to build the laboratory module, and claimed that the Russians had destroyed it on purpose as a warning to the Chinese. Allegations of sabotage were thrown around in the United Nations Security Council and on May 1, 1996, the Chinese declared war on the Russian Republic.

Opening Stages of World War III

China quickly consolidated its forces and declared the existence of the Sino-South East Asian Alliance. Members of the alliance included North Korea, Vietnam, Indonesia, and nearly all other countries in South East Asia, with the exception of Taiwan, Japan, and South Korea. The Chinese-led alliance quickly launched its armies against Taiwan and South Korea and before the end of the second month both countries were firmly under the control of the Chinese. The United States of America, living up to its position of defense for both South Korea and Taiwan, declared war on what became known as the Sino Alliance. With the United States distracted in the Far East, several Arab countries in the Middle East declare war on Israel and several neighboring former Russian Republics. As part of their war effort, these countries cut the world off from all oil produced they produced and force the surrender of all European, American, or Canadian forces within their borders. This sent oil prices skyrocketing and world economy began to collapse, but many western countries instituted special war bonds to keep their economies running for the war efforts.

To assist Israel, NATO organized an expeditionary force and sent it to the Middle East through the Persian Gulf, but the fleet was intercepted by a carrier group from India. Not wishing to start a war with India at this stage, NATO withdrew its expeditionary force from the Indian Ocean. The United States pulls most of its forces into the Pacific Ocean to wage its war against the Sino Alliance, but it has little chance of defeating the huge Chinese army.

Africa descends into chaos as several countries, bolstered by military arms sold by the former Soviet Union, declare war on their neighbors. Old tribal feuds, hidden for decades, resurface as leaders feel that the present is a perfect time for revenge.

As the interests of the United States pull it away from the interests of the European countries, NATO becomes sidetracked and the European countries give their full support into the European Union. As part of this new support, a common currency is brought into effect, as is the European Union Reaction Force.

China launches its invasion of Siberia and quickly captures Vladivostok. The degradation of the Russian military is exposed, as more troops run away from the Chinese army then try to fight it. China contains Japan by blockading the island by sea and constantly attacking the island with its massive air force. The United States is forced to operate further and further away from China, as the island bases it maintained since World War II are systematically destroyed by long range cruise missile attacks from China. Fortunately, the United States is using its own cruise missiles to directly attack China's industrial centers.

The War Grows

In September 1996, India joined the Sino Alliance and brought its army to bear against the nuclear-armed Pakistan. For unknown reasons, the government of Pakistan surrenders to the invading Indians without much of a fight. India proceeded to invade Bangladesh and Sri Lanka before moving its army into Kazakhstan. The Indian navy completely takes control of the Indian Ocean, forcing the remaining NATO ships to fall back into the Pacific and Atlantic Oceans. The European Union forms an alliance with the Russian Republic and deploys a large portion of the EU Reaction Force into Siberia to slow the advancing Chinese army. In an effort to increase the effectiveness of their troops, the United States, in conjunction with the Japanese and the Canadian, develop several prototype power armor suits, although many of these crude designs are eventually copied by the Sino Alliance.

After successfully completing their invasion of Israel, the Arab countries of Egypt, Saudi Arabia, Kuwait, Iran, Jordan, Syria, and Lebanon form the United Arab Empire. The United Arab Empire proceeds to invade the rest of the Arabian Peninsula and Iraq, which requires only two months to finish. Afterwards, the United Arab Empire turns its attention against Europe and begins its invasion through Turkey and into the Balkans. The European Union recalls much of its force back from Russia to stop the invasion from the Middle East.

The Tides of War Begin to Change

Advances in technology continue to shift the war in favor of the United States and the European Union. The European Union Reaction Force easily overpowers the invasion from the Middle East and successfully forces the United Arab Empire to pull back its troops. The EU is once again able to send its forces, now equipped with power armor designed in the United States and Canada, into Russia to slow the advancing Chinese army.

Through superior technology and tactics, the Americans are able to gain total supremacy in the Indian and Pacific Ocean, allowing them to increase their raids against the industrial centers of India, China, and the United Arab Empire. While the Chinese army is slowing in central Siberia and the Indian army is heavily engaged in Kazakhstan, the Americans are continuing to systematically destroy the industrial capabilities of both countries, and it is beginning to have a serious impact on their abilities to continue the war.

With the decreasing support from their industries back in China, the Chinese army is forced to stop its advance and begin to fall back as supplies begin running out along the Siberian front. While not quite the same feet as the storming of the beach at Normandy, the Americans and Canadians succeed in landing an army in northern Russia, which places the army behind the main Chinese army. The American and Canadian army is able to liberate Vladivostok and begin an invasion of northern China, where it finally meets resistance from hastily assembled Chinese reserves.

In February 1998, an experimental nuclear fusion reactor is successfully tested in Princeton University in the United States of America. This new reactor will allow for more powerful military equipment to be built, from tanks and airplanes to ocean ships and power armor. Seeing increasing opportunities for cooperation, the European Union, the Unites States, and Canada begin to coordinate their military actions through NATO.

The second-generation power armor troops from NATO land in Sri Lanka and capture it from the occupying Indian forces. This, coupled with disastrous defeats in Kazakhstan, forced the Indian government to reevaluate its position in the Sino Alliance and it begins to seek a way to end its involvement in the war. The main Chinese army fell back far enough that it had to engage the advancing Russian / European Union army and the American / Canadian army simultaneously.

The Visitor Arrives

It appears that at the current rate, the Sino Alliance would have been forced out of Siberia, but whether the advancing armies would have been able to successfully invade China itself is highly questionable. Even without the actual invasion of China, many soldiers had been killed in the three-year conflict, but nowhere near as bad as the wars that continued to tear Africa apart. What changed the course of the war and the destiny of humankind was a strange visitor from the stars. It passed through the atmosphere above the east coast of the United States and proceeded on a low orbit trajectory towards its final resting place on Macross Island. In its wake, every area that it passed over was devastated; the visitor accomplished in a single night what the Sino Alliance could not accomplish after three years of missile attacks. Hundreds of thousands of people died in the United States as the result of atmospheric disturbances, floods, and earthquakes that followed the visitor during its journey across the sky. The visitor leveled entire cities and the chaos that followed led to the deaths of thousands more.

An immediate ceasefire was called and World War III suddenly ended as the United Nations Security Council learned of a worse danger, a danger from the stars. But in the seeds of the armistice that ended World War III, laid the seeds for many new conflicts that would haunt the world struggling to rebuild and prepare for an invasion from above. As part of the armistice the Sino Alliance withdrew from Russia and Mongolia, but China still retained direct control over Taiwan, Hong Kong, and Macau. Also, India withdrew from the Sino Alliance and all of territory that it had conquered, which included Pakistan, Bangladesh, and most of central Asia. Many of countries in central Asia, already devastated by war, turned to the United Arab Empire to provide them with protection. The only change in the United Arab Empire, besides gaining new territory in central Asia, is the liberation of Israel and the formation of Palestine from the Gaza Strip, the West Bank, and East Jerusalem.

The United Earth Government

After the end of the Cold War, great efforts were made to integrate the world together in a process known as globalization. The end result would be that all parts of the world would be integrated economically so that no one would want for anything.

Unfortunately, after only a few years of globalization it became apparent that this would not occur at least for many years. Many companies shut down factories in prosperous counties and relocated them to poor countries where worker wages were lower and less money had to be spent on environmental protection or safety regulations.

This process was mostly put on hold during the Third World War, but it still continued in certain areas. For example, North American companies, cut off from the Asian market, turned to South America, Central America, and Mexico to establish low cost facilities, and over the course of the war, the general technological level in those areas rose dramatically. This culminated with the completion of one of the most advanced semiconductor factory in Costa Rica.

After the armistice that ended the World War III was signed and the true nature of the Visitor was revealed to the permanent members of the United Nations Security Council, serious talks began about creating a permanent defense force that would be controlled by the United Nations. This plan met with immediate problems, as countries that faced each other in war only months earlier attempted to decide how such a defense force would be controlled. After a long period of negotiations between the Sino Alliance, the European Union, the United States, Canada, and a coalition representing the countries of South America, a new international body called the United Earth Government (UEG) was established. This body would be responsible for controlling the new United Earth Defense Force, which would be used to protect the Earth from the alien invaders. The first Prime Minister of the UEG was a former democratic senator from the United States named Harlan J. Niven.

One of the major differences between the United Nations and the United Earth Government was its organization. The United Nations was organized as a collection of governments that were working together to create international committees, whereas the UEG was organized as a government, with a two tiered legislative body and headed by a Prime Minister. The first level of the body was called the Assembly and consisted of 3141 seats that would be distributed based on population to every country in the world with a population over one million and the second level was called the Senate and each country with a population of over a million was given two seats and each country with a population less then one million was given only one seat.

This two-tiered system created some balance, because together, the Sino Alliance and India held a third of the seats in the Assembly, but only four seats in the Senate. The only restriction on who could serve in the Assembly and the Senate is that they must have authority to make independent action. This restriction greatly sped up decisions within the United Earth Government. The Prime Minister was chosen from the Senate, but had to be approved by the Assembly. How the members of the Assembly and Senate were chosen was up to each individual country, but the disposition of seats in the Assembly was calculated every five years, corresponding with the global census held in the years 2000, 2005, and 2010 CE and a new Prime Minister was to be chosen at that time. The Prime Minister was chosen by first establishing a list of candidates, each of which must have been nominated by at least four other countries, and then having an election to choose the top two candidates, and then finally a second election was held to determine which of the two would become the new Prime Minister. Prime Ministers were only allowed to serve a single term, although former Prime Ministers couid remain in the Senate for as long as their country of origin chose to allow it.

During this time, the United Earth Defense Force was beginning construction on the Apollo Moon Base in 2000 and Mars Base Sara in 2001, and the decision had been made to use the Visitor, now called the Alien Space Ship-1 (ASS-1), as the flagship for a space fleet to protect the Earth and restoration efforts were beginning and a military base and a community for workers had been built on Macross Island, where the ship had crashed. Also, the United Earth Defense Force had acquired plans to build space ships capable of combat from the United States. These plans would eventually evolve into the Oberth Class Space Destroyer. Among the other technological discoveries related to the ASS-1 were the ground-combat anti-giant weaponry, or "Destroid System," and the all-purpose variable combat system, which would eventually become the Veritech Fighters. Major construction efforts by the United Earth Defense Force include their headquarters in a remote part of Alaska, and the Grand Cannons, which were located in Alaska, Australia, Brazil, the Central African Republic, and Luna (the moon) and began construction in 2002, 2004, 2004, 2005, and 2006 respectively.

The Formation of the Anti-Unification Movement

Within a span of a year, the UEG had established its presence on the world and built its headquarters in Sweden. The United Earth Defense Force was quickly becoming a force to be reckoned with and was spreading across the globe to ensure that every place was protected from alien invaders. But everything was not as perfect as it appeared to be. Across the globe those that had battled against globalization, fought against losing their independence as a country, and fought against becoming friends with those they considered to be their enemies, found that they all faced the same entity, the United Earth Government.

As these groups began joining together and staging protests, rallies, and demonstrations, a movement known as the Anti-Unification Movement was established. This movement was never a single group, but many groups sometimes working independently, sometimes working separately, and sometimes even working against each other. The movement located places in the world where they could gather and use as staging areas, these areas were in Africa and in the Middle East.

The United Arab Empire refused to participate in the United Earth Government in any way and sent its military might against Islamic countries of Northern and Central Africa, such as Libya, Sudan, and Somalia, that also refused to join the UEG. The rest of Africa was still struggling with chaos and many refused to join the

United Earth Government if it meant working with their enemies. To combat the situation in Africa, the UEG authorized the use of the United Earth Defense Force to invade the most violent and aggressive countries in hopes of convincing the weaker countries that joining the UEG was better then any other alternative. Unfortunately, the UEG was divided on how to deal with the United Arab Empire, so instead of military action, a trade embargo was established. Unfortunately, the trade embargo created a perfect place for the Anti-Unification Movement to establish a presence outside of UEG jurisdiction.

Outside of the efforts of the United Arab Empire, three major anti-unification groups were formed and laid the foundation for the peak of the movement, which would occur in 2005. The first group, known as Liberty Front, was an amalgamation of several militia groups in the United States and it was well supplied by dissident members of the United States military. The second group had no official name, but it was an ultra-violent faction of the Chinese military that broke from the People's Liberation Army following the end of the Third World War. The group, under the command of Colonel Long, was able to leave the Sino Alliance with a full strength brigade, including tanks, helicopters, and soldiers, and escaped into what was once Afghanistan, but now under the control of the United Arab Empire. The third group, and perhaps the most important, operated from deep within the European Union. The group, known only as the Black Group, consisted of many high ranked political figures throughout the European Union, and with their influence to secretly organize riots and protests.

The Rise of the Anti-Unification Movement

The first major action of the Anti-Unification Movement was staged in May of 2002, when a special-forces company from the United Arab Empire landed on Macross Island and attempted to destroy the ASS-1. The battle lasted several days, and while the soldiers were able to cause severe damage to the facilities around the ship, all of their efforts to actually damage the ASS-1 failed and they were eventually captured or killed by the United Earth Defense Force. This attack created a huge political nightmare for the United Arab Empire; the United Earth Government had evidence that the United Arab Empire had engaged in an act of war. The danger that the UEG was invade hung over the United Arab Empire for many months after the incident, but no invasion occurred as the United Earth Defense Force was still too occupied in Africa.

In 2003, the United Earth Defense Force established a special sub-division called the Robotech Defense Force (RDF), which would command all military forces that utilized the advanced alien technology, called Robotechnology. The RDF would control the new Destroids, the variable fighters, and even the space fleet, but the United Earth Defense Force retained command over the Grand Cannon projects and all suits of power armor. While 2004 saw a rise in violence against the United Earth Government, such as riots in Kazakhstan, Europe, and North America, and several military actions in Africa by the United Arab Empire, the Anti-Unification Movement peaked in 2005. During the month of January, the United Arab Empire sent another military force against Macross Island, and while this group was also destroyed, it cause much more damage to the island and the facilities located there. This battle also marked the first use of Destroids in a real combat situation. In April, 2005, just prior to the election for a new Prime Minister, the current Prime Minister, Harlan J. Niven, was assassinated by people working for the Black Group. Niven's chosen successor, Robert A. Rhysling from Britain, announced that the United Earth Defense Force would not rest until all anti-unification terrorists were stopped.

In July, 2005, Liberty Front began a campaign against the United States government. The group was responsible for attacks against military, political, and commercial targets in over 30 states and is directly responsible for the deaths of thousands. Because of secret internal support for Liberty Front within the US Government, the President called the RDF into America to deal with the terrorist group. By September, 2005, threats from several anti-unification groups forced the UEG to shut down Mars Base Sara to protect the population of the base. Much of the population of the base was brought onboard the Oberth, the first Oberth Class Space Destroyer, for the journey back to Earth. Unfortunately, the Black Group orchestrated the hijacking of the third Oberth Class Destroyer, the Koroljev, and used it to destroy the Oberth while it was still carrying the people from Mars Base Sara. On its way back to Earth, the Koroljev was attacked and destroyed by the Goddard, under the command of Captain Gloval, who would go on to command the ASS-1 / SDF-1. Suddenly exposed, nearly all members of the Black Group were quickly arrested by the United Earth Defense Force. The European Union also organized a massive internal investigation to clean out any remaining elements of the Black Group.

Following closely after the incident involving the Koroljev, the United Arab Empire launched an attack against the incomplete Grand Cannon II in Australia and the Grand Cannon IV in the Central African Republic. Both unfinished cannons were destroyed, but the United Arab Empire suffered huge riots protesting the current violence against the United Earth Government. Many groups operating against the regime in control of the United Arab Empire also began receiving secret aid from the United Earth Defense Force.

The Collapse of the Anti-Unification Movement

After many early successes in the United States, Liberty Front was forced into hiding by the Robotech Defense Force. Realizing that Liberty Front had supporters within the government, the President of the United States declared martial law. During the first few months of 2006, the President cleaned the government and congress of all those supporting Liberty Front or other anti-unification terrorists. By June, 2006, Liberty Front had been disbanded and its leaders were captured. Soon after, the President of the United States ordered an end to martial law and resigned from office.

Showing himself for the first time since he abandoned the Sino Alliance, Colonel Long began a three month long siege of Macross Island starting in April of 2006. His forces had occupied nearly all of the surrounding islands and established bases of operations for their attacks. Long's campaign against the United Earth Defense Force and the Robotech Defense Force almost succeed, except for the presence of the CVS-101 Prometheus and the SLV-101 Daedalus, which allowed the United Earth Defense Force to systematically capture each of Long's island bases. By the end of the siege, Colonel Long was killed and his forcers were captured or destroyed by the combined efforts of the Earth Defense Force and the Robotech Defense Force.

In September 2006, the last elements of the Black Group, now completely cut off from all support and hunted by the European Union and the United Earth Government, traveled to the Russian Republic with a small tactical nuclear weapon. The weapon was detonated in the city of St. Petersburg, Russia, and killed hundreds of thousands of people.

By the end of 2006, the last remaining countries in Africa that were rebelling against the UEG put down their weapons and negotiations begin to bring them peacefully into the Organization of African Unity and the United Earth Government.

Throughout 2007 the United Arab Empire struggled with internal dissident elements that were opposing the increasingly oppressive regime. Slowly, country after country separated from the United Arab Empire and declared its independence. Most of these countries sought immediate admittance into the United Earth Government and the Islamic League was formed within the United Earth Government. By the end of the 2007, the United Arab Empire had completely collapsed and from the ashes of the empire came many of the countries that had originally formed it.

Conclusion

The Global Civil War always consisted of two separate parts that have become merged into a single event in the eyes of history. The first part, World War III, was never actually stopped, and many sides were unsatisfied with the results of the war, but found a way to release these feelings through the Anti-Unification Movement, which forms the second part. It is strange to see, but the Anti-Unification Movement was almost successful in pulling apart the UEG. Nearly all militaries on Earth contributed to the movement, but never at the same time.

If it had not been for the Zentraedi Holocaust, which killed 98% of all Humans on Earth, the United Earth Government might have collapsed within a few years of the completion of the SDF-1. As we see from events following the start of the First Robotech War, even the United Earth Defense Force gained a life of its own and was positioning itself for a coup d'état to stay in power if it felt threatened. The only international organization that was successful was the RDF, which had NATO working side by side with former members of the Chinese, Indian, and Russian militaries. It is therefore fortunate that the RDF is one of the few organizations that withstood the Zentraedi Holocaust and served as a model for a world struggling to survive.

2

Use of Nuclear Weapons in War

An all-out nuclear war between Russia and the United States would be the worst catastrophe in history, a tragedy so huge it is difficult to comprehend. Even so, it would be far from the end of human life on earth. The dangers from nuclear weapons have been distorted and exaggerated, for varied reasons. These exaggerations have become demoralizing myths, believed by millions of Americans.

While working with hundreds of Americans building expedient shelters and life-support equipment, I have found that many people at first see no sense in talking about details of survival skills. Those who hold exaggerated beliefs about the dangers from nuclear weapons must first be convinced that nuclear war would not inevitably be the end of them and everything worthwhile.

Only after they have begun to question the truth of these myths do they become interested, under normal peacetime conditions, in acquiring nuclear war survival skills. Therefore, before giving detailed instructions for making and using survival equipment, we will examine the most harmful of the myths about nuclear war dangers, along with some of the grim facts.

- Myth: Fallout radiation from a nuclear war would poison the air and all parts of the environment. It would kill everyone. (This is the demoralizing message of On the Beach and many similar pseudoscientific books and articles.)
- Facts: When a nuclear weapon explodes near enough to the ground for its fireball to touch the ground, it forms a crater.

Many thousands of tons of earth from the crater of a large explosion are pulverized into trillions of particles. These particles are contaminated by radioactive atoms produced by the nuclear explosion. Thousands of tons of the particles are carried up into a mushroom-shaped cloud, miles above the earth. These radioactive particles then fall out of the mushroom cloud, or out of the dispersing cloud of particles blown by the winds thus becoming fallout.

Each contaminated particle continuously gives off invisible radiation, much like a tiny X-ray machine while in the mushroom cloud, while descending, and after having fallen to earth. The descending radioactive particles are carried by the winds like the sand and dust particles of a miles-thick sandstorm cloud except that they usually are blown at lower speeds and in many areas the particles are so far apart that no cloud is seen. The largest, heaviest fallout particles reach the ground first, in locations close to the explosion. Many smaller particles are carried by the winds for tens to thousands of miles before falling to earth. At any one place where fallout from a single explosion is being deposited on the ground in concentrations high enough to require the use of shelters, deposition will be completed within a few hours.

The smallest fallout particles those tiny enough to be inhaled into a person's lungs are invisible to the naked eye. These tiny particles would fall so slowly from the four-mile or greater heights to which they would be injected by currently deployed Soviet warheads that most would remain airborne for weeks to years before reaching the ground. By that time their extremely wide dispersal and radioactive decay would make them much less dangerous. Only where such tiny particles are promptly brought to earth by rain- outs or snow-outs in scattered "hot spots," and later dried and blown about by the winds, would these invisible particles constitute a long-term and relatively minor post-attack danger.

The air in properly designed fallout shelters, even those without air filters, is free of radioactive particles and safe to breathe except in a few' rare environments as will be explained later. Fortunately for all living things, the danger from fallout radiation lessens with time. The radioactive decay, as this lessening is called, is rapid at first, then gets slower and slower. The dose rate (the amount of radiation received per hour) decreases accordingly. Fallout meters called dosimeters measure the dose received by recording the number of R. Fallout meters called survey meters, or dose-rate meters, measure the dose rate by recording the number of R being received per hour at the time of measurement. Notice that it takes about seven times as long for the dose rate to decay from 1000 roentgens per hour (1000 R/hr) to 10 R/hr (48 hours) as to decay from 1000 R/hr to 100 R/hr (7 hours). (Only in high-fallout areas would the dose rate 1 hour after the explosion be as high as 1000 roentgens per hour.)

If the dose rate 1 hour after an explosion is 1000 R/hr, it would take about 2 weeks for the dose rate to be reduced to 1 R/hr solely as a result of radioactive decay. Weathering effects will reduce the dose rate further,' for example, rain can wash fallout particles from plants and houses to lower positions on or closer to the ground. Surrounding objects would reduce the radiation dose from these low-lying particles.

Within two weeks after an attack the occupants of most shelters could safely stop using them, or could work outside the shelters for an increasing number of hours each day. Exceptions would be in areas of extremely heavy fallout such as might occur downwind from important targets attacked with many weapons, especially missile sites and very large cities. To know when to come out safely, occupants either would need a reliable fallout meter to measure the changing radiation dangers, or must receive information based on measurements made nearby with a reliable instrument.

The radiation dose that will kill a person varies considerably with different people. A dose of 450 R resulting from exposure of the whole body to fallout radiation is often said to be the dose that will kill about half the persons receiving it, although most studies indicate that it would take somewhat less. Almost all persons confined to expedient shelters after a nuclear attack would be under stress and without clean surroundings or antibiotics to fight infections. Many also would lack adequate water and food. Under these unprecedented conditions, perhaps half the persons who received a whole-body dose of 350 R within a few days would die.

Fortunately, the human body can repair most radiation damage if the daily radiation doses are not too large. A person who is healthy and has not been exposed in the past two weeks to a total radiation dose of more than 100 R can receive a dose of 6 R each day for at least two months without being incapacitated.

Only a very small fraction of Hiroshima and Nagasaki citizens who survived radiation doses some of which were nearly fatal have suffered serious delayed effects.

The reader should realize that to do essential work after a massive nuclear attack, many survivors must be willing to receive much larger radiation doses than are normally permissible. Otherwise, too many workers would stay inside shelter too much of the time, and work that would be vital to national recovery could not be done. For example, if the great majority of truckers were so fearful of receiving even non-incapacitating radiation doses that they would refuse to transport food, additional millions would die from starvation alone.

- Myth: Fallout radiation penetrates everything; there is no escaping its deadly effects.
- Facts: Some gamma radiation from fallout will penetrate the shielding materials of even an excellent shelter and reach its occupants. However, the radiation dose that the occupants of an excellent shelter would receive while inside this shelter can be reduced to a dose smaller than the average American receives during his lifetime from X rays and other radiation exposures normal in America today. The design features of such a shelter include the use of a sufficient thickness of earth or other heavy shielding material. Gamma rays are like X rays, but more penetrating.

The actual paths of gamma rays passing through shielding materials are much more complicated, due to scattering, etc., than are the straight-line paths. But when averaged out, the effectiveness of a halving-thickness of any material is approximately as shown. The denser a substance, the better it serves for shielding material. Thus, a halving-thickness of concrete is only about 2.4 inches (6.1 cm). If additional halving-thicknesses of packed earth shielding are successively added to the five thicknesses, the protection factor (PF) is successively increased from 32 to 64, to 128, to 256, to 512, to 1024, and so on.

- ° Myth: A heavy nuclear attack would set practically everything on fire, causing "firestorms" in cities that would exhaust the oxygen in the air. All shelter occupants would be killed by the intense heat.
- ° Facts: On aclear day, thermal pulses (heat radiation that travels at the speed of light) from an air burst can set fire to easily ignitable materials (such as window curtains, upholstery, dry newspaper, and dry grass) over about as large an area as is damaged by the blast. It can cause second-degree skin burns to exposed people who are as far as ten miles from a one-megaton (1 MT) explosion. (A 1-MT nuclear explosion is one that produces the same amount of energy as does one million tons of TNT.) If the weather is very clear and dry, the area of fire danger could be considerably larger. On a cloudy or smoggy day, however, particles in the air would absorb and scatter much of the heat radiation, and the area endangered by heat radiation from the fireball would be less than the area of severe blast damage.

"Firestorms" could occur only when the concentration of combustible structures is very high, as in the very dense centers of a few old American cities. At rural and suburban building densities, most people in earth- covered fallout shelters would not have their lives endangered by fires.

- ° Myth: In theworst-hit parts of Hiroshima and Nagasaki where all buildings were demolished, everyone was killed by blast, radiation, or fire.

- Facts: InNagasaki, some people survived uninjured who were far inside tunnel shelters built for conventional air raids and located as close as one-third mile from ground zero (the point directly below the explosion). This was true even though these long, large shelters lacked blast doors and were deep inside the zone within which all buildings were destroyed. (People far inside long, large, open shelters are better protected than are those inside small, open shelters.)

Many earth-covered family shelters were essentially undamaged in areas where blast and fire destroyed all buildings. This shelter was essentially undamaged, although less than 100 yards from ground zero at Nagasaki. The calculated maximum overpressure (pressure above the normal air pressure) was about 65 pounds per square inch (65 psi). Persons inside so small a shelter without a blast doorwould have been killed by blast pressure at this distance from the explosion. However, in a recent blast test,5 an earth-covered, expedient Small-Pole Shelter equipped with blast doors was undamaged at 53 psi. The pressure rise inside was slight not even enough to have damaged occupants' eardrums. If poles are available, field tests have indicated that many families can build such shelters in a few days.

The great life-saving potential of blast-protective shelters has been proven in war and confirmed by blast tests and calculations. For example, the area in which the air bursting of a 1-megaton weapon would wreck a 50-psi shelter with blast doors in about 2.7 square miles. Within this roughly circular area, practically all them occupants of wrecked shelters would be killed by blast, carbon monoxide from fires, or radiation. The same blast effects would kill most people who were using basements affording 5 psi protection, over an area of about 58 square miles.

- Myth: Because some modern H-bombs are over 1000 times as powerful as the A-bomb that destroyed most of Hiroshima, these H-bombs are 1000 times as deadly and destructive.
- Facts: A nuclear weapon 1000 times as powerful as the one that blasted Hiroshima, if exploded under comparable

conditions, produces equally serious blast damage to wood-frame houses over an area up to about 130 times as large, not 1000 times as large.

For example, air bursting a 20-kiloton weapon at the optimum height to destroy most buildings will destroy or severely damage houses out to about 1.42 miles from ground zero.6 The circular area of at least severe blast damage will be about 6.33 square miles. (The explosion of a 20 kiloton weapon releases the same amount of energy as 20 thousand tons of TNT.) One thousand 20-kiloton weapons thus air burst, well separated to avoid overlap of their blast areas, would destroy or severely damage houses over areas totaling approximately 6,330 square miles. In contrast, similar air bursting of one 20- megaton weapon (equivalent in explosive power to 20 million tons of TNT) would destroy or severely damage the great majority of houses out to a distance of 16 miles from ground zero.6 The area of destruction would be about 800 square miles - not 6,330 square miles.

Today few if any of Russia's huge intercontinental ballistic missiles (ICBMs) are armed with a 20-megaton warhead. Now a huge Russian ICBM, the SS-18, typically carries 10 warheads, each having a yield of 500 kilotons, each programmed to hit a separate target. See Jane's Weapon Systems, 1987-88.

- Myth: A Russian nuclear attack on the United States would completely destroy all American cities.
- Facts: As long as Soviet leaders are rational they will continue to give first priority to knocking out our weapons and other military assets that can damage Russia and kill Russians. To explode enough nuclear weapons of any size to completely destroy American cities would be an irrational waste of warheads. The Soviets can make much better use of most of the warheads that would be required to completely destroy American cities; the majority of those warheads probably already are targeted to knock out our retaliatory missiles by being surface burst or near-surface burst on their hardened

silos, located far from most cities and densely populated areas.

Unfortunately, many militarily significant targets - including naval vessels in port and port facilities, bombers and fighters on the ground, air base and airport facilities that can be used by bombers, Army installations, and key defense factories - are in or close to American cities. In the event of an all-out Soviet attack, most of these '"soft" targets would be destroyed by air bursts. Air bursting a given weapon subjects about twice as large an area to blast effects severe enough to destroy "soft" targets as does surface bursting the same weapon. Fortunately for Americans living outside blast and fire areas, air bursts produce only very tiny particles.

Most of these extremely small radioactive particles remain airborne for so long that their radioactive decay and wide dispersal before reaching the ground make them much less life- endangering than the promptly deposited larger fallout particles from surface and near-surface bursts. However, if you are a survival minded American you should prepare to survive heavy fallout wherever you are. Unpredictable winds may bring fallout from unexpected directions. Or your area may be in a "hot spot" of life-endangering fallout caused by a rain-out or snow-out of both small and tiny particles from distant explosions. Or the enemy may use surface or near-surface bursts in your part of the country to crater long runways or otherwise disrupt U.S. retaliatory actions by producing heavy local fallout.

Today few if any of Russia's largest intercontinental ballistic missiles (ICBMs) are armed with a 20-megaton warhead. A huge Russian ICBM, the SS-18, typically carries 10 warheads each having a yield of 500 kilotons, each programmed to hit a separate target. See "Jane's Weapon Systems. 1987-1988." However, in March 1990 CIA Director William Webster told the U.S. Senate Armed Services Committee that ".... The USSR's strategic modernization program continues unabated," and that the SS-18 Mod 5 can carry 14 to 20 nuclear warheads. The warheads are generally assumed to be smaller than those of the older SS-18s.

- Myth: So much food and water will be poisoned by fallout that people will starve and die even in fallout areas where there is enough food and water.
- Facts: If the falloutparticles do not become mixed with the parts of food that are eaten, no harm is done. Food and water in dust-tight containers are not contaminated by fallout radiation. Peeling fruits and vegetables removes essentially all fallout, as does removing the uppermost several inches of stored grain onto which fallout particles have fallen. Water from many sources -- such as deep wells and covered reservoirs, tanks, and containers -- would not be contaminated. Even water containing dissolved radioactive elements and compounds can be made safe for drinking by simply filtering it through earth, as described later in this book.
- Myth: Most of the unborn children and grandchildren of people who have been exposed to radiation from nuclear explosions will be genetically damaged will be malformed, delayed victims of nuclear war.
- Facts: The authoritative study by the National Academy of Sciences, A Thirty Year Study of the Survivors qf Hiroshima and Nagasaki, was published in 1977. It concludes that the incidence of abnormalities is no higher among children later conceived by parents who were exposed to radiation during the attacks on Hiroshima and Nagasaki than is the incidence of abnormalities among Japanese children born to unexposed parents.

This is not to say that there would be no genetic damage, nor that some fetuses subjected to large radiation doses would not be damaged. But the overwhelming evidence does show that the exaggerated fears of radiation damage to future generations are not supported by scientific findings.

- Myth: Overkill would result if all the U.S. and U.S.S.R, nuclear weapons were used meaning not only that the two superpowers have more than enough weapons to kill all of each other's people, but also that they have enough weapons to exterminate the human race.

- Facts: Statements that the U.S. and the Soviet Union have the power to kill the world's population several times over are based on misleading calculations. One such calculation is to multiply the deaths produced per kiloton exploded over Hiroshima or Nagasaki by an estimate of the number of kilotons in either side's arsenal. (A kiloton explosion is one that produces the same amount of energy as does 1000 tons of TNT.) The unstated assumption is that somehow the world's population could be gathered into circular crowds, each a few miles in diameter with a population density equal to downtown Hiroshima or Nagasaki, and then a small (Hiroshima-sized) weapon would be exploded over the center of each crowd. Other misleading calculations are based on exaggerations of the dangers from long-lasting radiation and other harmful effects of a nuclear war.
- Myth: Blindness and a disastrous increase of cancers would be the fate of survivors of a nuclear war, because the nuclear explosions would destroy so much of the protective ozone in the stratosphere that far too much ultraviolet light would reach the earth's surface. Even birds and insects would be blinded. People could not work outdoors in daytime for years without dark glasses, and would have to wear protective clothing to prevent incapacitating sunburn. Plants would be badly injured and food production greatly reduced.
- Facts: Large nuclear explosions do inject huge amounts of nitrogen oxides (gasses that destroy ozone) into the stratosphere. However, the percent of the stratospheric ozone destroyed by a given amount of nitrogen oxides has been greatly overestimated in almost all theoretical calculations and models. For example, the Soviet and U.S. atmospheric nuclear test explosions of large weapons in 1952-1962 were calculated by Foley and Ruderman to result in a reduction of more than 10 percent in total ozone. (See M. H. Foley

and M. A. Ruderman, 'Stratospheric NO from Past Nuclear Explosions", Journal of Geophysics, Res. 78, 4441-4450.) Yet observations that they cited showed no reductions in ozone. Nor did ultraviolet increase. Other theoreticians calculated sizable reductions in total ozone, but interpreted the observational data to indicate either no reduction, or much smaller reductions than their calculated ones.

A realistic simplified estimate of the increased ultraviolet light dangers to American survivors of a large nuclear war equates these hazards to moving from San Francisco to sea level at the equator, where the sea level incidence of skin cancers (seldom fatal) is highest- about 10 times higher than the incidence at San Francisco. Many additional thousands of American survivors might get skin cancer, but little or no increase in skin cancers might result if in the post-attack world deliberate sun tanning and going around hatless went out of fashion.

Furthermore, almost all of today's warheads are smaller than those exploded in the large- weapons tests mentioned above; most would inject much smaller amounts of ozone-destroying gasses, or no gasses, into the stratosphere, where ozone deficiencies may persist for years.

And nuclear weapons smaller than 500 kilotons result in increases (due to smog reactions) in upper tropospheric ozone. In a nuclear war, these increases would partially compensate for the upper-level tropospheric decreases-as explained by Julius S. Chang and Donald J. Wuebbles of Lawrence Livermore National Laboratory.

° Myth: Unsurvivable "nuclear winter" surely will follow a nuclear war. The world will be frozen if only 100 megatons (less than one percent of all nuclear weapons) are used to ignite cities. World-enveloping smoke from fires and the dust from surface bursts will prevent almost all sunlight and solar heat from reaching the earth's surface. Universal darkness for weeks! Sub-zero temperatures, even in summertime! Frozen crops, even in the jungles of South

America! Worldwide famine! Whole species of animals and plants exterminated! The survival of mankind in doubt!

- Facts: Unsurvivable "nuclear winter" is a discredited theory that, since its conception in 1982, has been used to frighten additional millions into believing that trying to survive a nuclear war is a waste of effort and resources, and that only by ridding the world of almost all nuclear weapons do we have a chance of surviving.

Non-propagandizing scientists recently havecalculated that the climatic and other environmental effects of even an all-out nuclear war would be much less severe than the catastrophic effects repeatedly publicized by popular astronomer Carl Sagan and his fellow activist scientists, and by all the involved Soviet scientists.

Conclusions reached from these recent, realistic calculations are summarized in an article, "Nuclear Winter Reappraised", featured in the 1986 summer issue of Foreign Affairs, the prestigious quarterly of the Council on Foreign Relations.

The authors, Starley L. Thompson and Stephen H. Schneider, are atmospheric scientists with the National Center for Atmospheric Research. They showed " that on scientific grounds the global apocalyptic conclusions of the initial nuclear winter hypothesis can now be relegated to a vanishing low level of probability."

Their models indicate that in July (when the greatest temperature reductions would result) the average temperature in the United States would be reduced for a few days from about 70 degrees Fahrenheit to approximately 50 degrees. (In contrast, under the same conditions Carl Sagan, his associates, and the Russian scientists predicted a resulting average temperature of about 10 degrees below zero Fahrenheit, lasting for many weeks!)

Persons who want to learn more about possible post-attack climatic effects also should read the Fall 1986 issue of Foreign Affairs. This issue contains a long letter from Thompson and Schneider which further demolishes the theory of catastrophic "nuclear winter." Continuing studies indicate there will be even smaller reductions in temperature than those calculated by Thompson and Schneider.

Soviet propagandists promptly exploited belief in unsurvivable "nuclear winter" to increase fear of nuclear weapons and war, and to demoralize their enemies. Because raging city firestorms are needed to inject huge amounts of smoke into the stratosphere and thus, according to one discredited theory, prevent almost all solar heat from reaching the ground, the Soviets changed their descriptions of how a modern city will burn if blasted by a nuclear explosion. Russian scientists and civil defense officials realistically described - before the invention of "nuclear winter" - the burning of a city hit by a nuclear weapon.

Buildings in the blasted area for miles around ground zero will be reduced to scattered rubble - mostly of concrete, steel, and other nonflammable materials - that will not burn in blazing fires. Thus in the Oak Ridge National Laboratory translation (ORNL-TR-2793) of Civil Defense.

Second Edition (500,000 copies), Moscow, 1970, by Egorov, Shlyakhov, and Alabin, we read: "Fires do not occur in zones of complete destruction . . . that are characterized by an overpressure exceeding 0.5 kg/cm2 [- 7 psi]., because rubble is scattered and covers the burning structures. As a result the rubble only smolders, and fires as such do not occur."

Firestorms destroyed the centers of Hamburg, Dresden, and Tokyo. The old-fashioned buildings of those cities contained large amounts of flammable materials, were ignited by many thousands of small incendiaries, and burned quickly as standing structures well supplied with air. No firestorm has ever injected smoke into the stratosphere, or caused appreciable cooling below its smoke cloud.

The theory that smoke from burning cities and forests and dust from nuclear explosions would cause worldwide freezing temperatures was conceived in 1982 by the German atmospheric chemist and environmentalist Paul Crutzen, and continues to be promoted by a worldwide propaganda campaign.

This well funded campaign began in 1983 with televised scientific-political meetings in Cambridge and Washington featuring American and Russian scientists. A barrage of newspaper and magazine articles followed, including a scaremongering article by Carl Sagan in the October 30, 1983 issue of Parade, the Sunday tabloid read by millions.

The most influential article was featured in the December 23,1983 issue of Science (the weekly magazine of the American Association for the Advancement of Science): "Nuclear winter, global consequences of multiple nuclear explosions," by five scientists, R. P. Turco, O. B. Toon, T. P. Ackerman, J. B. Pollack, and C. Sagan. Significantly, these activists listed their names to spell TTAPS, pronounced "taps," the bugle call proclaiming "lights out" or the end of a military funeral.

Until 1985, non-propagandizing scientists did not begin to effectively refute the numerous errors, unrealistic assumptions, and computer modeling weakness' of the TTAPS and related "nuclear winter" hypotheses.

A principal reason is that government organizations, private corporations, and most scientists generally avoid getting involved in political controversies, or making statements likely to enable antinuclear activists to accuse them of minimizing nuclear war dangers, thus undermining hopes for peace. Stephen Schneider has been called a fascist by some disarmament supporters for having written "Nuclear Winter Reappraised," according to the Rocky Mountain News of July 6, 1986. Three days later, this paper, that until recently featured accounts of unsurvivable "nuclear winter," criticized Carl Sagan and defended Thompson and Schneider in its lead editorial, "In Study of Nuclear Winter, Let Scientists Be Scientists." In a free country, truth will out - although sometimes too late to effectively counter fast-hitting propaganda.

Effective refutation of "nuclear winter" also was delayed by the prestige of politicians and of politically motivated scientists and scientific organizations endorsing the TTAPS forecast of worldwide doom. Furthermore, the weakness' in the TTAPS hypothesis could not be effectively explored until adequate Government funding was made available to cover costs of lengthy, expensive studies, including improved computer modeling of interrelated, poorly understood meteorological phenomena.

Serious climatic effects from a Soviet-U.S. nuclear war cannot be completely ruled out. However, possible deaths from uncertain climatic effects are a small danger compared to the incalculable millions in many countries likely to die from starvation caused by disastrous shortages of essentials of modern agriculture sure to result from a Soviet-American nuclear war, and by the cessation of most international food shipments.

3

Warnings and Communications

Importance of Adequate Warning

When Hiroshima and Nagasaki were blasted by the first nuclear weapons ever to be used in war, very few of the tens of thousands of Japanese killed or injured were inside their numerous air raid shelters. The single-plane attacks caught them by surprise. People are not saved by having shelters nearby unless they receive warning in time to reach their shelters and unless they heed that warning.

Types of Warnings

Warnings are of two types, strategic and tactical.

- Strategic warning is based on observed enemy actions that are believed to be preparations for an attack. For example, we would have strategic warning if powerful Russian armies were advancing into western Europe and Soviet leaders were threatening massive nuclear destruction if the resisting nations should begin to use tactical nuclear weapons. With strategic warning being given by news broadcasts and newspapers over a period of days, Americans in areas that are probably targeted would have time to evacuate. Given a day or more of warning, tens of millions of us could build or improve shelters and in other ways improve our chances of surviving the feared attack. By doing so, we also would help decrease the risk of attack.

° Tactical warning of a nuclear attack on the United States 'would be received by our highest officials a few minutes after missiles or other nuclear weapons had been launched against our country. Radar, satellites and other sophisticated means of detection would begin to feed information into our military warning systems almost at once. This raw information would have to be evaluated, and top- level decisions would have to be made. Then attack warnings would have to be transmitted down to communities all over America.

Tactical warning (attack warning) of an out-of- the-blue, Pearl-Harbor-type attack would be less likely to be received by the average American than would an attack warning given after recognized strategic warning.

However, the short time (only 15 to 40 minutes) that would elapse between missile launchings and the resultant first explosions on targets in the United States would make it difficult for even an excellent warning system to alert the majority of Americans in time for them to reach the best available nearby shelter.

Strengths and weaknesses of the present official warning system are summarized in the following two sections. Then the life-saving warnings that the first nuclear explosions would give, especially to informed people, are described.

Official Warning System

The U.S. official warning system is designed to give civilians timely warning by means of siren signals and radio and television announcements. The National Warning System (NAWAS) is a wire-line network which is to provide attack information to official warning points nationwide. NAWAS is not protected against electromagnetic pulse (EMP) effects from nuclear explosions. When the information is received at warning points by the officials who are responsible, they will sound local sirens and initiate radio and TV emergency broadcasts - if power has not failed. Officials at NAWAS warning points include many local civil defense directors.

NAWAS receives information from our constantly improving military warning and communications systems.

Siren Warnings

The Attack Warning Signal is a wavering, wailing sound on the sirens lasting three to five minutes, or a series of short blasts on whistles or horns. After a brief pause, it is repeated. This signal means only one thing: take protective action- go promptly to the best available shelter.

Do not try to telephone for information; get information from a radio broadcast after you reach shelter. It is Federal policy that the Attack Warning Signal will not be sounded unless an enemy attack on the United States has been detected. However, since local authorities may not follow this policy, the reader is advised to check the plans in his community before a crisis arises.

The following limitations of attack warnings given by sirens and broadcasting stations should be recognized:

- Only a relatively small fraction of urban Americans could hear the sirens in the present city systems, especially if most urban citizens had evacuated during a crisis.
- Except in a crisis threatening the outbreak of nuclear war at any moment, most people who would hear the attack warning signal either would not recognize it or would not believe it was a warning of actual attack.
- A coordinated enemy attack may include the detonation of a few' submarine-launched ballistic missiles (SLBMs) at high altitudes over the United States within a few minutes of the launching of hundreds of SLBMs and intercontinental ballistic missiles (ICBMs). Such high-altitude bursts would produce electromagnetic pulse (EMP) effects primarily intended to knock out or disrupt U.S. military communications. These EMP effects also could knock out the public power necessary to sound sirens and could put most unprotected broadcasting stations off the air.

Radio warnings and emergency communications to the general public will be broadcast by the Emergency Broadcast System (EBS). This system uses AM broadcasting stations as the primary means to reach the public; selected FM and TV stations are included for backup. All stations during a crisis plan to use their normal broadcast frequencies.

EBS stations that are not put off the air by EMP or other effects of early explosions will attempt to confirm the siren warnings of a nuclear attack. They will try to give information to listeners in the extensive areas where sirens and whistles cannot be heard. However, EMP effects on telephones are likely to limit the information available to the stations.

The functioning EBS stations should be able to warn listeners to seek the best available nearby shelter in time for most of these listeners to reach such shelter before ICBMs begin to explode. Limitations of the Emergency Broadcasting System in February 1986 included the fact that EMP protection had been completed for only 125 of the approximately 2,771 radio stations in the Emergency Broadcast System. One hundred and ten of 3,000 existing Emergency Operating Centers also had been protected against EMP effects. Many of the protected stations would be knocked out by blast; most do not afford their operating personnel fallout protection that is adequate for continuing broadcasts for long in areas subjected to heavy fallout.

Warnings Given by the Attack Itself

The great majority of Americans would not be injured by the first explosions of a nuclear attack. In an all-out attack, the early explosions would give sufficient warning for most people to reach nearby shelter in time. Fifteen minutes or more before big intercontinental ballistic missiles (ICBMs) blasted our cities, missile sites, and other extensive areas, most citizens would see the sky lit up to an astounding brightness, would hear the thunderous sounds of distant explosions, or would note the sudden outage of electric power and most communications. These reliable attack warnings would result from the explosion of submarine-launched ballistic missiles (SLBMs). These are smaller than many ICBMs. The SLBM warheads would explode on Strategic Air Command bases and on many civilian airport runways that are long enough to be used by our big bombers. Some naval bases and high-priority military command and communication centers would also be targeted.

The vast majority of Americans do not know how to use these warnings from explosions to help them save their lives. Neither are they informed about the probable strategies of an enemy nuclear attack.

One of the first objectives of a coordinated enemy attack would be to destroy our long-range bombers, because each surviving U.S. bomber would be one of our most deadly retaliatory weapons. Once bombers are airborne and well away from their runways, they arc difficult to destroy.

To destroy our bombers before they could get away, the first SLBMs would be launched at the same time that ICBMs would be fired from their silos in Europe and Asia. U.S. surveillance systems would detect launchings and transmit warnings within a very few minutes. Since some enemy submarines would be only a few hundred miles from their targets, some SLBMs would explode on American targets about 15 or 20 minutes before the first lCBMs would hit.

Some SLBMs would strike civilian airport runways that are at least 7000 Ft long. This is the minimum length required by B-52s; there were 210 such runways in the U.S. in 1977. During a crisis, big bombers would be dispersed to many of these long runways, and enemy SLBMs would be likely to target and hit these runways in an effort to destroy the maximum number of bombers.

Today most Soviet SLBMs have warheads between 100 kilotons and one megaton. See Jane's Weapon Systems, 1987-88. Within 10 to 15 minutes of the beginning of an attack, runways 7000 feet or longer are likely to be hit by airbursts, to destroy U.S. aircraft and airport facilities. Later cratering explosions may be used to destroy surviving long runways, or at least to produce local fallout so heavy that they could not be used for several days for rearming and refueling our bombers. Therefore, homes within about 4 miles of a runway at least 7000 ft long are likely to be destroyed before residents receive warning or have time to reach blast shelters away from their homes. Homes six miles away could be lightly damaged by such a warhead, with the blast wave from a 1-megaton explosion arriving about 22 seconds after the warning light. Some windows would be broken 40 miles away. But the large majority of citizens would not be injured by these early SLBM attacks. These explosions would be life-saving "take cover warnings to most Americans, if they have been properly informed.

Sudden power and communications failures caused by the electromagnetic pulse (EM P) effects of nuclear explosions also could serve as attack warnings in extensive areas. An EMP is an intense burst of radio- frequency radiation generated by a nuclear explosion. The strong, quick-rising surges of electric current induced by EMP in power transmission lines and long antennas could burn out most unprotected electrical and electronic equipment. Also likely to be damaged or destroyed would be unprotected computers. The solid state electrical components of some aircraft and of some motors of modern autos, trucks, and tractors may be put out of commission. Metal bodies give some protection, whereas plastic bodies give little.

The usual means of protecting electrical equipment against surges of current produced by lightning are generally ineffective against EMP. The protective measures are known, but to date all too few civilian installations have been protected against EMP effects. Three or four nuclear weapons skillfully spaced and detonated at high altitudes over the United States would produce EMP effects that might knock out most public power, most radio and TV broadcasting stations lacking special protection against these effects, and most radios connected to long antennas. Nuclear explosions on or near the ground may produce damaging EMP effects over areas somewhat larger than those in which such equipment and buildings would be damaged by the blast effects.

HOW TO RESPOND TO UNEXPECTED ATTACK WARNINGS

Although a Pearl-Harbor-type of attack is unlikely, citizens should be prepared to respond effectively to unexpected warnings.

These warnings include:

° Extremely bright lights -more light than has been seen before. The dazzling, bright lights of the first SLBM explosions on targets in many parts of the United States would be seen by most Americans. One should not look to determine the source of light and heat, because there is danger of the viewer's eyes being damaged by the heat and light from a large explosion at distances as far as a hundred miles away, in clear weather. Look down and away from the probable source, and quickly get behind anything that will shield you from most of the thermal pulse's burning heat and intense light. A thermal pulse delivers its heat and light for several seconds- for more than 11 seconds if it is from a 1 -megaton surface burst and for approximately 44 seconds if from a 20- megaton surface burst.

If you are at home when you see the amazingly bright light, run out of rooms with windows. Hurry to a windowless hallway or down into the basement. If you have a shelter close to your house, but separate from it, do not leave the best cover in your home to run outdoors to reach the shelter; wait until about two minutes after first seeing the light.

If outdoors when you see the bright light, get behind the best available cover.

It would be impossible to estimate the distance to an explosion from its light or appearance, so you should stay under cover for about two minutes. A blast wave initially travels much faster than the normal speed of sound (about 1 mile in 5 seconds). But by the time its overpressure has decreased to 1 pound per square inch (psi), a blast wave and its thunderous sound have slowed down and are moving only about 3% faster than the normal speed of sound.

If no blast or sound reaches you in two minutes, you would know that the explosion was over 25 miles away and you would not be hurt by blast effects, unless cut by shattered window glass. After two minutes you can safely leave the best cover in your home and get a radio. Turn the dial to the stations to which you normally listen and try to find information. Meanwhile, quickly make preparations to go to the best shelter you and your family can reach within IS minutes the probable time interval before the first lCBMs start to explode.

At no time after an attack begins should you look out of a window or stay near a window. Under certain atmospheric conditions, window's can be shattered by a multi-megaton explosion a hundred miles away.

- The sound of explosions. The thunderous booms of the initial SLBM explosions would be heard over almost all parts of the United States. Persons one hundred miles away from a nuclear explosion may receive their first warning by hearing it about 7-1/2 minutes later. Most would have time to reach nearby shelter before the lCBMs begin to explode.
- Loss of electric power and communications. If the lights go out and you find that many radio and TV stations are suddenly off the air, continue to dial if you have a battery-powered radio, and try to find a station that is still broadcasting.

How to Respond to Attack Warnings During a Worsening Crisis

If an attack takes place during a worsening crisis, the effectiveness of warnings would be greater. Even if our government did not order an evacuation of high-risk areas, millions of Americans would already have moved to safer areas if they had learned that the enemy's urban civilians were evacuating or that tactical nuclear weapons were being employed overseas. Many prudent citizens would sleep inside the best available shelter and stay in or near shelter most of their waking hours. Many people would have made or improved family car small-group shelters and would have supplied them with most essentials. The official warning systems would have been fully alerted and improved.

During such a tense crisis period, neighbors or people sheltered near each other should have someone listen to radio stations at all times of the day and night. If the situation worsened or an attack warning were broadcast, the listener could alert the others.

One disadvantage of waiting to build expedient shelters until there isa crisis is that many of the builders are likely to be outdoors improving their shelters when the first SLBMs are launched. The SLBM warheads may arrive so soon that the civilian warning systems cannot respond in time. To reduce the risk of being burned, persons working outdoors when expecting an attack should wear shirts, hats, and gloves. They should jump into a shelter or behind a nearby shielding object at the first warning, which may be the sudden cut-off of some radio broadcasts.

Remaining Inside Shelter

Curiosity and ignorance probably will cause many people to come out of shelters a few hours after an attack warning, if no blast or obvious fallout has endangered their area. This is dangerous, because several hours after almost all missiles have been launched the first enemy bombers may strike. Cities and other targets that have been spared because missiles malfunctioned or missed are likely to be destroyed by nuclear bombs dropped during the first several days after the first attack. Most people should stay inside their shelters for at least two or three days, even if they are in a locality far from a probable target and even if fallout meter readings prove there is no dangerous fallout. Exceptions would include some of the people who would need to improve shelters or move to better shelters. Such persons could do so at relatively small risk during the interval between the ICBM explosions and the arrival of enemy bombers and; or the start of fallout deposition a few hours, later.

Fallout would cover most of the United States within 12 hours after a massive attack. People could rarely depend on information received from distant radio stations regarding changing fallout dangers and advising when and for how long they could go outside their shelters. Weather conditions such as wind speed would cause fallout dangers to vary with distance. If not forced by thirst or hunger to leave shelter, they should depend on their own fallout meter readings or on radiation measurements made by neighbors or local civil defense workers.

PSYCHOLOGICAL PREPARATIONS

Learning What to Expect

The more one knows about the strange and fearful dangers from nuclear weapons and about the strengths and weakness' of human beings when confronted with the dangers of war, the better chance one has of surviving. Terror, a self-destructive emotion, is almost always the result of unexpected danger. Some people would think the end of the world was upon them if they happened to be in an area downwind from surface bursts of nuclear weapons that sucked millions of tons of pulverized earth into the air. They might give up all hope if they did not understand what they saw. People are more likely to endure and survive if they learn in advance that such huge dust clouds, particularly if combined with smoke from great fires, may turn day into night as have some volcanic eruptions and the largest forest fires.

People also should expect thunder to crash in strange clouds, and the earth to shake. The sky may be lit with the flickering purples and greens of "artificial auroras" caused by nuclear explosions, especially those that are miles above the earth.

Fear

Fear often is a life-saving emotion. When we believe death is close at hand, fear can increase our ability to work harder and longer. Driven by fear, we can accomplish, feats that would be impossible otherwise. Trembling hands, weak legs, and cold sweat do not mean that a person has become ineffective. Doing hard, necessary work is one of the best ways to keep one's fears under control.

Brave men and women who are self-confident admit their fears, even when the threat of death is remote. Then they plan and work to lessen the causes of their fears. (When the author helped Charles A. Lindbergh design a reinforced-concrete blast shelter for his family and neighbors, Lindbergh frankly admitted that he feared both nuclear attack and being trapped. He was able to lessen both of these fears by building an excellent blast shelter with two escape openings.)

Terror

If the danger is unexpected enough or great enough, normal persons sometimes experience terror as well as fear. Terror prevents the mind from evaluating dangers and thinking logically. It develops in two stages, which have been described by Dr. Walo von Gregerz, a physician with much war experience, in his book Psychology of Survival. The first stage is apathy: people become indifferent to their own safety and are unable even to try to save themselves or their families. The second stage is a compulsion to flee.

Anxiety, fear, and terror can result in symptoms very similar to those caused by radiation injury: nausea, vomiting, extreme trembling, diarrhea. Dr. von Gregerz has described terror as being "explosively contagious." However, persons who learn to understand the nature of our inherent human traits and behavior and symptoms are less likely to become terrorized and ineffective in the event of a nuclear attack.

Emotional Paralysis

The most common reaction to great danger is not terror, but a kind of numbing of the emotions which actually may be helpful. Dr. von Gregerz calls this "emotional paralysis. "This reaction allows many persons, when in the grip of great danger, to avoid being overwhelmed by compassionate emotions and horrible sights. It permits them to think clearly and act effectively.

Help From Fellow Americans

The atomic explosions that destroyed most of Hiroshima and Nagasaki were air bursts and therefore produced no deadly local fallout. So we cannot be sure how people would behave in areas subjected to both blast and fallout from surface bursts. However, the reactions of the Japanese survivors are encouraging, especially in view of the fact that among them the relative number of horribly burned people was greater than is likely to be found among a population that expects a nuclear attack and takes any sort of shelter.

Dr. von Gregerz summarizes: "In most cases the victims were, of course, apathetic and often incapable of rational action, but open panic or extremely disorganized behavior occurred only in exceptional cases among the hundreds of thousands of survivors of the two atomic bombing attacks." Also encouraging: ". . . serious permanent psychological derangements were rare after the atomic bomb attacks, just as they were after the large-scale conventional bombings."

Atom Bomb Survivors

Some maintain that after an atomic attack America would degenerate into anarchy an every- man-for-himself struggle for existence. They forget the history of great human catastrophes and the self- sacrificing strengths most human beings are capable of displaying. After a massive nuclear attack starvation would afflict some areas, but America's grain-producing regions still would have an abundance of uncontaminated food. History indicates that Americans in the food-rich areas would help the starving. Like the heroic Russians who drove food trucks to starving Leningrad through bursting Nazi bombs and shells. Many Americans would risk radiation and other dangers to bring truckloads of grain and other necessities to their starving countrymen. Surely, an essential part of psychological preparations for surviving a modern war is a well- founded assurance that many citizens of a strong society will struggle to help each other and will work together with little regard for danger and loss.

How to Keep Radios Operating

Having a radio to receive emergency broadcasts would be a great advantage. The stations that would still be on the air after an attack would probably be too distant from most survivors to give them reliable information concerning local, constantly changing fallout dangers. However, both morale and the prospects of long-range survival would be improved in shelters with a radio bringing word of the large- area fallout situation, food-relief measures, practical survival skills, and what the government and other organizations were doing to help. Radio contact with the outside world probably can be maintained after an attack if you remember to:

- Bring all of your family's battery-powered, portable radios with you to shelter along with all fresh batteries on hand.
- Protect AM radios by using only their built-in short loop antennas. The built-in antennas of small portable radios are too short for EMP to induce damaging surges of current in them.
- Keep antennas of FM, CB, and amateur radios as short as practical, preferably less than 10 inches. When threatened by EMP, a danger that may continue for weeks after the initial attack because of repeated, high-altitude explosions, do not add a wire antenna or connect a short radio antenna to a pipe. Remember that a surge of current resulting from EMP especially can damage diodes and transistors, thus ending a radio's usefulness or reducing its range of reception.
- Keep all unshielded radios at least six feet away from any long piece of metal, such as pipes, metal ducts, or wires found in many basements and other shelters. Long metal conductors can pick up and carry large EMP surges, causing induced current to surge in nearby radios and damage them.
- Shield each radio against EMP when not in use by completely surrounding it with conducting metal if it is kept within six feet of a long conductor through which powerful currents produced by EMP might surge. A radio may be shielded against EMP by placing it inside a metal cake box or metal storage can, or by completely surrounding it with aluminum foil or metallic window screen.
- Disconnect the antenna cable of your car radio at the receiver or at least ground the antenna when not in use by connecting

it with a wire to the car frame. Use tape or clothespins to assure good metal-to-metal contact. The metal of an outside mirror is a convenient grounding-point. Park your car as near to your shelter as practical, so that after fallout has decayed sufficiently you may be able to use the car radio to get distant stations that are still broadcasting.

- Prevent possible damage to a radio from extreme dampness (which may result from long occupancy of some below ground shelters) by keeping it sealed in a clear plastic bag large enough so the radio can be operated while inside.
- Conserve batteries, because after an attack you may not be able to get replacements for months. Listen only periodically, to the stations you find give the most useful information. The batteries of transistor radios will last up to twice as long if the radios are played at reduced volume.

EVACUATION

Changed Evacuation Requirements

The most threatening Soviet nuclear warheads in the mid-1970s were multi-megaton, such as single warheads of approximately 20 megatons carried by each of over 250 SS-18s. About half of these huge Russian warheads would have hit within a quarter of a mile or less of their intended targets - close enough to destroy a missile in its hardened silo. Today's improved Russian warheads have a 50-50 probability of hitting within a few hundred feet of their aiming points. With such accuracy, multi- megaton warheads are not needed to destroy very hard targets, especially missiles in their blast-protective silos.

Soviet strategy continues to stress the destruction of military targets, in order to minimize Russian losses from retaliatory strikes. This logical, long-established Soviet strategy is emphasized in numerous authoritative Russian books, including the three editions of Soviet Military Strategy by Marshall of the Soviet Union V. D. Sokolovskiy.

One result of this logical strategy has been the replacement of huge Soviet warheads by numerous, much smaller, much more accurate warheads. In 1990 almost all large missiles have several Multiple Independently-targetted Reentry Vehicles (MIRVed) warheads. Soviet warheads - especially the 10 warheads of 500 kilotons each carried by most SS-18s - could destroy almost all important U.S. fixed military installations, and also almost all U.S. command and control facilities, airport runways longer than 7,000 feet, major seaports, and the factories and refineries that are the basis of our military power. (Although an all-out Soviet attack could destroy almost all missile silos and missiles in them, a first-strike attack is deterred in part by the possibility that most U.S. missiles in silos would be launched on warning and would be in space, on their trajectories toward Russian targets, before Soviet warheads could reach their silos.)

How should your plans either to evacuate during a worsening crisis, or to remain in your home area, be influenced by the dramatic changes in the Soviet nuclear arsenal? The air bursting of one of the probably few 20-megaton warheads carried by Soviet ICBMs would destroy typical American homes up to about 16 miles from ground zero. In contrast, the air bursting of an approximately 1-megaton warhead - one of the large warheads in today's Soviet arsenal - would destroy most homes within a roughly circular area having a radius of "only" about 5 miles. So, if you take into consideration the advantages to Soviets of arming their largest ICBMs with several very accurate smaller warheads, each capable of destroying a militarily important target, you may logically conclude that unless your home is closer than 10 miles from the nearest probable target, you need not evacuate to avoid blast and fire dangers.

Your planning to avoid incapacitating or fatal exposure to fallout radiation will involve more uncertainties than will your plans to avoid blast and fire dangers. The high altitude winds that carry fallout farthest before deposition usually blow from west to east. Therefore, in most areas your chances of avoiding extremely dangerous radiation dangers are improved if you evacuate westward to an area away from likely nearby targets. However, since no one can foretell with certainty in what directions future winds will blow, your plans to remain where you live, or your crisis evacuation plans should include building, improving, or utilizing high-protection-factor shelter, as explained in following chapters.

If you live near a target the destruction of which has high priority in Soviet war-winning strategy, then a decade or so ago it quite likely was targeted by a 20-MT warhead. This cloud would expand in minutes to this huge size in the thin air of the stratosphere, would contain only extremely small particles almost all of which would remain airborne for weeks to years, and would result in no fallout deposition that would promptly incapacitate exposed people.

A 20-MT surface burst or near-surface burst would produce a stabilized radioactive cloud extending almost as far in all directions from GZ as would a 20-MT air burst. Its tremendous fireball would "suck up" millions of tons of pulverized rock and would contaminate those particles with its radioactive material. Fallout particles as big as marbles6 would fall from the stabilized cloud to the ground in minutes. Very heavy fallout could be deposited as far as 18 miles upwind from such a 20-MT explosion, with heavy fallout, capable of causing fatalities within days to weeks, extending downwind for several hundred miles.

Clearly, the risk of your being endangered by very heavy fallout if you remain 6 miles from GZ of a 1-MT surface burst, and happen to be upwind or crosswind from GZ, is less than the risk you would have run a decade ago if you had stayed 18 miles upwind or crosswind from the same target, which had been destroyed by a 20-MT surface or near-surface burst.

Highest-risk and High-risk Areas

Highest-risk areas are those in which buildings are likely to be destroyed by blast and/or fire, and/or where a person in the open for the first two weeks after fallout deposition would receive a total radiation dose of 10,000 R or more. The largest highest-risk areas would be those within our five Minuteman missile fields, within a few miles all around them, and for up to about 150 miles downwind.

This outdated attack included 113 surface bursts of 20 megatons each on urban and industrial targets, an unlikely assumption similar to those used in making some official civil defense risk-area maps that assumed surface bursts on all targets nationwide. Employing all surface bursts makes little sense to the military, because air bursting the same weapons would destroy most military installations, as well as factories and other urban and industrial assets, over approximately twice as large an area.

As will be explained later, to survive in such areas people would have to stay inside very good shelters for several weeks, or, after two weeks or more, leave very good shelters and drive in a few hours to an area relatively free of fallout dangers. A "very good" fallout shelter is one that reduces the radiation dose received by its occupants to less than 1/200th of the dose they would have received outdoors during the same period. If the two-week dose outdoors were 20,000 R, such a shelter with a protection factor of 200 (PF 200) would prevent each occupant from receiving a dose greater than 100 R -- not enough to incapacitate.

High-risk fallout areas are those where the two- week dose outdoors is between 5,000 and 10,000 R. In such areas, good fallout shelters would be essential, supplied at least with adequate water and baby food for two weeks. Furthermore, survivors would have to remain inside shelters for most of each day for several additional weeks.

The radiation dangers in the shaded areas of the map are shown decreasing as the distances from the explosions increase. This generally is the case, although sometimes rain or snow' carries radioactive particles to the ground, producing 'rainouts" of exceptionally heavy fallout farther downwind. Furthermore, this computer-drawn map made at Oak Ridge National Laboratory does not indicate the very dangerous fallout near the isolated surface bursts. Although the most dangerous fallout would be carried by high- altitude winds that usually blow from west to east, such simplified fallout patterns as those shown should be used only as rough guides to help improve chances of evacuating a probable blast area or very heavy fallout area and going to a less dangerous area. Wind directions are undependable; an enemy's targeting can be unexpected; weapons can miss. A prudent citizen, no matter where he is, should try to build a shelter that gives excellent protection against fallout radiation.

A major disadvantage of all types of risk-area maps is the fact that poorly informed people often misinterpret them and conclude that if they are outside a mapped risk area, they are relatively safe from blast, fire, and even deadly fallout dangers.

Another reason for not placing much reliance on risk-area mapsis that such unclassified maps available in 1986 are based on the largest attacks considered possible a decade ago. In 1986 the sizes of Soviet warheads are much smaller, their numbers are much larger, and their total megatonage and cap ability to produce fallout remain about the same as 10 years ago.

The outdated attack scenario used in producing also involved the surface bursting of multi-megaton warheads totaling 3,190 megatons on military targets, including over 2,000 megatons logically surface bursted on our five Minuteman missile fields. Such an attack on our missile fields would produce about the same amount of fallout. Today, however, heavy fallout from our missile fields would extend somewhat shorter distances downwind, because of the lower heights of the stabilized radioactive clouds from one-megaton and smaller surface and near-surface bursts, as compared to those of multi-megaton warheads that would have been exploded 10 years ago, at a time when a 20-megaton warhead was typical of the Soviet nuclear ICBM arsenal.

In 1986 hundreds of targets besides those might be hit, but the total area of the United States subjected to lethal fallout probably would be less. To maximize areas of destruction by blast and fire, most targets in urban and/or industrial areas would be attacked with air bursts, which would produce little or no promptly lethal or incapacitating fallout - except perhaps in scattered "hot spots" where rain-outs or snow-outs could bring huge numbers of tiny, very radioactive particles to earth within hours after the air bursting of today's kiloton-range Soviet warheads. And since most Americans live far away from "hard" targets - especially far from missile silos, downwind from which extremely heavy fallout is likely - most of us living in or near high-risk areas probably would be endangered primarily by blast and fire, not fallout, in the event of a Soviet attack.

Whether to Evacuate

Let's assume that Russian cities were being evacuated, or that tactical nuclear weapons were beginning to be used in what had been an overseas conventional war involving the United States. In such a worsening crisis, most Americans could improve their survival chances by getting out of the highest-risk and high-risk areas.

U.S. capabilities for war-crisis evacuation are poor and tending to worsen. Several years ago, out of the approximately 3,100 evacuation plans required nationwide, about 1,500 had been made, and these involved only about one third of Americans living in risk areas. By 1986 some cities and states had abandoned their war-crisis evacuation plans; most still have plans that would save millions if ordered in time during a crisis lasting at least a few days and completed before the attack. Who would order an evacuation under threat of attack, and under what circumstances, remain unanswered questions. Furthermore, compulsory evacuation during a war crisis was not and is not part of any official American evacuation plan. So, if you believe that a nuclear attack on the United States is possible and want to improve your chances of surviving, then well before a desperate crisis arises you had better either make preparations to improve your and your family's survival chances at or near where you live, or plan and prepare to evacuate.

Spontaneous evacuations, in which Americans would make their own decisions without the authorities having recommended any movement, probably would occur during a worsening war crisis.

Traffic jams and other complications are less likely to occur if citizens start leaving high-risk areas on their own, over a period of several hours to a few days, rather than if almost everyone, on receiving recommendations from officials, at once begins a poorly controlled evacuation. (Spontaneous evacuation by Gulf Coast residents, begun under threat of an approaching hurricane, have lessened subsequent traffic problems in the evacuations ordered or recommended by officials several hours later.)

Except in areas where the local civil defense war-crisis evacuation plans are well developed, most Americans living farther than 10 miles from the nearest probable separate target probably can best improve their chances of surviving a nuclear attack by preparing to remain at or near their homes and there to make or improve good shelters. Exceptions include those living in the vicinity of targets of great military importance to the Soviets - especially our missile fields, on which many warheads would be surface or near-surface bursted, producing extremely heavy fallout for up to 150 miles downwind. Americans living in these greatly endangered areas would do well to make their plans in keeping with the local official civil defense evacuation plans, at least regarding directions and distances to localities not likely to be endangered by heavy fallout.

Nuclear submarine ports, Strategic Air Command bases, and Air Force installations with long runways also would be destroyed by even a limited Soviet counterforce or disarming attack. These prime strategic assets are likely to be blasted by Submarine Launched Ballistic Missiles (SLBMs) in the first 15 or 20 minutes of the war. SLBM warheads are not as accurate as ICBM warheads, and air bursts can destroy bombers and submarines in port over about twice as large areas as if these same weapons are exploded at or near the surface. Therefore, SLBM warheads probably would be air bursted on these prime "soft" targets, with little or no local fallout. (In an all-out Soviet attack, hours later long runways are likely to be cratered by accurate ICBM warheads and by bombs, to make sure our returning bombers could not use them.)

On the following page are listed considerations, favorable and unfavorable, to evacuation. These comparative lists may help you and your family make a more logical decision regarding evacuation:

Evacuation Factors Table:

Favorable to Evacuation:	Unfavorable to Evacuation:
You live in a highest-risk or high-risk area.	You live outside a highest-risk or high-risk area and could build an expedient fallout shelter and make other survival preparations where you live.
You have transportation (this means a car and enough gasoline), and roads are open to a considerably lower-risk area.	You have no means of transportation or you believe that roads are likely to be blocked by the time you make your decision.
You are in fairly good health or can evacuate with someone capable of taking care of you.	You are sick, decrepit, or lack the will to try to survive if things get tough.
Your work is not of the kind that your community depends on (such as a policeman, fireman, or telephone operator).	You cannot suddenly leave your home area for several days without hurting others.
You have some tools with which to build or improve a fallout shelter. You also have water containers, food, clothing, etc., adequate for life in the area to which you would go.	You lack the tools. etc., that would be helpful - but not necessarily essential - to successful evacuation.

Instructions for building expedient fallout and blast shelters and for making expedient life-support equipment are given in following chapters. The reader is advised to study all of this book carefully before making up his mind regarding basic survival action.

The Need for an Evacuation Checklist

A good flyer, no matter how many year she has flown, runs through a checklist covering his plane before taking off. Similarly, a citizen preparing under crisis pressures to do something he has never done before evacuate should use a checklist to be sure that he takes with him the most useful of his available possessions. A family planning to use an expedient shelter or basement at or near home also should use the Evacuation Checklist on the following page to make sure needed survival items are not overlooked.

Evacuation Checklist

(Includes items for building or improving shelters)

Loading Procedure: Make separate piles for each category (except categories 1 and 5). Then load the car with some items from each category, taking as much as can be safely carried and being careful to leave room for all passengers.

The Most Needed Items

- Category 1. Survival Information: Shelter building and other nuclear survival instructions, maps, all available small battery-powered radios and extra batteries, a fallout meter such as a homemade KFM, and writing materials.
- Category 2. Tools: Shovel, pick, saw (a bow- saw is best), ax or hatchet, file, knife, pliers, and any other tools specified in the building instructions for the shelter planned. Also take work gloves.
- Category 3. Shelter-Building Materials: Rain- proofing materials (plastic, shower curtains, cloth, etc.) as specified in the instructions for the type of shelter planned Also, unless the weather is very cold, a homemade shelter-ventilating pump such as a KAP, or the materials to build one.
- Category 4. Water: Small, filled containers plus all available large polyethylene trash bags, smaller plastic bags and pillow cases, water-purifying material such as Clorox, and a teaspoon for measuring.
- Category 5. Peacetime valuables: Money, credit cards, negotiable securities, valuable jewelry, checkbooks, and the most important documents kept at home. (Evacuation may be followed not by nuclear war, but by continuing unstable nuclear peace.)
- Category 6. Light: Flashlights, candles, materials to improvise cooking-oil lamps (2 clear glass jars of about 1-pint size, cooking oil, cotton string for wicks, kitchen matches, and a moisture-proof jar for storing matches.

- Category 7. Clothing: Cold-weather boots, overshoes, and warm outdoor clothing (even in summer, since after an attack these would be unobtainable), raincoats and ponchos. Wear work clothes and work shoes.
- Category 8. Sleeping Gear: A compact sleeping bag or two blankets per person.
- Category 9. Food: Food for babies (including milk powder, cooking oil, and sugar) has the highest priority. Compact foods that require no cooking are preferred. Include at least one pound of salt, available vitamins, a can and bottle opener, a knife, and 2 cooking pots with lids (4-qt size preferred). For each person: one cup, bowl, and large spoon. Also, a bucket stove, or minimum materials for making a bucket stove: a metal bucket, 10 all- wire coat hangers, a nail, and a cold chisel or screwdriver.
- Category 10. Sanitation Items: Plastic film or plastic bags in which to collect and contain excrement; a bucket or plastic container for urine; toilet paper, tampons, diapers, and soap.
- Category 11. Medical Items: Aspirin, a first-aid kit, all available antibiotics and disinfectants, special prescription medicines (if essential to a member of the family), potassium iodide (for protection against radioactive iodine), spare eyeglasses, and contact lenses.
- Category 12. Miscellaneous: Two square yards of mosquito netting or insect screen with which to screen the shelter openings if insects are a problem, insect repellents, a favorite book or two.

Some Useful Items (To take if car space is available):

1. Additional tools.
2. A tent, a small camp stove, and some additional kitchen utensils.

Evacuating by Car

To make room for supplies, the back seat was left at home. The load on top of the car included blankets, a small rug, and a small tent all made of springy materials which kept the load from becoming compacted and working loose under the 1/4-inch nylon ropes tightened around it. The two loop-ended ropes went over the load and around the top of the car, passing over the tops of the closed doors.

Using Muscle Power

Hazards of evacuation would include highways blocked by wrecks and stalled vehicles. If leadership and know-how were provided, the muscle power of people usually could quickly clear a highway. During a major Chinese evacuation before advancing Japanese armies in World War II. I observed Chinese, using only muscle power, quickly clear a mountain road of wrecks and other obstructions.

Americans can do the same, if someone convinces them that they can do it, as proved by a wintertime episode on Monarch Passover the Continental Divide in Colorado. At least 100 vehicles were held up after a large wrecking truck overturned on the icy highway. The patrolmen were doing nothing until I told them how the Chinese handled such a situation. The patrolmen then called for volunteers from among the delayed motorists to lift the overturned truck back onto its wheels. In less than 15 minutes, about50 people had combined their muscle power and opened Monarch Pass to traffic.

Citizens should take direct action to keep traffic moving during a crisis evacuation.

Making an Expedient or Permanent Shelter Instead of Evacuating

Millions of Americans have homes within very large urban-industrial areas, probably not all of which would be subjected to blast and fire dangers. Many, whose homes are in the suburbs or adjacent towns in these metropolitan areas, could logically decide not to evacuate, but to build earth-covered shelters at or very near their homes and to supply them with life-support essentials.

Likewise, people living even as close as 5 miles from an isolated probable target may decide to build a good shelter near their supplies, rather than to evacuate. This is a good idea, provided that (1) their homes are far enough away from probable aiming points to make such shelters practical, and (2) enough time, space, tools, materials, and supplies are available.

They succeeded, despite the necessity of working on cold November days with snow flurries. The top two inches of earth were frozen and the next two feet so dry that most of it had to be loosened with their dull pick. No member of this family had done any serious digging before, yet they built a shelter that would have given about 100 times as much protection against fallout radiation as would a typical small frame house and at least 25 times as much as a typical home basement.

(Fallout shelters are designed for protection against radiation from fallout particles. Although fallout shelters lack blast doors and other means for keeping out blast, the better types would prevent their occupants from being killed by blast effects in extensive areas where people in houses would have little chance of surviving. In this book, an "expedient shelter" generally means an expedient fallout shelter.)

Even as simple an earth-covered fallout shelter as this Door-Covered Trench Shelter, if built well separated from flammable buildings, usually would save its occupants' lives in extensive areas devastated by blast and/or fire. The area of probable survival in a good earth covered fallout shelter would extend from where blast damage would be light but fires likely to be numerous, inward toward GZ to where most homes would be collapsed by blast and/or destroyed by fire. This ring-shaped area of probable survival from blast and/or fire effects of a 1-MT air burst would extend from about 8 miles from GZ inward to approximately 5.5 miles. Its area would be about 105 square miles, more than the 95 square miles in the circular area with a radius of 5.5 miles centered on GZ and within which this simple a shelter probably would be collapsed by the blast overpressure of a 1-MT air burst. (Door-Covered Trench

Shelters and most of the other types of earth-covered expedient shelters described in this book have been proven dependable in test explosions conducted by the Defense Nuclear Agency.)

In many areas, this and even better types of expedient fallout shelters affording considerable blast protection could be built by untrained families, following the written, field-tested instructions in this book. Furthermore within a few days a small but significant fraction of the population could build expedient blast shelters complete with expedient blast doors and providing at least 15-psi blast protection.

4

Sheltering and Bunkers

ADEQUATE SHELTER

To improve your chances of surviving a nuclear attack, your primary need would be an adequate shelter equipped for many days of occupancy. A shelter that affords good protection against fallout radiation and weather would be adequate in more than 95% of the area of the United States. However, even in almost all areas not endangered by blast and fire during a massive nuclear attack, the fallout protection provided by most existing buildings would not be adequate if the winds blew from the wrong direction during the time of fallout deposition.

To remain in or near cities or other probable target areas, one would need better protection against blast, fire, and fallout than is provided by most shelters in buildings. Blast tests have proved that the earth-covered expedient fallout shelters described in this book can survive blast effects severe enough to demolish most homes.

This chapter is concerned primarily with expedient shelters that give excellent protection against fallout radiation. These earth-covered fallout shelters could be built in 48 hours or less by tens of millions of Americans following field-tested, written instructions. The special blast doors and other design features needed for effective blast protection require more work, materials, and skill than are needed for expedient fallout shelters. If average Americans are to do their best when building expedient shelters and life-support equipment for themselves, they need detailed information about what to do and about why it is to their advantage to do it. We are not a people accustomed to blindly following orders. Unfortunately, during a crisis threatening nuclear war, it would take too long to read instructions explaining why each important feature was designed as specified.

This family, like scores of other families recruited to build shelters or life-support equipment, was offered a sum about equivalent to laborers' wages if its members completed the experiment within a specified time. The test period began the moment the family received the written, illustrated instructions preparatory to evacuating by car, as mentioned in the preceding chapter. Like the other test families, this family was paid for all of its materials used. If a family worked hard and completed the project in half the specified time, it was paid a cash bonus. Throughout such tests workers were guided only by the written instructions, which were improved after each successive test.

The successful outcome of almost all the shelter building experiments indicates that tens of millions of Americans in a nuclear war crisis would work hard and successfully to build earth-covered expedient shelters that would give them better protection against fallout, blast, and fire than would all but a very small fraction of existing buildings. However, this belief is dependent on two conditions: (1) that in a desperate, worsening crisis our country's highest officials would supply strong, motivating leadership; and (2) that Americans would have received well in advance shelter-building and other practical, tested survival instructions.

Shelter Against Radiation

The family previously pictured evacuating by car drove 64 miles to build a shelter at the site. Although the August sun was very hot in this irrigated Utah valley, the family members did not build in the shade of nearby trees. To avoid digging through roots, they carried the poles about 150 feet and dug their trench near the edge of the cornfield.

The father and the oldest son did most of the work of making the shelter. The mother and second son had health problems; the two youngest children were not accustomed to work.

The family followed an earlier version of the plans and instructions given in Appendix A for building a Pole-Covered Trench Shelter. Because the earth was firm and stable, the trenches were dug with vertical walls. If the earth had been less stable, it would have been necessary to slope the walls increasing the width at the top of the main trench from 3-1/2 to 5 feet.

Before placing the roof poles, the workers assured themselves a more comfortable shelter by covering the trench walls. They had brought a large number of the plastic garbage bags required in their home community and split some bags open to make wall coverings. Bed sheets or other cloth could have been used.

The room of this 6-person shelter was 3-1/2 feet wide, 4-1/2 feet high, and 16-1/2 feet long. A small stand- up hole was dug at one end, so each tall occupant could stand up and stretch several times a day.

The trenches for entry and emergency exit were dug only 22 inches wide, to minimize radiation entering the shelter through these openings. The family sat and slept along the left wall, to be better shielded from radiation coming through the openings.

This shelter was designed so that its main trench could be enlarged to make a much more livable room without disturbing its completed roof. For this reason, the 9-foot roofing poles were placed off- center, with the two extra feet resting on the ground to the right of the main room.

Whenever practical, expedient shelters should be built so that they can be readily enlarged to make semi-permanent living quarters. After it becomes safe to emerge for limited periods, occupants could sleep and spend much of their waking time in such a rainproof dugout that affords excellent protection against continuing radiation. In cold weather, living in a dugout like this is more comfortable than living in a tent or shack. After the fallout radiation dose rate outdoors has decayed to less than about 2 R per hour, the small vertical entry could be enlarged and converted to a steeply inclined stairway.

The importance of giving inexperienced shelter builders detailed instructions is illustrated by the unnecessary work done by the young women. They had agreed to try to build a Pole- Covered Trench. Shelter, working unassisted and using only hand -tools. Because the summer sun in Utah was hot, they selected a shady site under a large tree. The brief instructions they received included no advice on the selection of a building site. Cutting and digging out the numerous roots was very difficult for them and required several of the 22 hours they spent actually working.

Another disadvantage of making a shelter under trees is that more of the gamma rays from fallout particles on the leaves and branches would reach and penetrate the shelter than if these same particles were on the ground. Many gamma rays from fallout particles on the ground would be scattered or absorbed by striking rocks, clods of earth, tree trunks, or houses before reaching a below ground shelter.

Types of Shielding

Shelters provide protection against radiation by utilizing two types of shielding: barrier shielding and geometry shielding.

- Barrier shielding is a simplified illustration. (In a real fallout area, a man in an open trench would have fallout particles all over and around him.) The 3-foot thickness of earth shown (or a 2-foot thickness of concrete) will provide an effective barrier, attenuating (absorbing) about 99.9%, of all gamma rays from fallout. (In the illustration, only a single fallout particle 3 feet from the edge of the trench is considered.) Only one gamma ray out of 1000 could penetrate the 3 feet of earth shown and strike the person in the trench. Rays from particles farther away than 3 feet would be negligible; rays from particles closer than 3 feet would be attenuated according to the thickness of earth between the fallout particle and the man in the trench.

However, the man in the trench would not be protected from "skyshine," which is caused by gamma rays scattering after striking the nitrogen, oxygen, and other atoms of the air. The man's exposed head, which is just below ground level, would be hit by about one-tenth as many gamma rays as if it were 3 feet above ground. Even if all fallout could be kept out of the trench and off the man and every part of the ground within 3 feet of the edges of the trench, skyshine from heavy fallout on the surrounding ground could deliver a fatal radiation dose to the man in the open trench.

Skyshine reaches the ground from all directions. If the man were sitting in a deeper trench, he would escape more of this scattered radiation, but not all of it. For good protection he must be protected overhead and on all sides by barrier shielding.

The barrier shielding of the Pole-Covered Trench Shelter was increased by shoveling additional earth onto its "buried roof." After father and son had mounded earth about 18 inches deep over the centerline of the roof poles, a large piece of 4-mil-thick polyethylene was placed over the mound. This waterproof material served as a "buried roof" after it was covered with more earth. Any rainwater trickling through the earth above the plastic would have run off the sloping sides of the "buried roof" and away from the shelter.

- Geometry shielding reduces the radiation dose received by shelter occupants by increasing the distances between them and fallout particles, and by providing turns in the openings leading into the shelter.

The farther you can keep away from a source either of light or of harmful radiation, the less light or other radiation will reach you. If fallout particles are on the roof of a tall building and you are in the basement, you will receive a much smaller radiation dose from those particles than if they were on the floor just above you. Likewise, if either visible light or gamma rays are coming through an opening at the far end of a passageway, less will reach you at the other end if the passageway is long than if it is short. Turns in passageways are very effective in reducing the amount of radiation entering a shelter through them. A right-angle turn, either from a vertical or horizontal entry, causes a reduction of about 90%.

Note: Fallout shelters need not provide additional shielding to protect occupants against initial nuclear radiation that is emitted from the fireballs of nuclear explosions. Large nuclear weapons would be employed in an attack on the United States. The initial nuclear radiation from the sizes of explosions that may endanger Americans would be greatly reduced in passing through the miles of air between the fireballs and those fallout shelters far enough away to survive the blast effects. The smaller an explosion, the larger the dose of initial nuclear radiation it delivers at a given blast overpressure distance from ground zero. (For a discussion of the more difficult shielding requirements of blast shelters that would enable occupants to survive blast effects much closer to explosions and therefore would be subjected to much larger exposures of initial nuclear radiation)

All of the earth excavated in digging the trenches was mounded over the roof poles, making a covering 30 inches deep. This shelter had a protection factor (PF) of over 300; that is, persons inside would receive less than 1 300th of the gamma-ray dose of fallout radiation that they would receive if they were standing outside in the open.

To have made the roof covering more than 36 inches thick would not have increased the protection against radiation very much, unless the entry trench and the air duct-emergency exit trench had been dug considerably longer. Field tests have shown that some families, given only 48 hours, cannot dig the longer trenches, cut the additional poles, and shovel on the additional earth necessary for a shelter that would offer significantly better protection than the shelter shown here.

Earth Arching Used to Strengthen Shelters

Several types of expedient shelters can be made to withstand greater pressures if their roofs are built of yielding materials and covered with enough earth to attain "earth arching." This arching results when the yielding of the roof causes part of the load carried by the roof to be shifted to the overlying earth particles, which become rearranged in such a way that an arch is formed. This arch carries the load to surrounding supports that are less yielding. These supports often include adjacent earth that has not been disturbed.

To attain earth arching, the earth covering the yielding roof must be at least as deep as half the width of the roof between its supports. Then the resultant earth arch above the roof carries most of the load.

(A familiar example of effective earth arching is its use with sheet metal culverts under roads. The arching in a few feet of earth over a thin-walled culvert prevents it from being crushed by the weight of heavy vehicles.)

Protective earth arching also results if a shelter is covered with a material that compresses when loaded, or if the whole roof or the whole shelter can be pushed down a little without being broken.

Shelter Against Beta and Alpha Particles

In addition to the invisible, light-like gamma rays, fallout particles radiate two types of hazardous invisible particles: beta and alpha particles. These radiations would be minor dangers to informed people in fallout areas, especially to those who had entered almost any kind of shelter before the fallout began to be deposited in their area.

- Beta particles are high-speed electrons given off by some of the radioactive atoms in fallout. Only the highest-energy beta particles can penetrate more than about 10 feet of air or about)1/8 inch of water, wood, or human body tissue. Any building that keeps out fallout particles will prevent injury from beta radiation.

The only frequently serious dangers are from (1) internal beta-radiation doses from fallout- contaminated food or drink, and (2) beta burns from fresh fallout particles. Fresh fallout particles are no more than a few days old and therefore very radioactive. If fresh particles remain for at least several tens of minutes in contact with the skin, beta burns are likely to result. If only thin clothing separates fresh fallout particles from the skin, a considerably longer time will elapse before their radiation causes beta burns.

In dry, windy weather, fresh fallout particles might get inside one's nose and ears, along with dust and sand, and could cause beta burns if not promptly washed off or otherwise removed.

Prompt washing will prevent beta burns. If water is not available, brushing and rubbing the fallout particles off the skin will help.

If a person is exposed outdoors where there is heavy, fresh fallout for a long enough time to receive a large dose of gamma radiation, the highest-energy beta radiation given off by fresh fallout particles on the ground may be a relatively minor danger to his eyes and skin. Even ordinary glasses give good protection to the eyes against such beta radiation, and ordinary clothing gives good protection to the skin. Ordinary clothing will shield and protect the body quite well from all but the highest-energy beta particles given off by fresh fallout deposited on the clothing. Fallout-contaminated clothing should be removed as soon as practical, or at least brushed and beaten before entering a shelter room, to rid it of as many fallout particles as possible. (Fallout particles that are many days old will not cause beta burns unless large quantities are on the body for hours.)

Most of the knowledge about beta burns on human skin was gathered as a result of an accident during the largest U.S. H-bomb test in the tropical Pacific.6 Winds blew the fallout in a direction not anticipated by the meteorologists. Five hours after the multimegaton surface burst, some natives of the Marshall islands noticed a white powder beginning to be deposited on everything exposed, including their bare, moist skin. Unknown to them, the very small particles were fresh fallout. (Most fallout is sand-like, but fallout from bursts that have cratered calcareous rock, such as coral reefs and limestone, is powdery or flaky, and white.) Since the natives knew nothing about fallout, they thought the white dust was ashes from a distant volcanic eruption. For two days, until they were removed from their island homes and cared for by doctors, they paid practically no attention to the white dust. Living in the open and in lightly constructed homes, they received from the fallout all around them a calculated gamma-ray dose of about 175 R in the two days they were exposed.

The children played in the fallout-contaminated sand. The fallout on these islanders' scalps, bare necks, and the tops of their bare feet caused itching and burning sensations after a time. Days later, beta burns resulted, along with extreme discoloration of the skin. Beta burns are not deep burns; however, it took weeks to heal them. Some, in spite of proper medical attention, developed into ulcers. (No serious permanent skin injury resulted, however.)

For survivors confined inside crowded, unsanitary shelters by heavy fallout, and without medicines, beta burns could be a worse problem than were similar burns to the Marshall Islanders.

All of the Marshall Islanders unknowingly ate fallout-contaminated food and drank fallout- contaminated water for two days. Mainly as a result of this, radioactive iodine was concentrated in their thyroid glands, and thyroid abnormalities developed years later.

In dry, dusty, windy areas the human nasal passages usually filter out much dust. A large part of it is swallowed and may be hazardous if the dust is contaminated with fallout. Under such dry, windy conditions, beta burns also could be caused by large amounts of dust lodged inside the nasal passages. Breathing through a dust mask, towel, or other cloth would give good protection against this localized hazard. In conclusion: persons under nuclear attack should make considerable effort to protect themselves from beta radiation.

- Alpha particles, identical to the nuclei of helium atoms, are given off by some of e radioactive atoms in fallout. These particles have very little penetrating power: 1 to 3 inches of air will stop them. It is doubtful that alpha particles can get through unbroken skin; they cannot penetrate even a thin fabric.6 Alpha particles are hazardous only if materials that emit them (such as the radioactive element plutonium) enter the body and are retained in bone, lung tissue, or other parts of the body. Any shelter that excludes fallout particles affords excellent protection against this radiation danger. Unless survivors eat or drink fallout-contaminated food or water in considerably larger quantities than did the completely uninformed natives of the Marshall Islands, danger from alpha particles would be minor.

PROTECTION AGAINST OTHER NUCLEAR WEAPONS EFFECTS

° Flash burns are caused by the intense rays of heat emitted from the fireball within the first minute following an explosion.6 This thermal radiation travels at the speed of light and starts to heat or burn exposed people and materials before the arrival of the blast wave. Thermal radiation is reduced but not eliminated if it passes through rain, dense clouds, or thick smoke. On a clear day, serious flash burns on a person's exposed skin can be caused by a 20-megaton explosion that is 25 miles away.

A covering of clothing preferably of white cloth that reflects light can reduce or prevent flash burns on those who are in a large part of an area in which thermal radiation is a hazard. However, in areas close enough to ground zero for severe blast damage, the clothing of exposed people could be set on fire and their bodies badly burned.

° Fires ignited by thermal radiation and those resulting from blast and other causes especially would endanger people pinned down by fallout while in or near flammable buildings. Protective measures against the multiple dangers from fire, carbon monoxide, and toxic smokes.

° Flash blindness can be caused by the intense light from an explosion tens of miles away in clear weather. Although very disturbing, the blindness is not permanent; most victims recover within seconds to minutes. Among the Hiroshima and Nagasaki survivors (people who had been in the open more than persons expecting a nuclear attack would be), there were a number of instances of temporary blindness that lasted as long as 2 or 3 hours, but only one case of permanent retinal injury was reported.

Flash blindness may be produced by scattered light; the victim of this temporary affliction usually has not looked directly at the fireball. Flash blindness would be more severe at night, when the pupils are larger. Retinal burns, a permanent injury, can result at great distances if the eye is focused on the fireball.

People inside any shelter with no openings through which light can shine directly would be protected from flash burns and eye damage. Persons in the open with adequate warning of a nuclear explosion can protect themselves from both flash blindness and retinal burns by closing or shielding their eyes. They should get behind anything casting a shadow quickly.

SKIN BURNS FROM HEATED DUST (THE POPCORNING EFFECT)

When exposed grains of sand and particles of earth are heated very rapidly by intense thermal radiation, they explode like popcorn and pop up into the air.6 While this dust is airborne, the continuing thermal radiation heats it to temperatures that may be as high as several thousand degrees Fahrenheit on a clear day in areas of severe blast. Then the shock wave and blast winds arrive and can carry the burning-hot air and dust into an open shelter.6,9 Animals inside open shelters have been singed and seriously burned in some of the nuclear air-burst tests in Nevada.

Thus Japanese working inside an open tunnel- shelter at Nagasaki within about 100 yards of ground zero were burned on the portion of their skin that was exposed to the entering blast wind, even though they were protected by one or two turns in the tunnel 4.4 (None of these Japanese workers who survived the blast-wave effects had fatal burns or suffered serious radiation injuries, which they certainly would have suffered had they been outside and subjected to the thermal pulse and the intense initial nuclear radiation from the fireball.)

Experiments conducted during several nuclear test explosions have established the amount of thermal radiation that must be delivered to exposed earth to produce the popcorning effect. Large air bursts may result in exposed skin being burned by hot dust and heated air produced at overpressure ranges as low as 3 or 4 psi.

However, calculations indicate that the large surface bursts most likely to endanger Americans would not result in the occupants of small, open shelters being burned by these effects except at somewhat higher overpressures.

Protection is simple against the heated dust and very hot air that may be blown into an open shelter by the blast. When expecting an attack, occupants of an open shelter should keep towels or other cloths in hand. When they see the bright light from an explosion, they should cover their heads and exposed skin. If time and materials are available, much better protection is given by making expedient blast doors. When occupants see the very bright light from a large explosion miles away, they can close and secure such doors before the arrival of the blast wave several seconds later.

Essential Life-support Equipment

Shelters can be built to give excellent protection against all nuclear weapon effects, except in places within or very close to cratered areas. But most shelters would be of little use in areas of heavy fallout unless supplied with enough life-support equipment to enable occupants to stay in the shelters until conditions outside become endurable. In heavy fallout areas most high-protection-factor shelters would be crowded; except in cold weather, most would need a ventilating pump to remove warmed air and bring in enough cooler outdoor air to maintain survivable temperature-humidity conditions. Means for storing adequate water is another essential life-support requirement. These and other essential or highly desirable life-support needs are covered in following chapters.

Basement Shelters

The blast and fire effects of a massive, all-out attack of the magnitude possible in 1987 would destroy or damage most American homes and other buildings and endanger the occupants of shelters inside them. Outside the blast and/or fire areas, the use of shelters inside buildings would not be nearly as hazardous. However, an enemy might also target some areas into which large numbers of urban Americans had evacuated before the attack, although such targetting is not believed to be included in Soviet strategy.

Earth-covered expedient shelters in a blast area give better protection against injury from blast, fire, or fallout than do almost all basements. But during the more likely kinds of crises threatening nuclear war most urban Americans, including those who would evacuate into areas outside probable blast areas, probably would lack the tools, materials, space, determination, physical strength, or time required to build good expedient shelters that are separate from buildings and covered with earth. As a result, most unprepared urban citizens would have to use basements and other shelters in existing structures, for want of better protection.

Shelters in buildings, including basement shelters, have essentially the same requirements as expedient shelters: adequate shielding against fallout radiation, strength, adequate ventilation-cooling, water, fallout radiation meters, food, hygiene, etc. Sketches and short descriptions of ways to improve the fallout protection afforded by home basements are to be found in widely distributed civil defense pamphlets, including two entitled "In Time of Emergency, and "Protection in the Nuclear Age."

In 1987, millions of copies of these pamphlets are stockpiled for possible distribution during a crisis. Unfortunately, most of such official instructions were written years ago, when the deliverable megatonnage and the number of Soviet warheads were small fractions of what they are today. Official civil defense instructions now available to average Americans do not inform the reader as to what degree of protection against fallout radiation (what protection factor) is given by the different types of do-it-yourself shelters pictured. There is no mention of dependable ways to provide adequate cooling-ventilation, an essential requirement if even a home basement is to be occupied by several families in warm or hot weather. Outdated or inadequate information is given about water, food, the improvement of shelter in one's home, and other survival essentials.

No field-tested instructions at present are available to guide householders who may want to strengthen the floor over a home basement so that it can safely support 2 feet of shielding earth piled on it. In areas of heavy fallout, such strengthening often would be needed to safely support adequate overhead shielding, especially if the house were to be jarred by a light shock from a distant explosion. In the following paragraphs, a way to greatly improve the fallout protection afforded by a typical home basement is outlined. If improved in this manner, a basement would provide excellent fallout protection for several families.

If earth is not available because the ground is frozen or because of the lack of digging tools, other heavy materials (containers of water, heavy furniture, books, etc.) should be placed on the floor above. These materials should weigh enough to produce a loading of about 90 pounds per square foot about the same weight as earth one foot thick. This initial loading of the floor joists causes them to carry some of the weight that otherwise would be supported by the posts that then are to be installed.

Cut posts to fit exactly under the beam. If trees at least 4 inches in diameter are not available, make posts by nailing boards together. Position the two outermost posts within 2 feet of the ends of the beam. Space the posts at even intervals, with each post under a floor joist. A post under every third joist is ideal; this usually means a spacing between posts of about 4-1/2 feet. If the basement is 20 feet long, 5 posts are enough. Nail each post to the beam, and secure the bases of each with brace boards laid on the basement floor, as illustrated. Finally, place a second 1-foot-thick layer of earth on the floor above. If the basement windows are protected with boards and if all but a part of one window and all the aboveground parts of the basement walls are covered with earth 2 feet thick, the basement shelter will have a protection factor of several hundred against fallout radiation.

Adequate ventilation and cooling should be assured by using a homemade air pump (a KAP), made and installed. Forced ventilation is especially necessary if more than one family occupies the basement in warm or hot weather.

More work and materials are - required to improve a home basement in this manner than are needed to build a covered-trench shelter for one family. An earth-covered shelter separate from buildings will provide equally good protection against radiation, better protection against blast, and much better protection against fire.

If a family cannot build a separate, earth- covered shelter outdoors, often it would be advisable to make a very small shelter in the most protected corner of the basement. Such an indoor shelter should be of sit-up height (about 40 inches for tall people) and no wider than 3 feet. Its walls can readily be built of chairs, benches, boxes, and bureau drawers. Interior doors make an adequately strong roof. Expedient shielding materials, to be placed on the roof and the two exposed sides, can be ordinary water containers and bureau drawers, boxes, and pillow cases filled with earth or other heavy materials. Or, if heavy-duty plastic trash bags or 4-mil polyethylene film are available, make expedient water containers and use them for shielding. To do so, first line bureau drawers, boxes, pillow cases, trash cans, etc. with plastic. Place the lined containers in position to shield your shelter, then fill these expedient water containers with drinkable water.

As demonstrated by hot-weather occupancy tests of such very small indoor shelters, a small KAP or other air pump must be operated to maintain a forced flow of air through such a crowded shelter, to prevent intolerable temperature-humidity conditions. In some basements a second small KAP would be needed in hot weather to pump outdoor air through the basement. This KAP could be operated by pulling a cord from within the small shelter, using an improvised pulley."

Public Shelters

In the event of an unexpected attack, many unprepared Americans should and would take refuge in nearby marked public shelters. Throughout the populated areas that would not be subjected to blast, fire, or heavy fallout, the use of public shelters could save millions of lives. All persons concerned with survival should remember that the large majority of officially surveyed and marked shelters give better protection against radiation than most unimproved home basements.

Persons preparing to go to public shelters should be aware that many lack forced ventilation and that the blowers and fans of most forced ventilation systems would be stopped by loss of electric power due to electromagnetic pulse effects or by other effects of nuclear explosions on electrical systems. A blast wave at an overpressure range as low as 1 psi (144 pounds per square foot) would wreck most shelter-ventilating fans.

In 1987, no water or food normally is stocked. A person who brought to a public shelter 10 large plastic trash bags and 10 pillow slips, to make 10 expedient water bags in which 60 gallons of water could be stored, would help both himself and dozens of other shelter occupants. If he hoped to share the basement in a strange family's home, his chances of being welcomed would be improved if he brought a small homemade shelter-ventilating pump and other survival items.

The same small pump would be impractical in a large public shelter. An Oak Ridge National Laboratory study completed in 1978 found that if all citizens were to go to National Shelter Survey (NSS) shelters within one mile of their homes, 69% of those who found space would be in shelters rated for 1000 or more occupants. The average number of shelter spaces in this largest class of public shelters was 3179. The prospect of living in an unequipped shelter crowded with this many unprepared people each of whom would have only 10 square feet of floor space is a strong motivation to work hard to build and equip a small, earth-covered shelter.

Deciding What Kind of Shelter to Build or Use

Before deciding what kind of shelter you and your family should build or use, it is best to read all of this book. Your final decision should include consideration of ways to provide life-support equipment discussed in following chapters. At this stage, however, the reader will find it helpful to review important reasons why different types of shelters offer the best hope of survival to different people, in different areas, and under different conditions.

This book is written primarily to improve the survival chances of people who cannot or do not build permanent shelters. The information which follows will help you select the best expedient or available shelter for your family.

Shelter Near or in Your Home

If your home is 10 or more miles from an average target such as a major airport with long runways, or is 20 or more miles from a great city with several strategic targets, you are fortunate: you can prudently build or use a shelter close to home. No one can foretell accurately which way the winds will blow or where weapons will explode, so, if practical, you should build a shelter that gives better protection against fallout, blast, and fire than shelters in buildings. Most people living outside targeted areas could build such a shelter in two days or less, using one of the designs of earth-covered expedient shelters detailed in Appendix A.

Even if you plan to evacuate, you should decide where you would take shelter nearby in case you were unable to do so. There is always a chance that an attack may be launched without warning, giving insufficient time to evacuate.

Or the missile aimed at the area in which you live may miss its target. If your targeted home area were not hit, moderately heavy fallout might be the only danger; even an improved basement shelter would be adequate in that case.

Earth-covered Expedient Family Shelters

Advantages of earth-covered, expedient family shelters:

* Better protection against heavy fallout, blast, and fire than afforded by the great majority of shelters in buildings.
* The possibility of building in favorable locations, including places far removed from target areas, and places where it is impractical to build or to improve large group-shelters giving good protection.
* The opportunity for men, women, and children to work together to provide good protection in minimum time.
* A better chance to benefit from thoughtful preparations made in advance than would be the case in public shelters where water, food, etc. must be shared.
* Less risk of personality clashes, hysteria under stress, exposure to infectious diseases, and other problems that arise when strangers are crowded together for days or weeks.

Disadvantages of earth-covered, expedient shelters:

* It may be difficult to meet the requirement for time, space, people able to work hard, materials, and tools and to get all these together at the building site.
* Building is difficult if heavy rain or snow is falling or if the ground is deeply frozen. (However, untrained Americans have built good fallout shelters with shielding provided by 5 or more feet of packed snow, including a winter version of the Crib-Walled Pole Shelter. The practicality of several Russian designs of snow-covered expedient shelters also has been demonstrated by winter construction tests in Colorado.
* The fewer occupants of family shelters could not provide as many helpful skills as would be found inmost public shelters, with tens-to-thousands of occupants.
* The lack of instruments for measuring changing radiation dangers. However, the occupants could make a homemade fallout meter by following the instructions, or buy a

commercial instrument before a rapidly worsening crisis arises.

Public and Other Existing Shelters

Advantages of the great majority of public and other existing shelters, most of which are in buildings:

* Their immediate availability in many localities, without work or the need to supply materials and tools.
* The provision of fair-to-excellent fallout protection generally much better than citizens have available in their homes.
* The availability in some shelters of fallout meters and occupants who know how to use them and who can provide other needed skills.
* The chance for persons who are not able to carry food or water to a public shelter to share some brought by the more provident occupants.

Disadvantages of the great majority of public and other existing shelters available to large numbers of people:

* The location of most of them in targeted areas.
* Poor protection against blast, fire and carbon monoxide.
* Lack of water and means for storing it, and lack of stocked food.
* No reliable air pumps, which are essential in warm or hot weather for supplying adequate ventilating-cooling air to maintain endurable conditions in fully occupied shelters especially belowground.
* Uncertainties regarding the availability of fallout meters and occupants who know how to use them.
* No dependable lights, sanitary facilities, or other life-support equipment, with few exceptions.
* The crowding together of large numbers of people who are strangers to each other. Under frightening conditions that might continue for weeks, the greater the number of people,

the greater would be the risks of the spread of infectious diseases and of hysteria, personality clashes, and the development of other conflicts.

BELOWGROUND EXPEDIENT EARTH-COVERED FALLOUT SHELTERS

Advantages of belowground, earth-covered expedient fallout shelters:

* They afford better protection than do aboveground, earth-covered types.
* Less time, work, and materials are required to build them than to build equally protective aboveground designs.
* If built sufficiently separated from houses and flammable woods, they provide much better protection against fire hazards than do shelters in buildings.
* If dug in stable earth, even types with unshored earth walls give quite good blast protection up to overpressure ranges of at least 5 psi where most homes and buildings would be destroyed by blast or fire.

Disadvantages of belowground expedient fallout shelters:

* They are not practical in areas where the water table or rock is very near the surface.
* It is impractical to build them in deep-frozen ground.
* They are usually more crowded and uncomfortable than improved basement shelters.

Expedient Blast Shelters

Advantages of expedient blast shelters:

* Occupants of expedient blast shelters could survive uninjured in extensive blast areas where fallout shelters would not prevent death or injury.
* Blast doors would protect occupants from shock waves, dangerous overpressures, blast winds, and burns on exposed skin caused by the popcorning effect and heated air.

* The expedient blast shelters were built and blast tested in Defense Nuclear Agency blast tests. Their air-supply systems were not damaged by blast effects that would have bent over or broken off the aboveground, vertical air-supply pipes typical of even expensive imported Swiss and Finnish permanent family blast shelters. (Notwithstanding this weakness, such permanent blast shelters will save many lives.) The horizontal blast doors of these tested expedient blast shelters were not damaged because they were protected on all sides by spiked-together blast- protector logs surrounded by ramped earth. (In contrast, the horizontal blast door of the most expensive blast shelter described in a widely distributed Federal Emergency Management Agency pamphlet (number H-12-3) is unprotected on its sides. This untested blast door probably would be torn off and blown away if struck by a strong blast wave, following blast winds, and pieces of houses and trees that would be hurled hundreds of feet.)
* The blast-tested expedient blast valve will prevent entry of blast waves through a shelter's ventilation pipes and resultant destruction of the ventilation pump and possible injury of occupants.

Disadvantages of expedient blast shelters:

* They require more time, materials, tools, skill, and work than are needed for building expedient fallout shelters.
* Especially expedient blast shelters should be well separated from buildings and woods that if burned are likely to produce dangerous quantities of carbon monoxide and toxic smoke.
* Their ventilation openings permit the entry of many more fallout particles than do the ventilation pipes with goosenecks and filters of typical permanent blast shelters. (However, deadly local fallout probably will not be a major danger in the blast areas where the great majority of Americans live, because a rational enemy will employ air bursts to destroy

> the mostly 'soft" targets found in those areas. Air bursts can destroy most militarily significant soft" targets over about twice as many square miles as can the surface or near-surface bursting of the same weapons. Fortunately, air bursts produce only tiny particles, and only a small fraction of these, while they still are very radioactive, are likely to be promptly brought to earth in scattered "hot spots" by rain-outs and snow-outs. Thus relatively few prompt fatalities or delayed cancer cases from air-burst fallout are likely to result- even from the air bursting of today's smaller Soviet warheads that would inject most of their particles into the troposphere at altitudes from which wet deposition can take place.

WARNING: Permanent home fallout and blast shelters described in widely available FEMA pamphlets have protection factors in line with the PF 40 minimum standard for public shelters in buildings. In heavy fallout areas a sizable fraction of the occupants of PF 40 shelters will receive radiation doses large enough to incapacitate or kill them later. Permanent shelters built specifically to protect against nuclear weapon effects should have PFs much higher than PF 40.

None of the permanent home or family shelters described in official OCD, DCPA, or FEMA free shelter-building instruction pamphlets have been built for evaluation and/or testing - a finding confirmed to the author in 1987 by a retired shelter specialist who for some 20 years served in Washington with FEMA and its predecessors.

VENTILATION AND COOLING OF SHELTERS

Critical Importance

If high-protection-factor shelters or most other shelters that lack adequate forced ventilation were fully occupied for several days in warm or hot weather, they would become so hot and humid that the occupants would collapse from the heat if they were to remain inside. It is important to understand that the heat and water vapor given off by the bodies of people in a crowded, long-occupied shelter could be deadly if fallout prevents leaving the shelter.

When people enter an underground shelter or basement in the summertime, at first the air feels cool. However, if most shelters are fully occupied for a few days without adequate ventilation, the floors, walls, and ceilings, originally cool, will have absorbed about all the body heat of which they are capable. Some shelters will become dangerously hot in a few hours. Unless most of the occupants body heat and water vapor from sweat are removed by air circulated through a typical shelter, the heat-humidity conditions will become increasingly dangerous in warm or hot weather. One of the most important nuclear war survival skills people should learn is how to keep occupied shelters adequately ventilated in all seasons and cool enough for many days of occupancy in warm or hot weather. Methods for ventilating with homemade devices and for keeping ventilating air from carrying fallout particles into shelters are described in Appendices A and B. Instructions for Directional Fanning, the simplest means for forcing adequate volumes of air to flow through shelters, are given at the end of this chapter.

MAKING AND USING AN EXPEDIENT AIR PUMP

The best expedient way to maintain livable conditions in a shelter, especially in hot weather, is to make and use a large-volume shelter-ventilating pump. Field tests have proved that average Americans can build the expedient air pump in a few hours, with inexpensive materials found in most households.

This simple pump was invented in 1962 by the author called it a Punkah-Pump, because its hand- pulled operation is somewhat like that of an ancient fan called a 'punkah", still used by some primitive peoples in hot countries. (Unlike the punkah, however, this air pump can force air to move in a desired direction and is a true pump.) It was named the Kearny Air Pump (KAP) by the Office of Civil Defense following tests of various models by Stanford Research Institute, the Protective Structures Development Center, and General American Transportation Company. These tests confirmed findings first made at Oak Ridge National Laboratory regarding the advantages of the KAP both as a manually operated pump for forcing large volumes of outdoor air through shelters and as a device for distributing air within shelters and fanning the occupants.

The air pump are the result of having scores of families and pairs of untrained individuals, including children, build and use this air pump. They were guided by successively improved versions of these detailed, written instructions, that include many illustrations. Some people who are experienced at building things will find these instructions unnecessarily long and detailed. However, shelter-building experiments have shown that the physically stronger individuals, usually the more experienced builders, should do more of the hard, manual work when shelters are built, and that those less experienced at building should do the lighter work including making shelter ventilating pumps. These detailed, step-by-step instructions have enabled people who never.

He carried the pump on top of his car to the shelter-building site. The pendulum-like, flap-valve pump was swung from two cabinet hinges (not shown) screwed onto a board. The board was nailed to roof poles of the narrow entry trench extending behind the girl in the photograph. The pull-cord was attached to the pump frame below its hinged top and extended along one trench wall for the whole length of the shelter. Any one of the six occupants could pull this cord and easily pump as much as 300 cubic feet per minute of outdoor air through the shelter and through the insect screens over both its entrances. (Without these screens, the numerous mosquitoes in this irrigated area would have made the family's shelter stay very unpleasant.)

During the 77 hours that the family continuously occupied their narrow, covered trench, the temperatures outside rose as high as 930 F. Without the air pump, the six occupants would have been driven from their shelter by unbearable temperature- humidity conditions during the day.

Numerous shelter occupancy tests have proved that modern Americans can live for weeks in an adequately cooled shelter with only 10 square feet of floor space per person.13Other tests, such as one conducted by the Navy near Washington, D.C. during an abnormally cool two weeks in August, 1962, have shown that conditions can become difficult even when summertime outdoor air is being pumped through a long-occupied shelter at the rate of 12 cubic feet per minute, per person.

This is four times the minimum ventilation rate for each occupant specified by the Federal Emergency Management Agency (FEMA) for American shelters: 3 cubic feet per minute (3 cfm). Three cfm is about three times the supply of outdoor air needed to keep healthy people from having headaches as a result of exhaled carbon dioxide. In hot, humid weather, much more outdoor air than 12 cfm per person must be supplied to a crowded, long-occupied shelter.

Maintaining Endurable Shelter Conditions in Hot Weather

The Navy test mentioned above showed how much modern Americans who are accustomed to air conditioning could learn from jungle natives about keeping cool and healthy by skillfully using hot, humid, outdoor air. While working in jungles from the Amazon to Burma, I observed the methods used by the natives to avoid unhealthful conditions like those experienced in the Navy shelter, which was ventilated in a conventional American manner.

These jungle methods include the first five of the six cooling methods listed in this section. During 24 years of civil defense research, my colleagues and 1 have improved upon the cooling methods of jungle people, primarily by the invention and thorough field-testing of the homemade KAP described in Appendix B, and of the Directional Fans covered by the instructions at the end of this chapter.

Even during a heat wave in a hot part of the United States, endurable conditions can be maintained in a fully occupied, belowground shelter with this simple pump, if the test-proven requirements listed below are ALL met.

Most basement shelters and many aboveground shelters also can be kept at livable temperatures in hot weather if the cooling methods listed below are ALL followed:

° Supply enough air to carry away all the shelter occupants' body heat without raising the "effective temperature ' of the air at the exhaust end of the shelter by more than 2 degrees F. The "effective temperature" of the air to which a person is exposed is equivalent to the temperature of air at 100% relative humidity that causes the same sensation of warmth or cold. "Effective temperature" combines the effects of the temperature of the air, its relative humidity, and its movement. An ordinary thermometer does not measure effective temperature. In occupancy tests of crowded shelters when the supply of outdoor air was hot and dry, shelter occupants have been surprised to find that they felt hottest at the air-exhaust end of their shelter, where the temperature reading was lower than at the air-intake end. Their sweaty bodies had acted as evaporative air coolers, but their body heat had raised the effective temperature, a reliable indicator of heat stress. If 40 cubic feet per minute (40 cfm) per person of outdoor air is supplied and properly distributed, then (even if the outdoor air is at a temperature which is typical of the hottest hours during a heat wave in a hot, humid area of the United States) the effective temperature of the shelter air will be increased no more than 2 degrees F by the shelter occupants' body heat and water vapor. Except for a relatively few sick people dependent on air conditioning, anyone could endure air that has an effective temperature only 2 degrees F higher than that of the air outdoors.

(There are exceptions to this ventilation requirement when the ceiling or walls of basement or aboveground shelters in buildings are heated by the sun to levels higher than skin temperature. In such shelters, more than 40 cfm of outdoor air per occupant must be supplied. However, if a shelter is covered by at least two feet of earth, it will be so well insulated that its ceiling and walls will not get hot enough to heat the occupants.)

- Move the air gently, so as not to raise its temperature. In the aforementioned Navy test, a high speed, electric ventilating pump and the frictional resistance of pipes and filters raised the temperature of the air supplied to the shelter by 3 degrees F. Under extreme heat wave conditions, an air supply 3 degrees F hotter than outdoor air could be disastrous especially if considerably less than 40 cfm per occupant is supplied, and body heat raises the air temperature several additional degrees.
- Distribute the air quite evenly throughout the shelter. In a trench shelter, where air is pumped in at one end and flows out the other, good distribution is assured.In larger shelters, such as basements, ventilating air will move from the air-supply opening straight to the air exhaust opening. Persons out of this air stream will not be adequately cooled. By using one or more additional, smaller KAPs, fresh air can be distributed easily throughout large shelter rooms, and the occupants will be gently fanned.
- Provide occupants with adequate drinking water and salt. In extremely hot weather, this means 4 quarts of water per day per person and 1 tablespoon (10 grams) of salt, including the salt in food.
- Wear as few clothes as practical. When the skin is bare, moving air can evaporate sweat more efficiently for effective cooling. Air movement can keep bare skin drier, and therefore less susceptible to heat rash and skin infections. In the inadequately ventilated Navy test shelter, 34 of the 99 initially healthy young men had heat rash and 23 had more serious skin complaints at the end of their sweaty two-week confinement, although their overall physical condition had not deteriorated.15 However, at sick call every day all of these Navy test subjects with skin complaints were treated by medical corpsmen. In a nuclear war, very few shelter

occupants would have medicines to treat skin diseases and infections, that if not taken care of usually worsen rapidly under continuously hot, humid conditions. Simple means for preventing skin diseases and infections-means proved very effective by jungle natives and by our best trained jungle infantrymen in World War.

- Keep pumping about 40 cfm of air per person through the shelter both day and night during hot weather, so that the occupants and the shelter itself will be cooled off at night. In the Navy test, the ventilation rate of 7 to 12 cfm was not high enough to give occupants the partial relief from heat and sweating that people normally get at night. In a National Academy of Sciences meeting on protective shelters, an authority stated: "Laboratory experiments and field investigations have shown that healthy persons at rest can tolerate daily exposures to ETs [effective temperatures] up to 900 F, provided they can get a good night's sleep in a cooler environment." An effective temperature 900 F is higher than the highest outdoor effective temperature during a heatwave in the South or in American deserts.

Adequate Ventilation in Cold Weather

In freezing weather, a belowground shelter covered with damp earth may continue to absorb almost all of its occupants' body heat for many days and stay unpleasantly cold. In one winter test of such a fully occupied shelter, the temperature of the humid air in the shelter remained around 50 degrees F. Under such conditions, shelter occupants should continue to ventilate their shelter adequately, to avoid the following conditions:

- A dangerous buildup of carbon dioxide from exhaled breath, the first symptoms of which are headaches and deeper breathing.
- Headaches from the carbon monoxide produced by smoking. When the ventilation rate is low, smoking should not be permitted, even near the exhaust opening.

° Headaches, collapse, or death due to carbon monoxide from open fires or gasoline lanterns that release gases into the shelter air.

Natural Ventilation

Enough air usually will be blown through an aboveground shelter if sufficiently large openings are provided on opposite sides and if there is any breeze. But if the weather is warm and still and the shelter crowded, the temperature-humidity conditions soon can become unbearable.

Adequate natural ventilation for belowground shelters is more difficult. Even if there is a light breeze, not much air will make a right-angle turn and go down a vertical entry, make another right-angle turn, and then flow through a trench or other shelter partially obscured by people and supplies.

In cool weather, occupants body heat will warm the shelter air and make it lighter than the outdoor air. If a chimney-like opening or vent-duct is provided in the ceiling, the warmed, lighter air will flow upward and out of the shelter, provided an adequate air-intake vent is open near the floor. An Eskimo igloo is an excellent example of how very small ventilation openings, skillfully located in the ceiling and at floor level, make it possible in cold weather for chimney-type natural ventilation to supply the 1 cfm per person of outdoor air needed to prevent exhaled carbon dioxide from becoming dangerously concentrated. In warm weather, chimney-type natural ventilation usually is inadequate for most high-protection factor shelters that are fully occupied for days. And in hot weather, when as much as 40 cfm per occupant is required, body-warmed shelter air is no lighter than the outdoor air. Chimney-type ventilation fails completely under these conditions.

Shelter Ventilation Without Filters

Numerous tests have shown that the hazards from fallout particles carried into shelters by unfiltered ventilating air are minor compared to the dangers from inadequate ventilation. A 1962 summary of the official standards for ventilating systems of fallout shelters stated: "Air filters are not essential for small (family size) shelters..." More recent findings have led to the same conclusion for large fallout shelters. A 1973 report by the Subcommittee on Fallout of the National Academy of Sciences on the radioiodine inhalation problem stated this conclusion: "The opinion of the Subcommittee is that inhalation is far less of a threat than ingestion [eating or drinking], and does not justify countermeasures such as filters in the ventilating systems of shelters."

Recommendations such as those above realistically face the fact that, if we suffer a nuclear attack, the vast majority of Americans will have only the fallout protection given by buildings and some expedient shelters. Consequently, how best to use available resources must be the primary consideration when planning for protection against the worst dangers of a nuclear attack; relatively minor hazards may have to be accepted. For unprepared people, inhalation of fallout particles would be a minor danger compared to being forced out of a shelter because of dangerously inadequate ventilation.

The most dangerous fallout particles are those deposited on the ground within the first few hours after the explosion that produces them. Typically, these 'hot" particles would be so large and fast-falling that they would not be carried into expedient shelters equipped with low-velocity air intake openings, such as those described in this book. Nor would these most dangerous '"hot" fallout particles be "sucked" into gooseneck air-intake pipes, or other properly designed air-intake openings of a permanent shelter.

For most shelters built or improved hurriedly during a crisis it will be impractical to provide filtered air. The Car-Over-Trench Shelter points up the overriding need for pumped air for occupants of crowded shelters during warm or hot weather. This simple shelter provides fallout protection about four times as effective as that given by a typical home basement. After the car was driven over the trench, earth was shoveled into the car and its trunk and on top of its hood. At one end was a combined crawlway entrance/air intake opening, at the other end, a 1-foot-square air exhaust opening. Each opening was covered by a small awning. To keep loose shielding earth from running under the car and into the trench, the upper edges of 5-foot-wide strips of polyethylene film first were attached with duct tape to the sides and ends of the car, about 2 feet above the ground. Then earth was piled onto the parts of the film strips that were lying on the ground, to secure them. Finally, earth was piled against the vertical parts of the attached film strips.

Inhalation Dangers

Only extremely small fallout particles can reach the lungs. The human nose and other air passages can filter out almost all particles 10 micrometers [10 microns] [or larger] in diameter, and about 95 percent of those exceeding 5 micrometers." Five micrometers equal 5 millionths of a meter, or 5 thousandths of a millimeter.

Using a dust mask or breathing through cloth would be helpful to keep from inhaling larger 'hot" fallout particles which may cause beta burns in noses, sinuses, and bronchial tubes. Many such retained particles may be swallowed when cleared from one's air passageways by the body's natural protective processes.

A relatively "large" particle - 40 microns (40 u m) in diameter, spherical, and with the sand-like density of most fallout particles - falls about 1300 feet in 8 hours. (A dark-colored particle 40 microns in diameter is about as small a speck as most people can see with the naked eye.) Most 40- u m-diameter fallout particles would take a few days to fall from the cloud of a one-megaton explosion down far enough into the troposphere to be occasionally scavenged and promptly brought to earth by rain or snow while still very radioactive. In 1987, however, most of the thousands of deployed Soviet ICBM warheads are 550 kilotons or smaller. (See Jane's Weapon Systems, 1987-88.)

The stabilized clouds of such explosions would be mostly in the troposphere, and some of even the tiniest particles - those small enough to be breathed into one's lungs - would be promptly scavenged and deposited in scattered "hot spots." Fortunately, most of the very small and tiniest fallout particles would not be deposited for days to months, by which time radioactive decay would have made them much less dangerous.

Breathing tiny radioactive particles into one's lungs would constitute a minor health hazard compared to other dangers that would afflict an unprepared people subjected to a large scale nuclear attack.

Scavenging of Radioactive Particles

Scavenging is most effective below about 30,000 feet, the maximum height of most rain and snow clouds. Because the Soviets have deployed thousands of ICBMs with warheads of "only" 100 to 550 kilotons, Americans face increased dangers from very radioactive particles scavenged by rain-outs or snow-outs.

The resultant "hot spots" of fallout heavy enough to kill unsheltered people in a few weeks could be scattered even hundreds of miles downwind from areas of multiple explosions, especially missile fields. Prudent Americans, even those living several hundred miles from important targets, whenever practical should equip their shelters with adequate ventilating pumps and dust filters.

This potential danger from extremely small fallout particles will be worsened if the United States deploys mobile ICBMs such as Midget- man, probably on large military reservations in the West. (The Soviet Union already has mobile ICBMs in its nuclear forces.) In the event of a Soviet attack, our hard-to-target mobile missiles probably would be subjected to a barrage of relatively small warheads air-bursted so as to blanket their deployment areas. The resultant large clouds of extremely small radioactive particles in the troposphere usually would be blown eastward, and resultant life-endangering "hot spots" from rain-outs and/or snow-outs could be scattered clear to the Atlantic coast.

Fortunately, even in many expedient shelters completed in a few days, filtered air can be provided by using a homemade KAP to pump air through furnace or air-conditioner filters. To learn how you can supply a shelter at low cost with air so well filtered that essentially all extremely small fallout particles and infective aerosols are removed.

These worsening potential dangers from extremely small "hot" fallout particles brought promptly to earth by scavenging are not likely to endanger nearly as many Americans' lives as would 24-hour fallout of much larger particles from surface and near-surface explosions. Providing enough outdoor air to shelters, rather than filtered air, will continue to deserve first priority.

Stopping or Restricting Shelter Ventilation

When instrument readings or observations show that heavy fallout has begun to be deposited, shelter occupants should decide whether to restrict or stop ventilation. If it is windy outside, even some sand-like fallout particles may be blown into a shelter with large ventilation openings. However, ventilation should not be restricted long enough to cause weaker occupants to be on the verge of collapse from overheating, or to result in headaches from exhaled carbon dioxide.

If a house is burning dangerously close to a separate, earth covered shelter, closing the shelter's ventilation openings for an hour or two usually will prevent the entry of dangerous concentrations of carbon monoxide, carbon dioxide, or smoke. (Most houses will burn to the ground in less than two hours.)

When an attack is expected, a shelter, occupied or soon to be occupied, should be kept as cool as practical by pumping large volumes of outdoor air through it when the outdoor air is cooler than the shelter air. This also will assure that the air is fresh and low in exhaled carbon dioxide. Then, if a need arises to stop or restrict ventilation, the shelter can be closed for longer than could be done safely otherwise.

Ventilation/Cooling of Permanent Shelters

A permanent family fallout shelter, built at moderate cost before a crisis, should have a ventilation system that can supply adequate volumes of either filtered or unfiltered air, pumped in through an air-intake pipe and out through an air-exhaust pipe. Provision also should be made for the grim possibility that fallout could be so heavy that a shelter might have to be occupied for weeks, or even part-time for months. A small or medium-sized permanent shelter should be designed so that most of the time after an attack it can have adequate natural ventilation through its entryway and emergency exit. During hot spells, forced ventilation through these same large air passageways should be provided by using a homemade KAP. This manual air pump, described in Appendix B, can force large volumes of air through low- resistance openings with minimum effort.

Warning: Many Official Instructions for Building and Ventilating Shelters are Life-endangering

The reader is advised not to read this section if pressed for time during a crisis, unless he is considering building an expedient or permanent shelter described in an official civil defense publication.

Because of the worldwide extreme fear of radiation, civil defense specialists who prepare official self-help instructions for building shelters have made radiation protection their overriding objective. Apparently the men in Moscow and Washington who decide what shelter-building and shelter-ventilating instructions their fellow citizens receive - especially instructions for building and improving expedient shelters-do not understand the ventilation requirements for maintaining endurable temperature/humidity conditions in crowded shelters. It must be remembered that shelters may have to be occupied continuously for days in warm or hot weather.

Russian small expedient shelters are even more dangerously under-ventilated than are most of their American counterparts, and can serve to illustrate similar ventilation deficiencies of American shelters. This booklet, published in a 200,000- copy edition, includes illustrated instructions for building 20 different types of expedient shelters. All 20 of these shelters have dangerously inadequate natural ventilation, and none of them have air pumps. Note that this high-protection-factor, covered-trench shelter depends on air flowing down through its "Dust Filter with Straw Packing (hay)" and out through its small "Exhaust Duct with Damper."

As part of Oak Ridge National Laboratory's participation in Defense Nuclear Agency's "Dice Throw" 1978 blast test, I built two Russian Pole- Covered Trench Shelters. As anticipated, so little air flowed through these essentially dead-ended test shelters that temperatures soon became unbearable.

Russian earth-covered expedient fallout shelters are based on military dugouts designed for brief occupancy during a conventional attack. Subsequently, they were improved for fallout protection but were made much less habitable by Soviet civil defense specialists. Apparently these specialists were ignorant of ventilation requirements, and almost certainly they did not field-test small expedient fallout shelters for habitability. Tens of millions of Russians have been taught to build such shelters.

Once any bureaucracy issues dangerously faulty equipment or instructions, it rarely corrects them except under pressure. I have experienced this reluctance even during wartime, when trying to improve faulty combat equipment that was causing American soldiers to lose their lives. Continuing proofs of such bureaucratic reluctance to correct dangerous errors are hundreds of thousands of potentially life- endangering civil defense pamphlets and booklets - especially the several editions of In Time of Emergency - kept nationwide in hundreds of communities, primarily for crisis distribution.

Some American official instructions for building expedient shelters have been slowly improved over the decades; the best are given in the June 1985 edition of Protection in the Nuclear Age, one of the Federal Emergency Management Agency's widely available free booklets. Yet even in this improved edition no mention is made of the crucial need for forced ventilation during warm weather, nor for expedient, simple means for providing pumped air. Also, in the June 1985 edition of Protection in the Nuclear Age, the second crawlway entry/exit of the Above- Ground, Door-Covered Shelter is replaced by a "4-6" DIA. "PIPE FOR VENTILATION," which makes this very small shelter essentially dead-ended and thereby eliminates adequate ventilation in warm weather. With only a 6-inch-diameter air-exhaust opening, not nearly enough air can flow naturally in warm weather through this crowded shelter's room (only about 39 inches wide by 34 inches high). As proved by habitability tests in Florida and elsewhere, a KAP or Directional Fan must be used, even with two crawlway entry/exits.

The essential second crawlway entry/exit of the Aboveground Door-Covered Shelter was eliminated as the result of a recommendation by a contractor for FEMA charged with field testing and evaluating expedient shelters, and improving abbreviated shelter-building instructions. No habitability tests were required. So the contractor concluded in his 1978 report to FEMA that the second entry/exit should be eliminated because "The building of entries is time consuming and with this small a shelter a second entry is really not justified."

In peacetime, bureaucracies of all nations tend to divide up responsibilities between specialists and to promote means by which non- prestigious wartime problems can apparently be solved with the least expense and work.

Directional Fanning to Ventilate Shelters

The Directional Fanning instructions on the following two pages may save more lives than any other instructions given in this book for a homemakeable survival item. I regret that no one rediscovered this premechanization, simple, yet effective way of manually pumping air until after the original Nuclear War Survival Skills was published.

In 1980, Dr. William Olsen, a NASA research engineer long concerned with improving self- help civil defense, rediscovered one kind of Directional Fanning. Since then, with the assistance of able Americans and others, I have designed and tested several types of Directional Fans. I have field-tested and repeatedly improved the instructions to enable average people to quickly learn how to make and use such fans effectively. The great advantage of Directional

Fanning is that almost anyone who is given the field-tested instructions can quickly make and use one of these simple fans. Only very widely available materials are needed. The main disadvantage is that Directional Fanning is a more laborious way to ventilate a shelter than using KAPs.

Americans are not likely to receive Directional Fanning instructions from the Federal Emergency Management Agency. FEMA's predecessors, the Office of Civil Defense and the Defense Civil Preparedness Agency, were unable to get the millions of dollars necessary to buy factory-made KAPs and other manual air pumps to ventilate officially designated fallout shelters, and FEMA has avoided shelter ventilating controversies. No widely available official American publication includes instructions for making and using any expedient airpumping device.

Thanks to Congressman Ike Skelton, Democrat of Missouri and strong civil defense advocate, in 1981 I was able to demonstrate Directional Fanning to Louis Giuffrida, at that time the Director of FEMA. I gave Directional Fans to the FEMA specialists concerned with shelter ventilation, all of whom have since left FEMA. To date, although Directional Fanning instructions have been reproduced in three private civil defense publications, and some 600 copies of a metric version of the instructions were distributed to British civil defense professionals at the 1984 Annual Study of Civil Defense and Emergency Planning Officers, FEMA has not even evaluated Directional Fanning.

In contrast, in 1981 I gave copies of instructions for both KAPs and Directional Fans to Dr. Yin Zhi-shu, the Director of the People's Republic of China's National Research and Design Institute of Civil Defense - and the next day he started evaluating these simple devices. (At that time I was traveling extensively in China as an official guest, exchanging civil defense information.) Dr. Yin, who heads all Chinese civil defense research and development, went with his top ventilation and shelter design specialists to a furniture factory in Beijing. There I watched workmen quickly build both a large and a small KAP, and also Directional Fans. Then Dr. Yin and his specialists began using their air-velocity meters to measure the volumes of air that these simple devices could pump. On the following days I participated in more ventilation tests using KAPs and Directional Fans in tunnel blast shelters in Beijing and in the port city of Dalien. While watching these top Chinese civil defense professionals make and test KAPs and Directional Fans, I kept thinking: 'This is the way Thomas Edison and Henry Ford would have evaluated simple devices of possible great importance to millions."

The reader is urged to keep the following two pages of Directional Fanning instructions ready for reproduction in a crisis. The sections on the small 2-handled Directional Fan and the large 1-Man Fan will be the most useful to unprepared people. Ventilation by pairs of men using Bedsheet Fans is an effective method for forcing very large volumes of outdoor air through tunnels, corridors and mines with ceilings at least 9 feet high - provided they have two large openings. However, this method requires organization and discipline.

Directional Fanning to Ventilate Shelters

Directional Fanning is the simplest way to force enough outdoor air through typical basement, trench, and other expedient shelters to maintain endurable conditions, even in extremely hot, humid weather.

During a worsening nuclear crisis most unprepared citizens probably will not have the time and/or materials needed to make a KAP or other efficient shelter-ventilating pump - even if they have the instructions. In contrast, tests with average citizens have indicated that if they have instructions for making and using Directional Fans and if there are a few hours of warning time before the attack, then the majority will be able to ventilate all of their expedient shelters, except some of the largest.

The principal disadvantage of Directional Fans is that they are more laborious to operate than are KAPs, that are manually powered, pendulum- like air pumps that conserve energy.

A. Directional Fanning to Ventilate and Cool Smaller Shelters

A 2-Handled Directional Fan of the size illustrated (14 in. x 16 in. with a 6 in. handle) is less tiring to use and requires less manual dexterity than does a 1-handled fan with the same size blade. With this small two handled fan you quite easily can force about 300 cubic feet per minute (300 cfm) of outdoor air through a crowded trench or basement shelter. This is enough air for up to 9 adults crowded into a small shelter in extremely hot humid weather, and enough for about 100 people in cold weather. By fanning vigorously, 500 to 600 cubic feet per minute have been forced through a small covered-trench shelter.

To make a durable 2-handled fan, first make its frame out of 2 sticks each 14 inches long and 2 sticks each 22 inches long. See sketch. To strengthen the corners, overlap the sticks about one-half inch, as shown.

When using sticks cut from a tree, select ones with diameters of about 3' inch, and make shallow notches in all 4 sticks before tying together the 4 corners of the blade. If you do not have strong string, use 1/2 inch-wide strips of bedsheet cloth, or other strong cloth, slightly twisted.

If using sawed sticks, he sure to use none smaller than 3/4 inch in cross section. If you have very small nails or brads, use only one to connect each corner: then tie each corner securely. To prevent possible blistering of hands, wrap cloth around the fan handles, or wear gloves.

To cover the fan's blade, any strong, light fabric, such as bedsheet cloth, serves well If you are going to sew on the cloth, first cuts 26 x 30-inch piece. Wrap the 30-inch width smoothly crosswise around the frame, after cutting 4 notches in the cloth's corners, so that the tied-together parts of the sticks will not he covered. Pin or tape the cloth to make a smooth blade: finally sew securely. (If waterproof construction adhesive is available, a smaller piece of cloth can be used and the blade can be covered in a very few minutes.) If time and/or materials are very limited, make a fan with its blade merely a piece of cloth connecting two 22-inch-long sticks. This very simple fan is reasonably effective, although tiring to use.

Cardboard covering a blade is likely to become damp and fragile in the humid air of a crowded shelter, very light sheetmetal makes a good fan blade and requires only 2 sticks. A blade of 4-inch plywood is too heavy.

If no sticks are available, a double thickness of heavy, stiff cardboard 22 inches long by 14 inches wide will pump almost as much air if used as a handleless fan. The pieces should he securely tied or taped together. If waterproof tape is available, cover the parts that you will grip with sweaty hands, thus preventing dampening and softening the cardboard.

For maximum ventilation, the air-intake opening of a shelter should heat least as large as its air-exhaust opening. (If the air-exhaust opening of your small shelter is much larger than that shown in the sketches, block part of it off to reduce it to approximately this 24-inch-high by 20-inch-wide size, for more effective use with this fan.)

The air should be fanned out of the shelter in the direction in which the air is naturally flowing. For maximum ventilation rate, fan about 40 strokes per minute.

With one or more Directional Fans, air inside a shelter can be distributed effectively and the occupants cooled. Also, if during the time of maximum fallout dose rate the occupants get close together in the most protective part of the shelter, they often will get unbearably hot unless fanned.

To fan air out through an air-exhaust opening, sit facing the opening with your elbows about 4 inches lower than the bottom of the opening. Then count 1, 2, 3 while you:

(1) Quickly raise the fan to a vertical position close in front of your face and immediately fan (push) a slug of air into the opening - ending the power stroke with your arms fully extended and with the fan almost horizontal and out of the

way of air that was "sucked" behind the fan and is still flowing out through the opening.

(2) After a slight pause, leisurely withdraw the almost horizontal fan until the bottom of its blade almost touches your stomach -- preparatory to the next power stroke.

To increase the flow of air through a shelter, while fanning the occupants:

Have two or more occupants sitting inside the shelter each use a fan of the size described above to fan the air so as to increase its velocity in the direction in which air already is flowing through the shelter. Such Directional Fanning is especially effective in increasing the air flow through small, narrow shelters.

To avoid higher radiation exposures near openings, build an essentially airtight partition across the shelter room, with a 24-inch-high x 20-inch-wide hole in it through which to fan. By fanning through a 24 x 20-inch hole in a cardboard partition built across a doorway inside a U- shaped permanent trench shelter 76 feet long, the air flow was increased by an average of :327 cubic feet per minute.

Directional Fanning to Larger Shelters Ventilate and Cool Larger Shelters

To ventilate larger basements, big covered trenches, and other large shelters lacking adequate ventilation, use one or more large 1-man fans. See sketch. Note that the 20 x :30-inch fan blade is made like a 2-stick kite, and that the upper end of the longer diagonal stick serves ass 10-inch handle.

The model illustrated is made of 2 nominal 1 x 2-inch boards, one 46 inches long and the other 35 inches long. These boards are connected at a point 17-1/2 inches from their lower ends, first with a single clinched nail, and then by being tied securely. The edges of the handle are rounded smooth

The blade frame is covered on both sides with strong bedsheet cloth, that is wrapped around and secured to the strong cords or wires tied to notches cut in the boards or sticks) near the 4 corners of the blade. (If cord or wire is not available. 4 2-inch-wide strips of strong cloth, slightly twisted, serve well.)

A durable but laboriously heavy fan can be made in a few' minutes using a 20 x 30-inch piece of 1/4 inch plywood nailed to a single 46-inch-long. 1 x 2- inch hoard. Or use a single round stick about 1-1/4 inches in diameter, flattened on one side.

A fan with its blade made of two sheets of very heavy cardboard tied on both sides of a 1 x 2-inch board is decidedly effective when dry. However, typical cardboard will become soft and worthless in most crowded, long-occupied humid shelters.

To fan directionally, it is best to stand just outside and to one side of a doorway, so that your body does not obstruct the air flow. Preferably stand opposite and facing the open door, which should be secured open and perpendicular to its doorway. Hold the fan like a golf club and swing it with your arms extended. Then slowly count 1, 2 while you:

1. Make the power stroke with the fan blade broadside until the end of the stroke, when you quickly turn it 90 degrees.
2. Make the pendulum-like return stroke with the fan blade kept edgewise)" feathered") to the air flow until the end, when you quickly turn it 90 degrees, preparatory.' to making the next power stroke.

To pump more air, block off the upper part of the doorway with cloth, cardboard, plywood, etc.. to prevent air from flowing back in the wrong direction through the upper part of the doorway. See sketch on preceding page.

Whenever practical, directionally fan the air in the same direction that the air is naturally flowing through the shelter. More air usually can be pumped through a shelter if the fan is used to force air out through the air exhaust opening. This reduces the air pressure inside the shelter and causes fresh outdoor air to be "sucked" into the shelter through the air-intake doorway, or through other large air-intake openings. Thus with one fan 1,000 cubic feet per minute can he pumped through a fully occupied shelter. This is enough outdoor air - if it is properly distributed within the shelter - to maintain tolerable conditions for weeks for 25 occupants during extremely hot weather, and for up to about 300 occupants during cold weather.

To ventilate and cool a room having only one doorway and no other opening, do not block off any part of the doorway. If air is fanned into such a room through the lower part of its completely open doorway, then air will flow back out of the room through the upper part of the doorway. However, this pumps much less air than when a separate, large air-exhaust opening is provided.

To increase the flow of outdoor air through a tunnel-shelter, several fanners equally spaced along its length should each fan in the direction of the natural air flow. This procedure was first proved practical during a 1981 ventilation test that Cresson H. Kearny participated in with Chinese civil defense officials in the port city of Dalien. In this test 5 fanners, each with a fan of approximately the size illustrated, forced air from the outdoors through a 395-foot section between two opened entrances of a typical Chinese tunnel-shelter. The air flow was increased from a natural flow of 290 cubic feet per minute to :3.680 cubic feet per minute. The 5 excellent Chinese fans each had a blade made of a piece of 3 mm (approx. 1/8th in.) plywood nailed to a single board.

With a Bedsheet Fan

Use a 2-man Bedsheet Fan to force thousands of cubic feet per minute of outdoor air through a tunnel or long corridor having at least a 9-foot ceiling and a large opening at each end. The most practical design tested was made from a strong double bedsheet cut down to 6-foot width, with the wide hem at its head-end left unchanged and with a similar- sized hem sewn in its opposite end, to give a finished length of 6 feet. A 6-foot-long, nominal 1 x 2-inch board (or an approximately 1-1/2 inch diameter stick) was secured inside each end hem of various models with waterproof construction adhesive, or with tacks, or by tying. Before a board was inserted, its edges were rounded. Round sticks were smoothed.

Two persons preparing to use a Bedsheet Fan see sketch) should stand facing each other, at right angles to the desired direction of air flow', with the cloth extended horizontally between them. Each fanner should grip his stick with one hand near its "downwind" end and with his other hand near its center.

A pair of Directional Fanners get ready to make a power stroke by leaning in the upwind direction, as illustrated. Then the pair of fanners should count 1, 2, 3 while they:

1. Make the power stroke by rapidly sweeping their sticks and the attached cloth in an arc, until they are leaning in the downwind direction and the sticks and cloth are again horizontal. See sketch.

2,3. Hold the sticks and cloth horizontal (to permit air that was "sucked" behind the cloth to continue flowing in the desired direction) while leisurely moving the Bedsheet Fan back to the starting position. During this move the fanners change hands, as illustrated. Note that what was the upper side of the fan at the beginning of the power stroke now has become the lower side.)

Two men thus fanning vigorously produced a net air flow of 5,500 cubic feet per minute through an empty school corridor that is 8 feet wide, has a 9- foot ceiling, and is 194 feet long. The doors at both ends were open. To adequately ventilate and cool people crowded into a long tunnel in hot weather, a pair of Bedsheet Fanners should be positioned about every 100 feet along its length.

The practicality of using Bedsheet Fans to ventilate some very large mines or caves having 2 or more large openings was proved by tests with members of the Citizens Preparedness Group of Greater Kansas City.

These tests were conducted in 1982 near Kansas City in a huge limestone mine that has a ceiling averaging about 17 feet high, corridors about 35 feet wide, columns of unexcavated rock about 15 feet square, and over 1,000,000 square feet of level, dry floor space.

The air inside is "dead", remarkably still, because the only openings are two truck-sized portals on one side of the mine. Five pairs of Bedsheet Fanners, spaced about 75 feet apart down a corridor, after fanning for several minutes produced a measured air flow of approximately 100,000 cubic feet per minute through this part of this corridor!

With many more pairs of Bedsheet Fanners working, enough air for at least 10,000 occupants could be "sucked" into this mine through one of its 17 x 20-foot portals, fanned down a corridor to the far "dead end" of the mine, then fanned through across corridor, and finally fanned back out through the corridor that has the second truck-sized portal at its outer end.

A pair of pre-mechanization coal miners produced a directed airflow' by holding apiece of canvas vertically between them while they quickly walked a short ways in the direction of the desired airflow; they walked back with the canvas held horizontally between them. Then they repeated.

Additional Advantages of Directional Fans

1. No installation is needed, thus saving working time and materials for making habitable shelters hurriedly built or upgraded during a crisis.
2. Directional Fans enable shelter occupants to quickly reverse the direction of air flow through their shelter when outdoor wind changes cause the direction of natural air flow' to be reversed.
3. Four or more Directional Fans when used to circulate air within a shelter room can serve like air ducts, while simultaneously fanning occupants.
4. Directional Fans are very unlikely to be damaged by blast effects severe enough to wreck bladed fans or other fixed ventilation devices placed at or near air-intake or air-exhaust openings, but not severe enough to injure shelter occupants.

PROTECTION AGAINST FIRES AND CARBON MONOXIDE

Relative Dangers

Fire and its consequences probably would be the third-ranking danger to unprepared Americans subjected to a massive nuclear attack. Direct blast effects would be first, covering a large fraction of densely populated areas and killing far more people. Considerably fewer fatalities seem likely to result from the second-ranking danger, fallout radiation.

The Facts About Fire Hazards

Firestorms would endanger relatively few' Americans; only the older parts of a few American cities have buildings close enough together, over a large enough area, to fuel this type of conflagration. Such fires have not occurred in cities where less than about 30% of a large area was covered with buildings. In the blast area of Hiroshima, a terrifying fire storm that burned almost all buildings within an area of about 4.4 square miles resulted from many fires being ignited almost simultaneously. Many were caused by heat radiation from the fireball. Even more fires were due to secondary effects of the blast, such as the overturning of stoves.

The buildings contained much wood and other combustible materials. The whole area burned like a tremendous bonfire; strong winds that blew in from all directions replaced the huge volumes of hot air that rose skyward from the intense fires.

Lack of oxygen is not a hazard to occupants of shelters in or near burning buildings or to those in shelters that are closed tightly to prevent the entry of smoke or fallout. Carbon monoxide, toxic smoke from fires, or high concentrations of carbon dioxide from shelter occupants' exhaled breaths would kill occupants before they suffered seriously from lack of oxygen.

Fires Ignited by Heat Radiation

Heat radiation will set fire to easily ignitable materials (dry newspapers, thin dark fabrics, dry leaves and dry grass) in about the same extensive areas over which blast causes moderate damage to frame houses. The blast wave and high-speed blast winds will blow out many flames. However, tests have shown that fire will continue to smolder within some materials such as upholstery and dry rotted wood, and after a while it often will burst into flame and will spread. The number of fires started by heat radiation in areas where blast is not severe can be reduced by whitewashing the insides of window panes and by removing flammable materials from places in and around houses where heat radiation could reach them. Also, occupants of shelters in some homes that would be only slightly damaged by blast could move quickly to extinguish small fires and throw out smoldering upholstered articles before fallout is deposited.

Earth-covered shelters can be protected against heat radiation from nuclear explosions and other causes by painting any exposed wood and other combustible materials at shelter openings with a thick coating of slaked lime (old-fashioned whitewash). The World War II firebombing of Kassel was less effective than were similar raids on other German cities because the roof timbers of buildings had been so treated. Chinese civil defense instructions recommend coating exposed wood with both slaked lime and mud. If only mud is available, a coating of it protects wood quite well. If kept damp, a mud coating is even more effective. (Simply keeping all exposed flammable materials damp is helpful.)

In blast areas, cloth or plastic canopies over the openings of expedient shelters usually would be ignited by the heat and certainly would be blown away by even moderate blast winds. If extra canopies and stakes could be made and kept inside the shelter, these replacements could be quickly erected after blast winds subside and before fallout begins at least 15 minutes after the explosion. If no spare canopies were available, it would be best to keep the available canopies and their stakes inside the shelter, if it were not raining.

Forest and Brush Fires

Unless forests or brushy areas are dry, it is difficult to start even scattered fires. Dangerous mass fires would be unlikely, except in blast areas where the heat radiation would be very intense. However, people building a shelter would do well to select a shelter site at least as far away from trees as the height of the tallest tree that could fall on the shelter because of fire and smoke hazards in dry weather, and because digging a shelter among tree roots is difficult.

Causes of Fire

If the blast-wrecked house shown in the illustration had had a furnace in operation when it was demolished, the chances of its being set on fire would have been high. In Hiroshima many of the first fires resulted from secondary effects of blast, especially the overturning of stoves, and not from heat radiation. Although the air burst produced no fallout, firefighters from undamaged, nearby communities were unable to reach most of the burning areas because of blast debris blocking the roads. Later they were kept from burning areas by the intense heat. Some water mains were broken, which made water unavailable for fire fighting in certain areas. In the event of an attack on the United States employing many surface bursts, fallout would prevent fire fighting for days to weeks in a large part of the most populated regions.

The basements of many substantial buildings will withstand 5-psi blast effects and can prevent occupants from suffering serious injuries from blast. Most home basements can be reinforced with stout boards and posts so as to give good protection against blast effects up to considerably higher than 5 psi. But considering the dangers of fires in probable blast areas, it is safer to build an earth-covered shelter well removed from buildings than it is to seek protection in shelters inside buildings.

Carbon Monoxide and Toxic Smoke

If an undamaged building is burning, people inside may be killed by carbon monoxide, toxic smoke, or fiery-hot air. Tests have shown that even fast-burning, rubble-free fires produce very high concentrations of carbon monoxide. If large-scale fires are burning near a shelter, the dangers from both carbon dioxide and carbon monoxide may continue for as long as 1)2 hours after ignition.22 Therefore, the ventilation pipes or openings of a shelter should not be placed close to a building that might be expected to burn.

In the smoldering rubble of a large test fire, after 24 hours the carbon monoxide concentration was still more than 1% and the air temperature was 1900 degrees F. A carbon monoxide concentration of only 0.08% (8 parts CO in 10,000 parts of air) will cause headache, dizziness, and nausea in 45 minutes, and total collapse in 2 hours.

Realization of carbon monoxide dangers to persons in simple fallout shelters and basements may have led the writers of Soviet civil defense publications to define the "zone of total destruction" as the blast areas where the overpressure exceeds 7 psi and "residential and industrial buildings are completely destroyed ... the rubble is scattered and covers the burning structures," and "As a result the rubble only smolders, and fires as such do not occur." Smoldering fires produce more carbon monoxide than do fiercely burning fires. Whether or not the occupants of basement shelters survive the direct blast effects is of little practical importance in those blast areas where the rubble overhead burns or smolders. So in the "zone of complete destruction," Russian rescue brigades plan to concentrate on saving persons trapped inside excellent blast shelters by the rubble.

About 135,000 Germans lost their lives in the tragic city of Dresden during three days of firebomb raids. Most casualties were caused by the inhalation of hot gases and by carbon monoxide and smoke poisoning.20 Germans learned that when these dangers were threatening an air raid shelter, the occupants best chance of survival was to run outside, even if the bombs were still falling. But in a nuclear war the fallout dose rate may be so high that the occupants of a shelter threatened by smoke and carbon monoxide might suffer a more certain and worse death by going outside. Instead, if they know from instrument readings and their calculations that they probably would receive a fatal dose before they could reach another shelter, the occupants should close all openings as tightly as possible. With luck, carbon monoxide in deadly concentrations would not reach them, nor would they be overcome by heat or their own respiratory carbon dioxide before the fire dangers ended.

Dr. A. Broido, a leading experimenter with fires and their associated dangers, reached this conclusion: "If I were building a fallout shelter I would spend a few extra dollars to build it in my backyard rather than in my basement, locating the intake vent as far as possible from any combustible material. In such a shelter I would expect to survive anything except the close-in blast effects."

This advice also applies to expedient shelters built during a crisis.

5

Pre-Crisis Preparations

Your chances of surviving a nuclear attack will be improved if you make the following low-cost preparations before a serious crisis arises. Once many Americans become convinced that a nuclear attack is a near certainty, they will rush to stores and buy all available survival supplies.

If you wait to prepare until a crisis does arise, you are likely to be among the majority who will have to make-do with inadequate supplies of water containers, food, and materials. Furthermore, even if you have the necessary materials and instructions to make the most needed survival items, you and your family are not likely to have time to make all of them during a few days of tense crisis.

The following recommendations are intended primarily for the majority who live in areas likely to be subjected to blast, fire, or extremely heavy fallout. These people should plan to evacuate to a safer area. (Many citizens living outside high-risk areas, especially homeowners with yards, can and should make better pre-crisis preparations. These would include building high-protection-factor permanent shelters covered with earth.)

SHELTER

Keep on hand the tools and materials your family or group will need to build or improve a high- protection-factor expedient shelter: One or more shovels, a pick (if in a hard-soil area), a bow-saw with an extra blade, a hammer, and 4-mil polyethylene film for rainproofing your planned shelter. Also store the necessary nails, wire, etc. needed for the kind of shelter you plan to build.

Keep instructions for shelter-building and other survival essentials in a safe and convenient place.

VENTILATION-COOLING

Make a homemade shelter-ventilating pump, a KAP, of the size required for the shelter you plan to build or use.

WATER

Keep on hand water containers (including at least four 30-gallon untreated polyethylene trash bags and two sacks or pillowcases for each person), a pliable garden hose or other tube for siphoning, and a plastic bottle of sodium hypochlorite bleach (such as Clorox) for disinfecting water and utensils.

FALLOUT METER

Make one or two KFMs and learn how to use this simple instrument.

FOOD

Store at least a 2-week supply of compact, nonperishable food. The balanced ration of basic dry foods, Food, satisfies requirements for adults and larger children at minimum cost. If your family includes babies or small children, be sure to store more milk powder, vegetable oil, and sugar. Continuing to breast-feed babies born during an impending crisis would greatly simplify their care should the crisis develop and worsen

For preparing and cooking basic foods:

- Make a 3-Pipe Grain Mill like the one, Food, or buy a small hand-cranked grain mill, which grinds more efficiently than other expedient devices.
- Make a Bucket-Stove. During evacuation, the stove can be used as a container. Store some kitchen-type wooden matches in a waterproof container.

- Keep essential containers and utensils on hand for storing and transporting food and for cooking and serving in a shelter.

Sanitation

A hose-vented 5-gallon can, with heavy plastic bags for liners, for use as a toilet. Include some smaller plastic bags and toilet paper with these supplies. Tampons. Insect screen or mosquito netting, and fly bait.

Medicines

- Any special medications needed by family members.
- Potassium iodide, a 2-oz bottle, and a medicine-dropper, for prophylactic protection of the thyroid gland against radioactive iodines.
- A first-aid kit and a tube of antibiotic ointment.

Light

- Long-burning candles (with small wicks) sufficient for at least 14 nights.
- An expedient lamp, with extra cotton-string, wicks, and cooking oil.
- A flashlight and extra batteries.

Radio

A transistor radio with extra batteries and a metal box in which to protect it.

Other Essentials

Review the EVACUATION CHECKLIST (developed primarily for persons who make no preparations before a crisis) and add items that are special requirements of your family. Permanent Family Fallout Shelters for Dual Use

The Need

Having a permanent, ready-to-use, well supplied fallout shelter would greatly improve millions of American families' chances of surviving a nuclear attack. Dual use family shelters - shelters that also are useful in peacetime - are the ones that Americans are most likely to build in normal peacetime and to maintain for years in good condition for use in a nuclear war. The longer nuclear peace lasts, the more difficult it will be, even during a recognized crisis, to believe that the unthinkable war is about to strike us and that we should build expedient shelters and immediately take other protective actions. The lifesaving potential of permanent, ready-to-use family shelters will increase with the years.

Americans who decide to build permanent shelters need better instructions than can be obtained from official sources or from most contractors. This chapter brings together fallout shelter requirements, based on shelters and shelter components that have been built and tested in several states and nations. The emphasis is on permanent fallout shelters that many Americans can build for themselves. The author believes that millions of Americans can build good permanent fallout shelters or have local contractors build them - if they learn the shelter requirements outlined in the following sections of this chapter and the facts about nuclear weapon effects and protective measures given in preceding chapters. Builders can use their skills and available local resources to construct permanent, dependable fallout shelters at affordable cost. Requirements for a permanent, dual-use family fallout shelter follow.

A HIGH PROTECTION FACTOR, AT AFFORDABLE COST

A permanent fallout shelter should be built - and can easily be built - to have a high enough protection factor to prevent its occupants from receiving fatal or incapacitating radiation doses, and also from receiving doses large enough to seriously worsen their risks of developing cancer in the years following an attack. Shelters with a protection factor of 40 (PF 40) meet the minimum standard of protection for public shelters throughout the United States, and permanent family fallout shelters described in official pamphlets provide at least PF 40 protection. In almost all fallout areas, PF-

40 shelters would prevent occupants from receiving fatal or incapacitating radiation doses while inside these shelters. However, in areas of heavy fallout the occupants of PF-40 shelters could receive radiation doses large enough to significantly contribute to the risk of contracting cancer years later. Furthermore, the larger the dose you receive while in a shelter, the smaller the dose you can receive after you leave shelter without being incapacitated or killed by your total dose.

If you build a permanent shelter, you would be foolish to build a shelter with a PF of only 40 when additional protection is so easy to obtain. By making a shelter with a 6-inch-thick concrete roof covered by 30 inches of shielding earth, and with other easily attained design features, you can have a shelter with a protection factor of about 1000. (An occupant of a PF 1000 shelter will receive a radiation dose only 1/1000th as large as he would receive if he were standing outside in an open field during the same time interval.)

To attain PF 1000 protection near the inner door of the illustrated shelter, its occupants must place containers full of water and/or other good shielding material against the door. They can do this easily and quickly if the shelter is supplied with filled water containers such as described in the Water section of this chapter.

The illustrated shelter room has 106 square feet of floor space - room enough for 5 adults and the survival essentials they will need for long occupancy, if shelter furnishings like those described in this chapter are provided. For each additional occupant, increase this shelter's length by 2 feet. To increase room size, increase length and not width. This retains maximum roof strength at minimum cost.

The 12-inch-thick concrete wall between the landing at the foot of the stairs and the end of the shelter room. Only a very small fraction of the radiation coming through the outer do· rs and down the stairs will make the 90 degree turn through the inner door, and most of this radiation will not strike shelter occupants if they place containers filled with water and other shielding material against the door.

Also note the homemakeable, low cost Double-Action Piston Pump and filter, that even in a heat wave will supply adequate air through the 5-inch-diameter air- intake pipe.

Few survival-minded Americans, before a recognized international crisis arises, either can afford or believe that they can afford to build a permanent family fallout shelter costing around $10,000 in 1987. A small reinforced concrete, below-ground shelter of the type specified in official Federal Emergency Management Agency pamphlets costs about $100 per square foot of floor space, if built by a contractor in a typical suburban area. Those with the needed skills and time can save about half of this cost by doing their own work. Also, at many building sites where gravity drainage of the earth around a shelter's walls can be assured and hydrostatic earth pressure against the walls thus prevented, no steel reinforcement in the poured concrete or concrete block walls is needed - unless required by the local building code.

Caution: Steel reinforcement in the walls and floor is needed in some clay soils that swell when wet and exert sufficient inward and upward pressure to crack unreinforced walls and floor slabs. Consult local builders who have learned from experience whether wall and floor reinforcement is needed in the type of soil where you plan to build. If needed, a grid of 1/2-inch rebars, spaced at 12 inches, usually is adequate.

To save money on steel reinforcement, check prices in salvage yards for used rebars and substitute reinforcing materials such as junked cable and small pipes.

How to safely pour a shelter's concrete roof slab without using a contractor's usual forms and equipment. These drawings show 8-ft.-long sheets of 3/4-inch plywood supported at their ends on shelter walls 7 feet-6 inches apart. Preparatory to pouring the concrete, the plywood sheets should be supported along the centerline of the shelter by 4"x4"s and other lumber, which can be used later to build seats and overhead bunks. Plywood left on the ceiling reduces condensation and heating problems in cold weather, but increases the volume of outdoor air that must be pumped through the shelter to maintain tolerable temperatures when it is occupied in hot weather. This was clearly demonstrated in the summer of 1963 when the author used SIMOCS (simulated occupants that produce heat and water vapor like people) to determine the habitability of a six-roomlet below ground group shelter, with a reinforced concrete roof that had been built in this manner by six New Jersey farm families. They had left ordinary 3/4-inch exterior plywood on the ceiling. Because the hollow concrete wall-blocks and the well drained gravel under the floor also kept heat from escaping into the surrounding soil, and because only natural ventilation was provided, the temperature/humidity became dangerously high within a few hours.

Insulating a shelter's walls and ceiling can be disadvantageous, because insulation makes unavailable the "heat sink" of the shelter and its surrounding earth. In hot weather insulation reduces the time during which ventilation can be stopped or restricted without disastrously overheating the occupants.

Today, for such a shelter it would be better to use pressure-treated, rot-proof plywood and lumber, approved by leading building codes. For information, write to the American Plywood Association, P.O. Box 11700, Tacoma, WA 98411, inquiring about rot-proof plywood, dimensional lumber, and other material used in building the All-Weather Wood Foundation. Most lumber yards will obtain treated plywood on order, and sell it for about 50% more than ordinary exterior grade plywood.

Big savings in shelter construction costs are made by using salvaged and/or used materials. Manufacturers of pre-cast reinforced concrete beams and floor sections often sell rejects for very little.

Most salvage yards have steel beams and other material that make excellent roofing for earth-covered shelters. (Shortly before the Cuban Missile Crisis, when living near New York, I built for myself at modest cost a very small shelter on a well drained hillside. I made it almost entirely of steel channels bought and cut to order at a salvage yard.) Used cylindrical steel tanks with closed ends often make good low-cost permanent shelters. One of the best low-cost family shelters that I ever went into was on a hillside overlooking San Francisco Bay. It was made of a salvaged steel brewing tank that had been installed after a vertical cylindrical entrance with a door had been welded on it. The tank's exterior had been protected with a bituminous coating. Its survival-minded owner was a brilliant Hungarian refugee who, as a boy, had survived in a deep wine cellar throughout the Russian siege and shelling of Budapest. Nothing equals war experience to teach the lifesaving value of shelters.

MINIMIZATION OF FIRE AND CARBON MONOXIDE DANGERS

Many shelter designers and builders do not realize the probable extent of fires after a major nuclear attack. Nor do the big majority of them provide shelters built under or close to a house with adequate protection against the entry of deadly amounts of carbon monoxide if the house burns. Although the areas of fires resulting from a nuclear explosion generally will be about as extensive as the areas of significant blast damage, on a clear day a house up to about 8 miles from ground zero can be ignited by the thermal pulse of a 1-megaton airburst. This photograph indicates how a thermal pulse can go through window glass and ignite curtains, upholstery, or dry paper, even if flammable material outdoors is too damp to be ignited. Furthermore, fires from any cause can spread, especially in fallout areas following a nuclear attack when firefighters may be unable or unwilling to expose themselves outdoors to radiation.

Good protection against carbon monoxide is provided by a permanent earth-covered shelter, built with its entry outdoors and well separated from a house and other flammable structures, and constructed so that it can be closed gas-tight. Both the air-intake and the air-exhaust pipes should be installed so that they can be quickly closed air-tight, as with screw-on fittings. Such closures should be kept well greased and securely attached close to where they would be used. If a shelter's entry is through a passageway from a house, a gasketted steel firedoor, insulated on the shelter side, should be installed near the house end of the passageway. The shelter should be further protected by a second gas.tight door, to prevent the entry of carbon monoxide and smoke if heat from the burning house destroys the gasket on the firedoor. If special firedoor gaskets are not available, rubber weather-stripping will serve. To lessen the risk of carbon monoxide being pumped into the shelter if the house burns and air must be pumped into the shelter while the fire still is smoldering, the air-intake and pump should be at the far end of the shelter, and the air-exhaust pipe and emergency exit should be near the passageway from the house.

Be sure to seal electrical conduits leading from a basement to a connected shelter, so that if the house burns carbon monoxide can not flow through the conduits into the shelter when fresh outdoor air is not being pumped into the shelter. The author, while conducting ventilation and habitability tests of an earth-covered blast shelter connected through a tunnel to a house's basement, observed air flowing out through unsealed conduits, the reverse of such a possible life-endangering flow of carbon monoxide. When the shelter was being maintained at a slight overpressure by cranking its blower to pump in outdoor air, a little air flowed through the unsealed conduit into the basement.

For ways to minimize carbon monoxide dangers arising from cooking, heating, lighting, and smoking, see following sections in this chapter.

Remember that air contaminated with only 0.16% carbon monoxide can kill you in 2 to 3 hours, and 0.04% carbon monoxide causes frontal headaches and nausea in 2 to 3 hours. The Navy sets its safe allowable carbon monoxide concentration in air at 0.01%.

PREVENTION OF CRACKS AND WET SHELTER PROBLEMS

If wet basements are a problem in your locality, below ground shelters are likely to be wet and unsatisfactory unless appropriate preventative measures are taken during their design and construction.

When making plans, you should consult local builders of satisfactory basements. You also should question persons who at various times of the year have observed excavations, holes, and/or basements in your immediate vicinity, or have noted seasonal swampy places or springs.

The most difficult type of shelter to keep dry for decades is one that is wholly or partially below the water table for part or all of the year. Concrete is not completely watertight. Waterproof coatings and coverings often are damaged during construction, or deteriorate with age. Shelter walls sometimes crack due to settling and earth movements. Metal shelters usually develop small leaks long before they become dangerously weakened.

A 100-occupant, below ground shelter, built in 1984 near Dallas, Texas as a prototype blast shelter for industrial workers, was flooded when the water table rose. The poorly sealed opening of this shelter's emergency exit was below ground level, and after heavy rains was below the water table. A prudently designed shelter has the top of its emergency exit slightly above the surface of the surrounding earth. All underground electric conduits leading down into a shelter must be well sealed to prevent entry of water.

To prevent a wholly or partially below water-table shelter from becoming wet inside sooner or later, it should have a sump and an automatic sump pump to discharge water to the ground outside. If at any time you find that the sump pump is discharging an appreciable amount of water, you may have a serious wet- shelter problem if electric power fails after an attack. Shelter roof surfaces should be gently sloped, no matter how good a waterproof coating is to be applied. By making a concrete shelter roof as little as 1 inch thicker along its centerline than along its sides, so that it slopes to both sides, the prospects are improved for having an earth-covered coated roof that will not leak for decades.

* Put a layer of gravel or crushed rock in the bottom of the excavation, and install perforated drainage pipes if gravity drainage is practical.

* Cover the gravel or crushed rock in the floor area with a plastic vapor barrier before pouring a concrete floor.
* Coat the outer surfaces of roof and walls withbituminous waterproofing or other coating that has proved to be most effective in your locality.

Backfill with gravel or crushed rock against the walls, to keep the soil from possibly becoming saturated. Saturated soil exerts hydrostatic pressure against walls, and may crack them and cause them to leak. In some areas it is more economical to cover a shelter's coated walls with a subsurface drainage mattin. This will eliminate the costs of backfilling with gravel or crushed rock.

NON-FLOATABLE SHELTERS

In most localities the water table usually is below the depth of excavation needed to build or install a belowground shelter. In some areas, however, after rainy periods the water table may rise until it is only a foot or two below the surface. Then a watertight shelter may float upward through the surrounding saturated soil, unless its weight plus the weight of its covering earth is sufficient to withstand its buoyancy.. (In many places swimming pools are kept full to prevent them from being cracked by uneven buoyant forces if the water table rises.)

Dramatic examples of floating shelters were steel blast shelters, guaranteed by contractors to be watertight, that were installed under the lawns of some Houston, Texas homes shortly after the Cuban Missile Crisis. When the water table rose after heavy rains, these shelters came up to the surface like giant mushrooms, to the frustrated dismay of their owners and the satisfaction of anti-defense newspaper feature writers. The most expensive permanent family fallout shelter described in a Federal Emergency Management Agency free handout (pamphlet H-12-1) is floatable. Itis designed to be built of reinforced concrete covered by a flagstone patio only about 3 inches above the ground. Its 6-inch- thick concrete roof is covered by a total thickness of only 6 inches of sand and flagstone. Like the rest of FEMA's permanent shelters, no prototype of this approximately PF-40 shelter was built, nor is there any record of anyone actually having built this shelter.

ADEQUATE, DEPENDABLE VENTILATION/ COOLING

Basic facts that you need to provide adequate, dependable ventilation for a small or medium sized shelter, Ventilation and Cooling of Shelters. A good permanent shelter has two ventilation systems:

- The primary ventilation system of a small permanent shelter should utilize a manually operated centrifugal blower, or a homemade Plywood Double-Action Piston Pump. A satisfactory air pump must be capable of supplying adequate outdoor air through an air-intake pipe, a filter, and an air exhaust pipe. "Adequate outdoor air" for a small shelter means at least 15 cubic feet per minute per occupant for the cooler parts of the United States, and at least 30 cfm per occupant in most of the country. Most permanent shelters have centrifugal blowers that can not deliver an adequate volume of air in hot weather for each planned occupant. For a medium sized permanent shelter, installing two or more manually powered air pumps is both more dependable and more economical than providing an emergency generator and its engine to supply power to an electric blower. The Swiss, who have made the world's best and most expensive per capita preparations to survive a war, use one or more hand-cranked centrifugal blowers to ventilate most of their shelters.
- The multi-week and/or emergency ventilation system of a permanent shelter that has an emergency exit should depend on a homemade KAP, made before a crisis and kept ready to use. By opening both the entrance and the emergency exit, the shelter is provided with two large, low- resistance openings through which a KAP can pump large volumes of air with minimum work.

Warning: Keep screen doors and/or screen panels ready to protect all openings against the swarms of flies and mosquitoes likely to become dangerous pests in fallout areas. Use your KAP to pump adequate air through screens. Insect screens greatly reduce natural ventilation, as the author first noted in Calcutta while a bedridden patient in a stifling hot ward of a hastily constructed Army hospital. Because there were no fans or blowers to pump in outdoor air or circulate the air inside, window screens were opened in the daytime when malaria mosquitoes were not flying. The doctors correctly concluded that the temperature reduction when the screens were opened helped the patients more than they were endangered by the entering filthy flies. Adequate ventilation is more important than protection from flies, but with a KAP and insect screens you can have both. Flies, mosquitoes, and other insects can be killed very effectively by occasionally spraying or painting screens and other alighting surfaces with water solutions of insecticides containing permithin and sold in many farm stores.

ADVICE ON VENTILATION OPENINGS AND FITTINGS

- Install ventilation pipes large enough to reduce resistance to airflow, thus increasing the volume of air that the shelter's pump can deliver. A shelter with a 200-cfm pump (such as the homemakeable Plywood Double-Action Piston Pump described in Appendix E) should have 5-inch galvanized steel pipe. The pumps that are installed in most family shelters deliver only about 100 cfm or less. Four-inch pipe is adequate for use with pumps this small, provided that the pipes have no more than two right-angle turns below each gooseneck. (A 90- degree L gives about as much resistance to airflow as 12 feet of straight pipe.)
- Make and install a gooseneck with its mouth about twice the diameter of the pipe. The purpose of such a gooseneck is to prevent more of the larger descending fallout particles from being pumped or blown into the shelter. For example,

if 200 cfm of air is being pumped into a shelter through a gooseneck of 5-inch-diameter pipe with its mouth also 5 inches in diameter, the velocity of the air up into the mouth of the gooseneck is about 1,440 feet per minute, and sand-like spherical particles smaller than approximately 500 microns in diameter also are "sucked" up. But if the 5-inch gooseneck's mouth is 10 inches across, then the upward air velocity is reduced to about 360 feet per minute, and only particles smaller than approximately 180 microns across are "sucked" up. Particles in the 180 to 500 micron-diameter range are relatively large and fall to earth in about 40 to 70 minutes from 35,000 feet, the base of the mushroom cloud of a 1-megaton explosion. These particles are very dangerous because their radioactivity has had little time to decay, and should be kept out of a shelter's ventilation system. Furthermore, large particles retained in a shelter's filter restrict airflow sooner than do small ones. (If an appropriately curved piece of 5-inch steel pipe cannot be found in a salvage yard or elsewhere, a good welder can use 5-inch steel pipe to make a substitute gooseneck with two 90-degree turns.)

° Do not use air intake hoods on a permanent shelter's pipes, because hoods are not as effective as goosenecks in preventing fallout particles from entering ventilation pipes. Also, pumping a given volume of air through a hood is more work than pumping the same volume through a gooseneck with equal cross-sectional areas.

° Never install any screen inside a gooseneck or air intake hood, because spider webs and the debris that sticks to webs will greatly reduce airflow. The author saw a gooseneck with a blast valve built inside it; spider webs and attached trash on this blast valve had consequentially reduced the volume of air that this shelter's pump could deliver. Of course a screen is much more easily obstructed than a blast valve. Yet FEMA's widely distributed pamphlets on a permanent Home

Fallout Shelter (H-12-1) and on a Home Blast Shelter (H-12-3) continue in successive editions to give detailed instructions for making an air intake hood with a screen soldered inside it. But these shelters that never have been built have much more serious weaknesses, including the likelihood that the aboveground parts of the ventilation pipes of the blast shelter would be bent over or broken off by blast-wind-hurled parts of buildings and trees, even in suburbia. (350 mph is the maximum velocity of the blast wind where the blast overpressure is 15 psi from a 1-megaton air burst.6 The ventilation openings of the blast- tested expedient blast shelters are much more likely to remain serviceable after being subjected to severe blast effects, because blast-protector logs are placed around their openings, that are only a few inches above ground level.)

PREVENTION AND CONTROL OF CONDENSATION

A shelter can be watertight, yet at certain seasons of the year its walls, ceiling, and floor can be dripping wet with water condensed from entering outdoor air. (This is a serious problem, except in arid parts of the West.) During the winter months a shelter and its surrounding earth get cold; then especially on some spring days the dew point of entering outdoor air is higher than the temperature of the shelter's interior surfaces. As a result, condensation occurs on those surfaces that are cooler than the dew point of the pumped-through air.

The most dramatic example that I have observed of the seriousness of this condensation problem was the dripping ceiling and wet walls of a reinforced-concrete, family-sized shelter that I inspected on an early spring day at the Civil Defence College in Yorkshire, England.

Such condensation also can occur in above- ground structures. Before World War II I had a 600-year-old bedroom in Queen's College, Oxford University. My bedroom's outer wall was made of solid limestone blocks about 15 inches thick, simply plastered and painted on the inside. On some spring days moisture condensed on the inside of the cold outer wall, ran down, and collected in little puddles on the floor. The occasional small coal fire in my adjacent study was barely sufficient to gradually evaporate the water and reduce my bedroom's humidity enough to prevent mold frorn forming. This often-repeated occurrence proves the inadequacy of merely keeping an electric light turned on for heat to prevent condensation inside an uninsulated shelter built in a cool, frequently humid locality.

Condensation and resultant 100 percent humid air can rust and eat away most steel pipes. Ventilation pipes should be made of galvanized steel or other materials that are undamaged by seasonal condensation and 100 percent humidity. In Connecticut I saw shelter ventilation pipes made of steel protected with twocoats of marine paint; they were badly rusted only two years after installation.

Operating a dehumidifier with automatic controls is the most practical way for most people to prevent condensation and other dampness problems in a shelter during peacetime. Almost all of the Chinese shelters that I inspected in six cities are dual-use shelters and typically are equipped with large dehumidifiers. A small dehumidifier adequate for a family shelter can be bought from a dependable mail order company, such as Sears, for about $250 in 1987. To save floor space and facilitate removal of water, a dehumidifier should be installed near a shelter's ceiling. Then water from the dehumidifier can be disposed of most easily through a pipe or tube providing gravity drainage, best to the outdoors, second best to the sewer. (After a nuclear attack the sewer system may become clogged and sewage may back up and flow into a belowground room having pipes that normally discharge into the sewer, and that lack check valves.) If the above mentioned ways of removing water are not possible, a sump and an automatic sump pump discharging water to the ground outdoors can solve the peacetime water disposal problem.

After an attack, electric power can be expected to fail and shelter humidity will have to be controlled as much as possible by ventilation with outdoor air. A simple way to learn when to ventilate a shelter to dry it was described in a Russian article on shelter management: Keep several small cans of water in the shelter.

They will be at about the same temperature as the shelter walls when the shelter is closed and is not being ventilated. If a filled can is exposed to outdoor air for about 10 minutes and moisture condenses on it (as a glass filled with an iced drink "sweats" on a humid summer day), do not ventilate the shelter. If no moisture condenses on the can, ventilate.

A WALK-IN ENTRANCE

Only a small fraction of permanent family shelters without a walk-in entrance have been kept in good condition for many years. Permanent family shelters with vertical or crawl- in entrances are found so inconvenient that the big majority of owners do not use them even for rotated food storage. In normal peacetime, most well informed Americans concerned with protecting their families conclude that only a shelter skillfully designed for dual use justifies the cost of building and maintaining it. Significantly, Chinese civil defense has come to the same conclusion regarding Chinese permanent public shelters: those that have been built, and that still are being built, are almost all useful both in peacetime and in wartime.

If a family can use its shelter without having to go outside and be exposed to rain, snow, cold, or night problems, its dual use shelter will be a more valuable peacetime asset than a shelter not directly connected to the house. Furthermore, a directly connected shelter can be entered more quickly in a crisis, and probably will reduce post-attack exposures to fallout radiation received by persons carrying things into the shelter, or by those moving about post-attack to protect the home. The main disadvantages of a directly connected shelter are that it usually provides poorer protection against heat, smoke and carbon monoxide if the house burns and that it is more expensive to build than an earth-covered shelter with an outdoor walk-in entrance.

AN EMERGENCY EXIT THAT ALSO PROVIDES A SECOND LARGE VENTILATION OPENING

Having an emergency exit in a fallout shelter is not as important as having one in a blast shelter, unless the fallout shelter is under or connected to a building. (Since buildings are likely to burn, it is important to have a means of escape.) However, an emergency exit makes any shelter more practical to live in than a shelter with only one large opening - especially in a heavy fallout area where it may be necessary to stay inside most of the time for weeks or months. Occupants of a shelter with only one large opening will not have adequate natural ventilation and will have to keep laboriously pumping air - at least intermittently - through the air-supply pipes to maintain liveable temperature and/or humidity conditions.

By opening both a shelter's entrance and its emergency exit, and taking measures to prevent the entry of rain, snow, and all but the smallest fallout particles, natural ventilation will be adequate most of the time, except in hot, calm weather. With two large openings, a homemade KAP can be used to pump enough outdoor air through the shelter, with much less work than is required to pump less air with a relatively high-pressure pump through typical ventilation pipes.

A DEPENDABLE, HIGH-PROTECTION FACTOR EMERGENCY EXIT

Occupants of a shelter with a dependable emergency exit will have less fear of being trapped if the main entry is blocked. If they open the exit, they also will be able to ventilate the shelter with natural ventilation through the entry and the exit, or with forced ventilation by operating a KAP.

To provide excellent radiation protection, a typical high-PF emergency exit is filled with sand. Such an exit has a bolted-on steel plate on its bottom inside the shelter, and an easily cut, waterproof, plastic-film covering over its top, which is a few inches below ground level. Obvious disadvantages of this typical sand- filled emergency exit include the difficulty of safely removing the bottom plate while sand is pressing down on it, and the impossibility of cutting the plastic film over the top of the exit without having fallout-contaminated earth fall on the person who does the cutting, and into the shelter room. Furthermore, if the earth covering the top of an emergency exit is frozen, occupants may be unable to break through it and get out.

An improved design of sand-filled emergency exit was conceived by Dr. Conrad V. Chester of Oak Ridge National Laboratory and in 1986 was further improved, built, and tested in a full-scale model by the author. The sand in this 26 x 26-inch square vertical exit was supported by a piece of 3/4- inch exterior plywood, that should be of the previously mentioned rot-proof type, pressure impregnated with wood preservative.

In the center of this 25-1/2 x 25-1/2-inch plywood sand-support was an 8-inch-diameter hole covered with two thicknesses of strong nylon cloth.

The double thickness of cloth was firmly attached to the plywood by being folded over four 3/16-inch galvanized steel rods, that were stapled to the plywood with galvanized poultry- netting staples. The nylon cloth covering the hole can be easily and quickly cut with a knife, permitting sand to fall harmlessly into the shelter room.

The square 26 x 26-inch plywood sand-support rests on a 1-1/2-inch-wide rim or ledge around the 23 x 23- inch square hole in the shelter's reinforced concrete roof slab. After a shelter occupant has cut out the nylon cloth covering the hole and all but about 30 lbs of sand has fallen or been pushed by his hand down into the shelter room, he can tilt the plywood sand-support up into a vertical position, and then turn it 45 degrees. The 26-inch width of the sand-support permits it to beeasily lifted down through the 32.5-inch-long diagonal of the 23 x 23-inch square hole in the shelter's roof slab.

Because the exit of this shelter was not made perfectly square, the sand-support could be tilted most easily from its horizontal position into the vertical position if it was oriented so that its side marked "N" was to the north. A similar 'N" arrow on the lower side of this sand-support enabled a man below it, after the exit's lid was tied down and before the exit was filled with sand, to position the sand-support for easy tilting and removal when the last of the sand was being cleared from this exit. The sand support should be cut to fit the exit after the exit is completed, because it is difficult to build an exit exactly to specified dimensions.

The top of the emergency exit should be a few inches above the earth around it, to prevent rainwater on the ground from possibly running in. Securely cover the exit's top with a lid of 1/8-inch galvanized steel having a threaded plug-hole (cut from a steel barrel) welded over a hole cut in the lid's center. Such a lid can be closely fitted to the top of a concrete exit by oiling it and pressing it against the concrete before the concrete begins to set.

Before filling the exit with sand, while inside the exit tie the lid down on each of its four sides with nine loops of 3/32-inch nylon cord repeatedly tightened between four galvanized steel loops welded to the lower side of the lid, and four loops set in the shelter's walls and roof slab. Use pliers to tighten, stretch, and hold the nylon cord while making the loops. Then after the plywood sand- support is positioned in the bottom of the exit, the exit can be filled by pouring dry sand through the plug-hold in the steel lid. Finally, the plug-hole should be closed so that it cannot be opened, and then made waterproof. To make doubly sure that the lid will not rust, paint it with a cement paint, and then with whatever color outdoor paint you want.

A shelter occupant can cut out the nylon cloth covering the hole in the sand-support, remove all sand and the plywood sand-support from this exit, cut the four tightened nylon-cord multiple loops holding down the lid, push off the lid, and then climb up and step outside - all in less than 5 minutes, even if damp sand has been used to fill the exit. (To make removal of the sand more difficult, in his tests the author used damp sand that does not flow freely and makes it necessary to loosen it repeatedly, with one's hand and arm thrust up through the 8-inch hole in the plywood sand-support.)

In a well designed blast shelter this sandfilled emergency exit will provide excellent protection against severe blast. Blast tests have proved that a 1/8-inch steel lid (the equivalent of a blast door) the size of this exit's lid will withstand blast effects of at least 50 psi. Furthermore, sand arching will transfer blast loadings on the sand outward from the slightly downward deflecting plywood sand-support to its edges, and thence to the supporting reinforced concrete rim or ledge around the 23 x 23-inch hole in the shelter's roof slab.

A small shelter with an emergency exit near its far end has additional advantages: It can be supplied with adequate natural ventilation most of the time, with easy forced ventilation by a KAP when forced ventilation is needed, and with daylight illumination.

ADEQUATE STORAGE SPACE FOR ESSENTIALS

As will be shown in the following sections of this chapter, about 20 square feet of shelter floor area per family member is needed for shelter furnishings and to store adequate water for a month, a year's supply of compact dry foods, cooking and sanitary equipment, blankets, tools, and other post-attack essentials. Twenty square feet per family member also provides enough space per person to store winter clothing and footwear, camping equipment, and foods normally kept on hand and rotated as consumed in the course of ordinary family living. Additional space is needed if you plan to use your shelter as a workshop, or as a fallout shelter to save a few of your unprepared friends without endangering your own family.

SEATS/BUNKS/SHELVES

Seats and overhead bunks built like those enable more shelter occupants to sit and sleep more comfortably in less space than when using any other shelter furnishings known to the author. Note that the seat has an adjustable backrest. This backrest is similar to the finemesh nylon fishnet backrests tested in a prototype of an expensive blast shelter designed and furnished at Oak Ridge National Laboratory. Shelter habitability tests have proved the need for backrests. Even some young German soldiers had painfully sore backs after sitting on ordinary benches during a 2-week shelter occupancy test.

Backrests should be installed in peacetime and kept ready for crisis use, rolled up against their upper attachments and covered. Then easily removable storage shelves, if needed, can be installed between benches and overhead bunks.

To sit or sleep comfortably, pull the bedsheet forward and then sit on about the outer foot of the 2-foot-wide seat.

Although this 5-occupant shelter is illustrated with a bunk for each family member, it is prudent to count on stored supplies making some bunks unusable, and to realize that in a desperate crisis it might be hard to refuse shelter to an unprepared good neighbor. Note that with four persons seated on a 6.5-foot-long seat and one person on the overhead bunk, five persons can be quite comfortably accommodated on 25 square feet of floorspace, including plenty of room for the sitters' legs.

To store the most supplies in a shelter, you should install shelves after you know the heights of the items to be stored. Often the space between an overhead bunk and the ceiling can best be used by making easily removable additional shelves.

WATER

- Water needs: Even most well-maintained shelters do not have enough water for prolonged occupancy. A permanent shelter should provide each occupant with at least 30 gallons of safe water - enough for an austere month, except in very hot weather.
- Containers: The most practical water container for shelter storage is a 5-gallon rigid plastic water can with a handle, a large diameter opening for quick filling and emptying, and a small spout for pouring small quantities. A 5- gallon water can of this type sells for about $5 in discount stores.

The plastic bottles that household chlorine bleach is sold in also are good for multi-year storage of drinking water, as are glass jugs. Plastic milk jugs are not satisfactory, because after a few years they often become brittle and crack.

Some shelter owners do not realize that, although a shelter can be kept dry in peacetime, except in the arid West its air is likely to become extremely humid after a few days of crowded occupancy. Very humid air soon softens and weakens cardboard containers of food and flexible water bags.

- Disinfecting for multi-year storage: To store safe water and keep it safe for years, first disinfect the container by rinsing it with a strong solution of chlorine bleach. Then rinse it with safe water before filling it with the clear, safe water to be stored. Next, disinfect by adding household bleach that contains 5.25% sodium hypochlorite as its only active ingredient, in the quantities specified in this book's Water chapter for disinfecting muddy or cloudy water. To 5 gallons, add 1 scant teaspoon of bleach. Finally, to prevent possible entry of air containing infective organisms through faulty closures, seal the container's closures with duct tape.
- Making efficient use of storage space: A 5- gallon rigid plastic water container typically measures 7 x 12 x 21 inches, including the height of its spout. Nine such 5-gallon containers can be placed on a 2 x 3-foot floor area. Twenty-seven 5-gallon containers, holding 135 gallons of water, can be stored on and over 6 square feet of floor if you make a water storage stand 24 x 42 x 48 inches high, built quite like the seat with overhead bunk described in the Seats/ Bunks/ Shelves section of this chapter. This easily moveable storage stand should have two plywood shelves, one 24 inches and the other 48 inches from the floor.
- Using filled containers for shielding: Filled 5-gallon water containers can be moved quickly to provide additional shielding where needed to increase the protection factor of

all or part of a shelter. For example, near the inner door of the shelter illustrated by Figs. 17.1 and 17.2 the protection factor is less than 1000. But if enough filled water containers are placed so as to cover the door with almost the equivalent of an 18- inch-thick "wall" of shielding water, the PF of the part of the shelter room near the door can be raised to about PF 1000.

If a shelter has twenty-seven 5-gallon cans of water stored on and under the above-described 2-shelf water storage stand, then in less than 3 minutes 2 men can shield the shelter door quite adequately. All they have to do is take the 18 cans off the shelves, put 9 of them on the floor against the door and doorway, move the storage stand over the 9 door-shielding cans, and place the remaining 18 cans on the stand's 2 shelves.

Equally good doorway shielding can be provided by placing at least a 24-inch thickness of containers full of dense food, such as whole- grain wheat or sugar, against the doorway. Two 55-gallon drums of wheat, each weighing about 400 pounds, can be quickly "walked" on a concrete floor and positioned so as to shield the lower part of a doorway. Heavy containers on the floor can provide a stable base on which to stack other shielding material.

° A water well: The best solution to the water problem quite often is a well inside the shelter. In many areas the water table is less than 50 feet below the surface, and a 50-foot well, cased with 6-inch steel pipe, can be drilled and completed for about $2000. Well drilling should be done after the shelter excavation has been dug and before the concrete shelter floor has been poured. An in-shelter well would be of vital importance not only to the occupants of a family shelter, but later on probably to nearby survivors.

Even if only a gallon or so an hour could be bailed from a well too weak to be useful in peacetime, it wouldbe a tremendous family asset post-attack. If infective organisms are found in water from a well drilled to provide water during and after an attack, safe water for months can be assured by merely storing a few gallons of household chlorine bleach.

If enough water for worthwhile peacetime use can be pumped from a well, install a submersible electric pump, with plastic pipe in the well. Then in an emergency the pipe and the attached pump can be pulled by hand out of the well, with only a saw being needed to cut off lengths of the plastic pipe as it is pulled. After thewell casing has been cleared of pump, pipe and wires, a homemade 2-foot-long bail-bucket on a nylon rope can be used to draw plenty of water.

- Local water sources: Most Americans' normal piped water would not run for months after a large nuclear attack. A month's supply of water stored in your shelter should be adequate, because, even if your area has heavy fallout, in less than a month radioactive decay will make it safe to haul water from nearby sources.

An important part of your shelter preparations is to locate nearby wells, ponds, streams, and streambeds that when dry frequently have water a foot or two below the surface. The author has found that digging a water pit in an apparently dry streambed often supplies enough filtered water to satisfy several families' basic needs. To keep the sides of a water pit dug in unstable ground from caving in, you should drive a circle of side-by-side stakes around the outside of your planned pit before starting to dig. With more work and materials, you and other survivors needing filtered water could dig a well like the Chinese water source. If you are in a fallout area, before drinking water from a water pit you should filter it through clayey soil to remove fallout particles and dissolved radioactive isotopes, as described in the Water chapter. Of course it is prudent to chlorinate or boil all surface and near-surface water after it has been filtered.

FOOD

- Advantages of a one-year supply: A family that expends the money and work to build and provision its own shelter should store a year's supply of long-lasting foods. If post-attack conditions enable you to continue living and making a living near your home, having a year's food supply will be a tremendous advantage. And if your area is afflicted with such dangerous, continuing fallout radiation and/or other post-attack conditions that surviving unprepared residents are soon forced to evacuate to better areas, then your and your family's chances will be better if hunger does not force you to move during the chaotic first few months after a nuclear attack.

The delivered costs listed in the right hand column include UPS shipping charges in the nearest and least expensive of UPS's 8 zones. For UPS shipping costs to the most distant points in the 48 states, add 34 cents per pound delivered.

All the foods in this survival ration, if stored in moisture-proof and insect-proof containers (the non-fat milk powder should be in nitrogen-packed cans), will provide healthful nutrition for at least 10 years. The exception is themulti-vitamin tablets, which should be replaced every 2 or 3 years, depending on storage temperature. So a family that spends about $300 per member on such a one year survival ration can consider that each of its members has been covered by famine insurance for $30 a year.

Scurvy will be the first incapacitating, then lethal vitamin deficiency to afflict unprepared, uninformed Americans. A multi-vitamin tablet contains enough vitamin C to fully satisfy the daily requirement.

However, a prudent shelter owner also should store vitamin C tablets, that keep for years. One hundred 500-mg generic vitamin C tablets -50,000 mg of vitamin C - in 1987 typically cost about $1.20 in a discount store; a 10 mg daily dose prevents scurvy. After a nuclear war in some areas vitamin C will be worth many times its weight in gold.

Wheat: If you live in a wheat producing area, the least expensive sources of ready-to- store wheat usually are local seed-cleaning firms. A hundred pounds or more of hard wheat, dried, bagged, and ready to store in moisture proof containers, costs about 10 cents a pound. (Today the wheat farmer receives about 4.5 cents a pound for truckloads, usually straight out of the field, not dry enough to store except in well ventilated granaries, and containing trash that makes weevil infestations more likely.) In some communities a few stores sell big bags of dry, cleaned hard wheat for 20 to 35 cents a pound.

Shelter owners who are unable or unwilling to obtain wheat from such sources can buy high protein hard wheat at higher prices from health food stores and a few mail order companies. The lowest mail order FOB price known to the author for hard western wheat in 1990 is $3.17 for 10 pounds, in a vacuum-packed metallized plastic bag similar to the containers used for some U.S. Army combat rations. This long-lasting wheat, as well as other grains and legumes, is sold by Preparedness Products, 3855 South 500 West, Salt Lake City, Utah 84115. Another reliable mail order source of wheat and other dry foods packaged for multi-year storage is The Survival Center, 5555 Newton Falls Rd., Ravenna, Ohio 44266.

* Beans, like wheat, in many communities can be purchased from local farmers' co-ops or local stores at much lower delivered cost than from mail order firms. In one small Colorado town the co-op sold 25 pounds of pinto beans in a polyethylene bag for $1 1.25-45 cents a pound. Local supermarkets sell bulk pinto beans for around 60 cents a pound.
* Non-fat milk powder in 1990 is sold nationwide in the larger cardboard packages for around $2.85 per pound. A better buy for multi-year storage is the instant non-fat milk powder sold by Preparedness Products. This Mormon-owned firm's 1990 FOB price is $57.95 for a case of 6 nitrogen-packed cans, containing a total of 22.5 pounds. The author bought a case three years ago and found this non-fat instant milk powder to be excellent. At $2.58 a pound, plus UPS shipping charges, the cost is considerably less than for comparable

milk powder packaged for multi-year storage and sold by other companies.

* Vegetable oil, sugar, salt, and multi-vitamin tablets are best bought at discount supermarkets. In cities such stores often sell large plastic containers of vegetable oil as "loss leaders" to attract customers, at prices as low as wholesale. Vegetable oil prices in small communities typically are much higher. For an economical survival ration, buy the lowest priced vegetable oil. Remember that one of the worst post-attack nutritional deficiencies will result from chronic shortages of fats (including oils), and that babies and little children cannot survive for a year on a diet of only grains and beans, with no oil or fat. See the Food chapter.

Cautions: Typical health food stores and most firms that specialize in survival foods sell basic foods at high prices, especially grains, beans, and milk powder. Investigate several other sources before buying.

To make sure that an advertised "one year supply" of survival foods actually will keep an adult well nourished for a whole year, require the seller to inform you by mail what his "one year supply" provides a typical adult male in: (1) calories, k cal; (2) protein, g; and (3) fat, g. Then you can use the values in the "Emergency Recommendations" to determine whether the advertised "one year supply" is adequate.

° Transitional foods: The emotional shock of suddenly being forced by war to occupy your shelter will be even worse if you have to adapt suddenly to an unaccustomed diet. It would be a good idea to occasionally practice eating only your survival rations for a day or two, and to store in your shelter a two week supply of canned and dry foods similar to those your family normally eats. Then it will be easier if war forces you to make the changeover. Of course the transitional foods that you store should be rotated and replaced as needed, depending on their shelf lives.

- A hand-cranked grain mill: Whole kernel grains and soybeans must be processed into meal or flour for satisfactory use as principal components of a diet. If unprepared America suffers a nuclear attack, unplanned, local food reserves and/or famine relief shipments will consist mostly of unprocessed wheat, corn, and soybeans. Then a family with a manual grain mill will have a survival advantage and will be a neighborhood asset.

Many health food stores at least have sources of hand-cranked grain mills. Mills with steel grinding plates are more efficient and less expensive than "stone" mills. A mail order firm that still sells hand-cranked grain mills of a make that the author has bought and found to be well made and efficient is Moses Kountry Health Foods, 7115 W. 4th N.W., Albuquerque, New Mexico 87107. It sells a serviceable Polish mill (Model "OB" Hand Grain Mill) for $;35.73 FOB, plus UPS shipping charges.

This mill cranks easily and grinds wheat into coarse meal or fine flour more efficiently than any of the American manual grain mills that the author has bought and used over the decades. Apparently manual grain mills no longer are manufactured in the U.S. Before buying a grain mill be sure to learn whether it grinds corn, our largest food reserve. In 1987 the author bought an advertised West German mill. Only after receiving it by mail order did he learn by reading the accompanying directions that it is not made for grinding corn.

COOKING AND HEATING

- Safety precautions: The first rule for safe cooking and/or heating in a shelter is to do it as near as practical to the exhaust opening. If the fire is under an exhaust pipe, install a hood over the fire. Operate the shelter ventilating pump when cooking, unless a natural airflow out through the exhaust opening can be observed or felt. Keep flammable materials, especially clothing, well away from any open fire.
- Hazardous fuels: Charcoal is the most hazardous fuel to burn in confined spaces, because it gives off much carbon

monoxide. In a crowded shelter there are obvious dangers in using the efficient little stoves carried by backpackers and in storing their easily vaporized and ignited fuels.

- "Canned heat": These convenient fuels are expensive. Sterno, widely used to heat small quantities of food and drink, typically retails in 7-ounce cans for what amounts to about $9.00 per pound.
- Wood: The safest fuel to burn in a shelter is wood, the most widely available and cheapest fuel. Furthermore, wood smoke is irritating enough to usually alert shelter occupants to sometimes accompanying carbon monoxide dangers. Scrap lumber cut into short lengths, made into bundles and stored in plastic bags, occupies minimum space and stays dry. Keep a saw and a hatchet in your shelter.
- Bucket Stove: The most efficient, practical and safe stove with which to cook or heat for weeks or months in a family shelter is a Bucket Stove, that burns either small pieces of wood or small "sticks" of twisted newspaper. Especially if you believe that you may have to live in your shelter for months or that your normal fuel will not be available after a nuclear attack, you should make and store at least two Bucket Stoves.
- An improved Fireless Cooker: Tosave a great deal of fuel and time, particularly with slow-cooking grains and beans, make a very well insulated Fireless Cooker similar to the expedient one. Make a plywood box, first measuring carefully to insure that, when completely lined with4 inches of styrofoam, the styrofoam will fit closely around a large, lidded pot wrapped in a bath towel. An excellent Fireless Cooker is a war survival asset that also is useful for peacetime cooking.

(To boil about twice as much wheat flour- meal in a given pot as can be boiled when making wheat mush, and to use the minimum amount of water and fuel, salt a batch of the flour-meal, add enough water while working it to make a stiff dough, then make dough balls about 1-1/2 inches in diameter, and roll them in flour-meal. Drop the wheat balls into enough boiling water to cover them, and boil at a rolling boil for 10 minutes. Then put the boiling-hot pot in a well insulated Fireless Cooker for several hours. Corn balls can be made and boiled in this manner, also without the almost constant stirring required when boiling a mush made of home-ground flour-meal.)

- A sturdy work bench: Inthe corner under the emergency exit build a work bench, secured to a wall, on which to cook and to which you can attach your grain mill. A bench 36 inches high, 42 inches wide, and 30 inches deep will serve. (The other corner at the air-exhaust end of the shelter should be the curtained-off toilet and bathing area.)
- Very warm clothing, footwear, and bedding: Heating a well ventilated shelter usually is unnecessary even in freezing weather if the occupants have these essentials for living in the cold, or if they have the materials needed to make at least as good expedient means for retaining body heat. The author has felt the warm hands of little Chinese children wearing padded clothing while living in their below freezing homes, where there was scarcely enough straw, grass, and twigs to cook with. If you store plenty of strong thread and large needles in your shelter, you can make warm clothing out of blankets - as some frontier settlers did to survive the subzero winters of Montana.

LIGHT

- White paint: To make a little light go a long way, paint the walls, ceiling, floor, and furnishings pure white.
- Candles: The most dependable and economical lights for a family shelter are long-burning candles. The best candle tested by the author is the 15-hour candle manufactured by the Reed Candle Company of San Antonio, Texas and sold by the millions in New Mexico each Christmas season for

use in outdoor decorative "luminaries". This votive-type, short candle is not perfumed and has a wick supported by a small piece of metal attached to its base, so that the wick remains upright and continues to burn if the wax melts and no longer supports it. If burned in one of the candle-lamps described below, this candle gives enough light to read by for 15 hours.

Persons who stock a permanent shelter should realize that after a nuclear war fats, oils, paraffin, and all other sources of light will be in extremely short supply for at least many months. Light at a delivered cost of about two cents per hour will be a bargain blessing.

* The second-best shelter candle tested by the author is a standard Plumber's Candle, that retails for about 60 cents in many stores nationwide, and that burns for about 10 hours with a brighter flame than a votive-type candle. Two types of expedient candle-lamps were proved by multi-day tests to be the most practical:
* The best expedient candle-lamp is made of a 1-pint Mason jar, identical to the cooking-oil lamp pictured on page 102 of the Light chapter except for the substitution of a short candle for the oil and wick. To make a stable candle base on a glass jar's rounded bottom, cover it with hot candle wax. To be able to light the candle and then put it inside the glass jar, make tongs out of an 18-inch length of coathanger wire bent in the middle, with each of its two ends bent inward 90 degrees and cut off to make 1/4-inch- long candle grippers.
* The second-best candlelamp is made by cutting a standard aluminum pop or beer can, as illustrated. Use a sharp small knife. To make a stable base for a short candle, put enough sand across the can's rounded bottom to barely cover its center. The first candle burned will saturate and then harden the sand, making a permanent candle base or holder.

Caution: Although candles are the safest non-electric lights for shelter use, they produce enough carbon monoxide to cause headaches in a poorly ventilated, long-occupied shelter. In a 2-week habitability test of a family shelter in Princeton, the father and mother did not smoke, yet they had persistent headaches. Specialists later concluded that their headaches were caused by the small amounts of carbon monoxide produced by the candles used both for light and to heat food and drink.

- Expedient lamps: The very economical lamp that burns cooking oil in a 1-pint glass jar is the better of the two expedient lamps. For use in a shelter, however, long- burning candles, that are serviceable after decades of storage, are more practical. Among the disadvantages of expedient lamps is the fact that untreated, soft cotton string needed to make excellent wicks is no longer available in some communities, and making wire-stiffened wicks is a time consuming chore.

Nylon Hammock-chairs

To enable the maximum number of additional people to occupy a shelter for days to months, nylon Hammock-Chairs should be made before a war crisis arises, and should be kept stored for emergency use. The best field-tested model for use in shelters that are at least 7 feet wide is similar to the expedient Hammock- Chair described on pages 120 through 124, is made of strong nylon cloth, and is 40 inches wide by 9 feet long along its center line, with each of its long sides being 8 feet-4 inches long. At each end is a curved hem 3-1/2 inches wide, through which a loop-ended nylon hammock rope is run, to draw the slung hammock into a boat-like, secure shape with adequate head and shoulder room. The breaking strength of a hammock rope should be at least 600 pounds.

To attach the nylon ropes that support the suspended chair's two "arms," a loop of nylon webbing, or of folded and stitched nylon cloth, should be sewn to each side edge of the hammock 52 inches from the end of the hammock that will serve as the top of the back of the chair. See the illustrations on page 124. Especially in permanent family shelters, support points both for the hammocks, and for the hammocks when they are converted into suspended chairs, should be made when the shelter is being built.

OFTEN OVERLOOKED SANITATION AND OTHER SHELTER NEEDS

Store enough soap to last your family for at least a year. After a major nuclear attack the edible fats and oils, used in past generations to make soap, will almost all be eaten. Production of detergents is based on inter-dependent, vulnerable chemical industries not likely to be restored for years.

A chemical toilet would help bridge the gap between modern living and surviving in a crowded shelter. For months-long occupancy, however, a more practical toilet is likely to be a 5-gallon can with a seat, a plastic trash bag for its removable liner, a piece of plastic film for its tie-on cover, and a hose to vent gasses to the outdoors. See page 104. Store at least 200 large plastic trash bags.

The author knows from his experiences in primitive regions that using anything other than paper in place of toilet paper or cloth is hard to get accustomed to. A hundred pounds of newspaper, stored in plastic trash bags to prevent it from getting damp, takes up only about 3 cubic feet of storage space and would be useful for many purposes.

Keep several thousand matches, in Mason jars, so that they will be sure to stay dry even if your shelter becomes very humid post-attack.

Store most of your radiation monitoring instruments in your shelter, along with paper and pencils with which to keep records of radiation exposures, etc. A steel or reinforced concrete shelter should have a transistor radio with extra batteries, and a vertical pipe through which an antenna can be run up to improve reception.

No one can remember all the needed survival facts and instructions given even in this one book, so keep Nuclear War Survival Skills and other survival guidance in your shelter, and also other books that you believe may improve your family's morale and survival chances.

PRACTICE SHELTER LIVING

A family that spends a weekend living in its completed small shelter will learn more about unrecognized shelter needs - and more about each other - than members are likely to learn if they all read civil defense information for two whole days. Furthermore, after this educational experience family members old enough to have nuclear fears will know for sure that anti-defense activists are talking nonsense when they maintain that if most Americans had shelters they would become less heedful of nuclear war dangers and more likely to support aggressive leaders.

TRANS-PACIFIC FALLOUT

Potential Dangers to Americans

Many strategists believe that if a nuclear war is fought in the next few decades it probably will not involve nuclear explosions on any of our 50 states. Perhaps the first nuclear war casualties in the United States will be caused by fallout from an overseas nuclear war in which our country is not a belligerent. As the number of nations with nuclear weapons increases - especially in the Middle East - this generally unrecognized danger to Americans will worsen. Trans-Pacific war fallout, carried to an America at peace by the prevailing west-to-east winds that blow around the world, could be several hundred times more dangerous to Americans than fallout from the worst possible overseas nuclear power reactor accident, and many times more dangerous than fallout from a very improbable U.S. nuclear power reactor accident as lethal as the disastrous Chernobyl accident was to Russians.

It produced fallout that by January 1, 1967 resulted in the fallout cloud covering most of the United States. This one Chinese explosion produced about 15 million curies of iodine- 131 - roughly the same amount as the total release of iodine- 131 into the atmosphere from the Chernobyl nuclear power plant disaster. (The

Lawrence Livermore National Laboratory's preliminary estimate is that 10-50 million curies of iodine- 131 were released during the several days of the Chernobyl disaster; in contrast, its estimate of the iodine- 131 released during the Three Mile Island nuclear power plant accident, the worst commercial nuclear power plant accident in American history, is about 20 curies.)

Later in 1970 a final draft of this report was submitted to Washington for approval before publication. It was promptly classified. Publication without censorship was not permitted until after it was declassified in its entirety in 1973. None of the recommendations in this pioneering report were acted upon, but many of them are given in this chapter.

Fallout from the approximately 300 kiloton Chinese test explosion caused milk from cows that fed on pastures near Oak Ridge, Tennessee and elsewhere to be contaminated with radioiodine, although not with enough to be hazardous to health. However, this milk contamination (up to 900 picocuries of radioactive iodine per liter) and the measured dose rates from the gamma rays emitted from fallout particles deposited in different parts of the United States indicate that trans-Pacific fallout from even an overseas nuclear war in which "only" two or three hundred megatons would be exploded could result in tens of thousands of unprepared Americans suffering thyroid injury.

Unprepared Americans do not have potassium iodide, the very effective prophylactic medication to prevent thyroid injury from radioiodine, and few could get it during the several days that it would take trans-Pacific war fallout to reach the United States. Fortunately, removal of even a cancerous thyroid rarely is fatal to people blessed with modern medical facilities.

Only about 7,500 Americans (people living within a few miles of a nuclear power plant in Tennessee) have been given prophylactic potassium iodide to keep in their homes. No government organization has advised even Americans living near other nuclear facilities to buy and keep any kind of prophylactic medicine to protect their thyroids in case of a peacetime nuclear accident. As expected, official warnings and advice to the public continue not even to mention preparations that individual Americans could make to protect themselves and their families against thyroid injury either from trans-Pacific war fallout deposited on an America at peace, or as a result of war fallout if our country is subjected to a nuclear attack.

The worst danger to Americans from trans- Pacific fallout from a large nuclear war would be the whole-body gamma radiation doses that millions would receive from fallout particles deposited on the ground, on streets, on and in buildings. Protective countermeasures would include both sheltering some pregnant women and small children living in "hot spot" areas of abnormally high rain-out of fallout, and evacuating others. Unless such unavoidably time-consuming and expensive countermeasures were taken, several thousand additional Americans might die from cancer in the following 20 or 30 years. The largest total doses would be received by people who would live normal unsheltered lives for the first month or so after fallout deposition, while the dose rates would be highest.

Several thousand additional cancer deaths would be extremely difficult to detect, if caused by whole-body gamma radiation from fallout deposited nationwide, with these scattered deaths occurring over the 20 or 30 years following a Trans-Pacific war fallout disaster. For during these same decades about 15 million Americans normally would die from cancers indistinguishable from those caused by wholebody radiation from war fallout deposited on an America at peace.

An authoritative risk estimate of getting cancer from low doses of radiation is given in Report No. 77 (March 15, 1984) of the National Council on Radiation Protection and Measurement, "Exposures from the Uranium Series with Emphasis on Radon and Its Daughters": "The low dose model for total excess cancer mortality is one hundred cases per million people exposed to one rem uniform whole body radiation. This would make the overall risk of cancer to the average individual in the population about one in ten thousand per rem, i.e., if ten thousand persons are exposed to a dose of one rem (one thousand mrem), one excess fatal cancer would be expected within the lifetime of the group."

Many radiation specialists have concluded from studies of the effects of extremely low doses that the above and similar conservative estimates of excess cancer deaths overestimate the number of fatalities likely to result from low radiation doses, such as would be received by millions of Americans from trans-Pacific war fallout.

TO PROTECT YOURSELF AGAINST TRANS-PACIFIC FALLOUT, START BY REALIZING THAT:

° The dangers from trans-Pacific war fallout have been increased by the continuing trend toward deployment of more accurate, smaller, more numerous nuclear weapons, because:

* A large nuclear explosion (half a megaton, or more) injects most of its fallout particles and gases into the stratosphere, above the tops of clouds and above the altitudes at which quite prompt removal of contaminants from the atmosphere by scavenging takes place. Very small particles in the stratosphere do not reach the ground before they are blown at least several thousand miles. Most of these tiny particles remain airborne for weeks to years, are very widely dispersed, and are blown around the world several to many times before being deposited. By then the radioactivity of iodine-131 (that has a half life of only a little more than 8 days) is so greatly reduced that it is not nearly as dangerous as is radioactive iodine deposited much sooner with the fallout from smaller weapons of several hundred kilotons, or less, explosive power.
* Nuclear explosions smaller than about half a megaton (500 kilotons) inject all or most of their fallout to lower altitudes - within the troposphere, below the stratosphere. Most of such fallout is deposited during the radioactive

cloud's first world-circling trip, when even quite rapidly decaying radioiodine still is dangerously radioactive. This greater danger from smaller nuclear weapons has been proved by numerous measurements of fallout from many nuclear test explosions, both foreign and American.

- The dangers from trans-Pacific fallout produced by peacetime nuclear accidents are not nearly as serious as many Americans have been led to believe. For example, the Chernobyl nuclear power reactor accident injected as much radioactive iodine into the atmosphere as would the explosions of several kiloton-range nuclear weapons totaling perhaps as much as half a megaton in explosive power. But not nearly as much of the radioactivity caused by this reactor accident reached the United States as would reach us from several nuclear explosions in the same area, capable of injecting an equal amount of radioactivity into the atmosphere, because:
  - The cloud from the steam explosion that blew off the roof and otherwise damaged the Chernobyl reactor building, may have risen quite soon to 20,000 feet or more and was partially blown eastward clear across Asia and the Pacific Ocean. However, the top of the radioactive smoke cloud over the Chernobyl power plant, that burned for days, rose only about 3,000 feet above the ground. As a result, much of the airborne Chernobyl radiation stayed at relatively low altitudes where scavenging (removal) of smoke and fallout particles and gasses is most effective and rapid, due to aggregation on cloud droplets, rain-out, and dry deposition. In contrast, almost all of the fallout particles and radioactive gasses from a nuclear explosion are injected much higher, to altitudes where scavenging is less effective; there, the generally prevailing west-to-east winds promptly start transporting very small particles and radioactive gasses (that originate in the mid- latitudes of the northern hemisphere) around the world.

* Variable winds for days carried much of the Chernobyl radioactive material northward to Scandinavian countries, then westward and southward to other European countries. The resultant wide dispersal of this fallout allowed time for both scavenging and radioactive decay before a small fraction of these invisible radioactive clouds rose and also were blown eastward by the prevailing high-altitude winds. These west winds carried an extremely small fraction of the radioactive emissions from the burning Chernobyl plant clear across Asia and the Pacific to America.

° The media habitually exaggerate dangers from nuclear accidents, and exploited the Chernobyl disaster. For example, when Dr. Robert Gale, the leading bone marrow transplant specialist who helped save a few Chernobyl victims, first returned from Russia, an Associated Press article quoted him as saying: "I think we can say there are at least 50,000 to 100,000 people who have had some dose of radiation which might be of long-term concern.

There will, unfortunately, be additional casualties. We hope the number will be small." The Rocky Mountain News headlined" 100,000 SOVIETS TO SUFFER FROM RADIATION, DOCTOR SAYS". Mary McGrory, the syndicated liberal columnist, also misinterpreted Dr. Gale's risk estimate and misinformed her readers by writing: "He [Dr. Gale] estimated that there could be 100,000 cases of radiation sickness . Such dramatic news items give the impression that 100,000 Russians - not just a small fraction of that number - are likely to suffer sickness or death from the Chernobyl radiation. So additional typical Americans, reading misinformation of this type and knowing very little about statistical evaluations of risks based on probabilities, have had their worst nuclear fears strengthened.

The public's exaggerated fears of extremely small amounts of radiation also are worsened by the media's use without explanations of very small units of radiation measurement, including the picocurie. (The picocurie is used to express the radioactive contamination of milk, water, etc., and is only one millionth of a millionth [1/ 1,000,000,000,000] of a curie.) One episode in which fears of radiation were thus worsened occurred shortly after the invisible fallout cloud from the Chernobyl disaster first reached the United States. Some listeners were frightened when a radio announcer merely stated that milk samples in northwest Oregon showed 118 picocuries per liter of radioactive iodine. Few Americans know that they will not be advised to stop using fresh milk unless its contamination is 15,000 picocuries or more per liter - as specified in the Food and Drug Administration's official, very cautious "Protective Action Guidance", published in the Federal Register of October 22, 1982.

The maximum measured radioactive contamination of milk in the United States by iodine-131 from the Chernobyl disaster was in milk produced by cows grazing on pasture in Washington: 560 picocuries per liter. The much greater potential danger from trans-Pacific war fallout is brought out by the fact that the approximately 300-kiloton Chinese test explosion of December 28, 1966 resulted in worse iodine- 131 contamination of milk produced by a cow grazing on pasture near Oak Ridge, Tennessee: 900 picocuries per liter. Even asmall overseas nuclear war with only 20 or so kiloton-range nuclear explosions could cause high enough contamination of milk to result in the Government's warning Americans to refrain from using fresh milk. Most Americans would heed this warning and would not drink or otherwise use fresh milk for weeks. In addition, a small overseas nuclear war possibly would cause a few American casualties years to decades later.

TWO SUMMARY CONCLUSIONS

1. Trans-Pacific war fallout deposited on an America at peace surely would be a disaster, but not an overwhelming one. The economic and psychological impact probably would be more damaging than the losses of health and life.
2. Prudent individuals should make preparations to enable them to use the low cost protective countermeasures described in this book, especially those in Chapter 13. Some

of the most effective countermeasures, such as getting enough prophylactic potassium iodide to prevent thyroid damage even if war fallout dangers from explosions in the United States or overseas were to continue for a couple of months, cannot be accomplished after even an overseas nuclear war begins.

INSTRUCTIONS FOR SIX EXPEDIENT FALLOUT SHELTERS

Shelter-building Instructions

The following step-by-step instructions for building 6 types of earthcovered expedient shelters have enabled untrained families to build even the most difficult of these shelters in less than 2 days. The only families who took longer --up to 4 days-- were the few who were delayed by very heavy rains. Each of these shelters has been built by several different families or groups of families. Only widely available materials and hand tools are required. They have been built under simulated crisis conditions in environments typical of large regions of the United States: covered-trench types have been built in forested clay hills of Tennessee, in a bare Colorado valley in snowy November, in an irrigated Utah valley in hot August. Most of the aboveground shelters were built by families in Florida, where the water table is within 18 inches of the surface.

All of these test families used instructions that contained general guidance to help inexperienced persons build almost any type of earth-covered shelter. In this appendix, general instructions which apply to all types of shelters will be given first, to avoid repetition. (However, if the instructions for building one type of shelter are reproduced separately, the pertinent parts of these general instructions should be given before the step-by-step instructions for building that shelter.

Warning

Earth-covered shelters built of green poles can become unsafe within a few months, because of fungi and/or boring insects. In damper parts of the U.S., earth-covered shelters built of dry poles or untreated lumber can become unsafe after several months. An exception is very dry areas of the West, where some pioneers lived for years in earth-covered dugouts with pole roofs.

GENERAL INSTRUCTIONS FOR BUILDING AN EXPEDIENT SHELTER

1. Read all the instructions and study the drawings before beginning work. (Most families have found it helpful first to read the instructions aloud and then to discuss problems and work assignments.)
2. Sharpen all tools, including picks and shovels. Dull tools waste time and energy, if no file is available, tools can be sharpened by rubbing them hard on concrete or a rough stone.
3. Wear gloves from the start. Blisters can lead to serious infections, especially if antibiotics cannot be obtained.
4. Whenever practical select a building site that:
   - Will not be flooded if heavy rains occur or if a large dam farther up a major valley is destroyed by a nuclear explosion.
   - Is in the open and at least 50 ft away from a building or woods that might be set afire by the thermal pulse from an explosion tens of miles away. (Keep well away from even a lone tree; it is hard to dig through roots.)
   - Has earth that is firm and stable, if the planned shelter is to be a trench type with unshored (unsupported) earth walls To make sure that the earth is firm and stable enough so that the walls will not cave in, make a "thumb test" by digging an 18-in.-deep hole and trying to push your bare thumb into the undisturbed earth at the bottom. If you can push your thumb no farther than 1 in the earth should be safe enough. If the earth does not pass the thumb-test, move to another location and repeat the

test. Or build a below ground shelter with shored walls, or an aboveground shelter.

- Has a sufficient depth of earth above rock or the water table for a trench to be dug to the depth required.

(To find out, try to dig a pit to the required depth before excavating the whole trench. Or, if you are quite sure there is no water- table problem, try driving down a sharpened rod or pipe to the required depth in several places along the planned length of the trench.)

5. If the shelter must be built on sloping ground, locate it with its length crosswise to the direction of the slope.
6. Before staking out the shelter, clear the ground of brush, weeds and tall grass over an area extending about 10 ft beyond the planned edges of the excavation. (If loose earth is shoveled onto tall plants, the earth will be difficult to shovel the second time when covering the completed shelter roof.)
7. Stake out the complete shelter, and then dig by removing layers of earth.
8. When digging earth that is too firm to shovel without first breaking it up, start picking (or breaking with a shovel) in a line across the center of the trench. Next, shovel out a narrow trench 6 or 8 in. deep all the way across the width of the trench. Then with pick or shovel break off row after row of earth all the way across the width of the trench, as illustrated.
9. When digging a trench, to avoid having to move the excavated earth twice more to get it out of the way, first pile all earth about 8 ft away from the trench. Later, pile additional earth you are excavating at least 3 ft away.
10. Never risk a cave-in by digging into lower parts of an earth wall. It is dangerous to produce even a small overhanging section of wall or to dig a small, cave-like enlargement of a shelter.

11. When making a "sandbag" of a pillowcase or sack to hold earth shielding in place around the sides of shelter openings or along the edges of a shelter roof, fill it so that it will be only about two-thirds full after its opening is tied shut securely. Avoid dropping the sandbag.
12. If sufficient sandbags are not available, make earth-filled "rolls." Bed sheets or any reasonably strong fabric or plastic film can be used to make these rolls as described below. (To make a longer roll than the one illustrated below, several persons should make one together, standing side- by-side.)

To make an 8-in.-high earth-filled roll:

(1) Select a piece of cloth at least as strong as a new bed sheet, 2 ft longer than the side of the opening to be protected, and 5 ft wide.

(2) Place 2 ft of the width of the cloth on the ground.

(3) While using both hands to hold up and pull on 3 ft of the width of the cloth and pressing against the cloth with your body, have another person shovel earth onto and against the cloth.

(4) While still pulling on the cloth, pull the upper part down over the earth that covers the lower part of the cloth.

(5) Cover the upper part of the cloth with earth so as to form an earth-filled 'hook" near the upper edge, as illustrated.

(6) If a greater thickness of rolls is needed, level the earth on top of a roll; then make another earth-filled roll on this level surface.

13. Cut and haul poles and logs more easily by doing the following:

(1) Take time to sharpen your tools before starting to work no matter how rushed you feel.

(2) When sawing green trees that have gummy resin or sap, oil your saw with kerosene or diesel fuel. If you don't have these, use motor oil, grease, or even soap.

(3) When felling a small tree, the following method will help make a square cut, keep your saw from being pinched, and help make the tree fall in the desired direction:

   (a) Saw the tree about one-third through on the side toward which you want it to fall.

   (b) Then start sawing the opposite side, while another person pushes on the tree with a 10-ft push- pole, pressing the end of the push-pole against the tree about 10 ft above the ground. A push-pole with a forked end or with a big nail on the end is best when you get ready to move it, or to use it for building your shelter. Make and use a measuring stick to speed up measuring and cutting poles and logs to the right lengths.

(4) After a tree has been felled, trim off all limbs and knots so that the pole or log is smooth and will require no additional smoothing

(5) It usually is best first to cut the poles exactly two or three times the final length of the poles to be used in the shelter.

(6) When you are ready to move the poles to the shelter site, drag them rather than trying to carry them on your shoulders. Shouldering them is more tiring, and you could injure yourself severely if you should trip. To drag a log or several poles by hand: (a) Cut a stick 2 to 2-1/2 in. in diameter and about 3-1/3 ft long; (b) Tie a short piece of 1/4-in. (or stronger) rope to the center of the stick; (c) Make a lasso-like loop at the free end of the rope, so that when it is looped around the log and two people are pulling (see illustration), the front end of the log is raised about 6 in. above the ground. The loop should be tightened around the log about 2 ft. from its end, so that the end of the log cannot hit the backs of the legs of the two people pulling it.

CAUTION: If you drag a log down a steep hill, one person should tie a rope to the rear end of the log, and then follow the dragger, ready to act as the brake if needed.

(7) When you get the poles or logs to the location where you will build the shelter, cut them to the desired minimum diameters and specified lengths, and put all those of one specified type together.

Be sure that the diameter of the small end of each pole of one type is at least as large as the minimum diameter specified for its type. Make and use a measuring stick, as previously described.

14. Use snow for shielding material for aboveground shelters if the earth is so deep-frozen that digging is impractical. For a Ridge-Pole Shelter, cover the entire shelter with 5 ft of wetted or well-packed snow. For a Crib- Walled Shelter, fill the cribs and then cover and surround the entire shelter with snow at least 5 ft thick. With wetted or well- packed snow 5 ft thick, the protection factor is about 50. Families have completed these winter shelters within 2 days. Several hundred pounds of snow can be moved at a time by sledding it on a piece of canvas or other strong material 6 to 8 ft wide. Attach a stick across one end of the material and tie a rope to the ends of the stick, so as to form a 'Y" bridle on which a person can pull. To keep the occupants of a snow-covered expedient shelter dry and tolerably warm in subfreezing weather, provide sufficient ventilation openings to maintain inside temperatures at a few degrees below freezing.
15. Make a reliable canopy over the shelter entry. A on the following page, you can make a dependable canopy that ordinary winds will neither tear nor blow down and that will not catch rainwater even if you have no waterproof material stronger than 4-mil polyethylene film.
16. Take to your shelter enough window screen or mosquito netting to cover its openings. Except in freezing-cold weather, flies and mosquitoes would soon become a problem in most localities soon after an attack.
17. Work to complete (1) an expedient ventilating- cooling pump (a KAP) and (2) the storage of at least 15 gallons of water

per person. This work should be accomplished by the time your shelter is completed. Especially in an area of heavy fallout during warm or hot weather, an earth- covered, high-protection-factor shelter when full of people would be useless unless adequately ventilated and cooled and provided with enough water.

18. In cold weather, restrict air flow through the shelter by hanging curtains of plastic or tightly woven fabric, or by otherwise partially obstructing its two openings. Always be sure to leave at least a few square inches open at the floor level of one opening and at the ceiling height of the other, to provide enough ventilation to prevent a harmful concentration of exhaled carbon dioxide. To prevent exhaled water vapor from wetting clothing and bedding and reducing its insulating value, keep the ventilation openings as wide open as possible without causing shelter temperatures to be intolerably cold.

DOOR-COVERED TRENCH SHELTER

Protection Provided

Against fallout radiation: Protection Factor 250 (PF 250) a person in the open outside this shelter would receive 250 times as much fallout radiation as he would if inside.

Against blast: Better protection than most homes, if built in very stable earth. Blast tests have indicated that this shelter would be undamaged up to at least the 5-psi overpressure range from large explosions. Without blast doors, the shelter's occupants could be injured at this overpressure range, although probably not fatally.

Against fire: Excellent, if sufficiently distant from fires producing carbon monoxide and toxic smoke.

Where Practical

In a location where at least one hollow-core door per occupant is available, and where the earth is very stable and a dry hole or trench 41/2 feet deep can be dug without difficulty. (A family evacuating in a pickup truck or large station wagon can carry enough doors, with doorknobs removed.

Strong boards at least 6 feet long and at least one full inch thick, or plywood at least 3/i-inch thick, also can be used to roof this 36-inch-wide trench and to support its overhead earth shielding.)

Warning: Some doors with single-thickness panels if loaded with earth will break before they bend enough to result in protective earth arching.

For Whom Practical

For a typical family or other group with two or more members able to work hard for most of 36 hours. (Stronger-than-average families with most members able to work hard have completed this type of shelter is less than 24 hours after receiving step-by-step, well illustrated instructions.)

Capacity

The shelter illustrated is roofed with 3 doors and is the minimum length for 3 persons. (If you have additional doors, or boards and sticks at least 3 ft long, make the entryway trenches 3 or 4 ft longer than illustrated if not pressed for time.)

For each additional person, add an additional door. (If more than about 7 persons are to be sheltered, build two or more separate shelters.)

Building Instructions

1. Before beginning work, study the drawings and read ALL of the following instructions.
2. Divide the work; CHECK OFF EACH STEP WHEN COMPLETED.
3. By the time the shelter is finished, plan to have completed (1) a ventilating pump (a KAP 16 in. wide and 28 in. high), essential for this shelter except in cool weather, and (2) the storage of at least 15 gallons of water per occupant.
4. Start to assemble materials and tools that are listed.

Essential Materials and Tools for a 3-Person Shelter

- Three hollow-core doors.
- A shovel (and a pick, if the earth is very hard).
- Two to three square yards per person of waterproof materials for rain proofing the roof. Use materials such as 4-mil polyethylene film, shower curtains, plastic table-cloths, plastic mattress covers, or canvas.
- Two pieces of plastic or tightly woven cloth (each about 6-1/2 X 6-1/2 ft) to make canopies over the two shelter openings. Also sticks and cords or strips of cloth to support the canopies.

  Materials and tools for building a simple shelter-ventilating pump, a KAP 16 in. wide and 28 in. high. Only in cold or continuously breezy, cool weather can tolerable temperatures and humidities be maintained in a crowded underground shelter without an air pump.
- Containers for storing adequate water.

Useful Materials and Tools

- Large cans, buckets, and; or pots with bail handles in which to carry earth and later to store drinking water or human wastes.
- Two pillowcases and one bedsheet per person-to make "sandbags" around shelter openings and to cover trench walls. (If available, large sheets of 4-mil polyethylene are better than bedsheets, because they keep earth walls damp and stable. They also help keep shelter occupants dry and clean and prevent earth from falling into their eyes.)
- File, knife, pliers, hammer.
- Measuring tape, yardstick, or ruler.
- Expedient life-support items.

5. To save time and work, SHARPEN ALL TOOLS AND KEEP THEM SHARP.

6. Wear gloves from the start even tough hands can blister and become painful and infected after hours of digging.
7. Check to be sure the earth is stable and firm enough so that a trench shelter with unshored (unsupported), vertical earth walls will be safe from cave-ins. (Interior doors are not strong enough to roof an earth-covered trench wider than 3 ft.) As a test of the stability of earth, dig a small hole about 18 in. deep. Remove all loose earth from the bottom of the hole. Then make a "thumb test" by pushing your bare thumb into the undisturbed surface at the bottom of the hole. If you can push your thumb into the earth no farther than one inch, the earth should be suitable for this type of shelter. If the earth does not pass the "thumb test," move to another location and try the test again. Continue to relocate and repeat until suitable earth is found, or build a shored-trench or aboveground shelter.
8. Prepare to dig a vertical-walled trench 4-1/2 ft deep and 3 ft wide. To determine the length of the trench, add together the widths of all the doors to be used for roofing it, then subtract 8 in. from the sum. (To avoid arithmetical errors, it is best to lay all the doors side by side on the ground.)
9. Clear any brush, grass, or weeds that are more than a few inches high from the area where the trench will be dug. Also clear the ground around all sides of the trench, to a distance of about 8 ft from the sides and ends of the trench.
10. Stake out a rectangular trench 36 in. wide, with its length as determined above. Also stake out the entrance at one end.
11. Dig the main trench, the entryway trench, and the ventilation trench. Place the excavated earth along both lengthwise sides of the trench, starting at the outside edges of the cleared space. Be sure that no earth is piled closer than 3 ft to the sides of the trench.
12. To be sure that unstable, unsafe earth is not encountered at depths below 18 in., repeat the "thumb test" each time

the trench is deepened an additional foot. If the earth does not pass the test, do not dig the trench any deeper; try another location.

13. To keep each trench its full width as it is dug, cut a stick 36 in. long and another 18 in. long; use them repeatedly from the start to check the widths of the main trench and the entry trenches. Keeping the trenches full width will save much work and time later.
14. Carefully level and smooth the ground to a distance of 2-1/2 ft from the sides of the trench, so that the doors will lie flat on the ground up to the edges of the trench.
15. If plenty of sheets, bedspreads, plastic, and: or other materials are available, cover the trench walls with them. Wall coverings should stop one inch from the floor of the trench to prevent their being stepped on and pulled down. Plastic wall coverings keep some types of damp earth walls from drying out and crumbling.
16. To be able to place an adequate thickness of shielding earth all the way to and around the entryway and ventilation hole, stack improvised 'sandbags" around these two openings before placing the earth on the roof. Or use cloth or plastic material to make rolls" of earth.
17. Shovel earth around the rolls, sandbags, or other means used to raise the level of the earth around the two shelter openings. Slope this earth outward, and pack it, so that rainwater on the ground cannot run into the shelter.
18. To rainproof the shelter and to prevent the roofing doors from being dampened and weakened, use available waterproof materials as follows:
    a. If the earth is dry, the easiest and best way to make a rainproof roof is to place the doors directly on the ground, with each of the end doors overlapping an end of the main trench by 4 or 5 in. (Be sure again to level the ground surface as you place each door, so that each

lies flat against the ground all the way to the edges of the trench.) Next, mound dry earth over the doors. First place a few inches of earth on the doors near their ends: then mound it about 12 in. deep above the centerline of the trench. Slope the earth to both sides so as to just cover the ends of the doors. Next, smooth off the earth mound, being careful to remove sharp stones that might puncture rainproof materials. Then place waterproof material over the smooth mound, making the "buried roof". Finally, carefully mound an additional 12 to 15 in. of earth on top of the buried roof, again placing it first over the doors near their ends. The earth over the trench should be at least 2 ft thick, so that effective earth arching will support most of the weight of the earth covering and will provide considerable protection if struck by blast.

b. If the earth is wet, place the waterproof material directly on top of the doors, to keep them dry and strong. To make water run off this waterproof covering and to keep water from collecting on a horizontal surface and leaking through, slope the doors toward one side of the trench by first making one side of the trench about 3 in. higher than the other side. A way to raise one side without increasing the distance the doors must span is to place an earth-filled roll" of bed sheets or other material along one edge of the trench. To keep the waterproof material used to cover the doors from sliding down the slope of the doors when earth is shoveled on, tuck the upper edge of the material under the higher ends of the doors. Finally, mound earth over the doors, first placing it near their ends. The mound should be at least 2 ft deep above the centerline of the roof and about 3 or 4 in. deep over both ends of the doors. If more waterproof material is available than is required to make a buried roof (or to cover the doors) and to make the illustrated canopies over the two shelter openings, use this excess material to cover the wet ground on which the doors are placed.

19. Dig small drainage ditches around the completed shelter, to lead runoff water away.
20. To keep rain and/or sand-like fallout particles from falling into the shelter openings, build an open-sided canopy over each opening.
21. Install the air pump (a KAP) in the shelter opening into which air is already naturally moving.
22. If the shelter has a KAP, protection against radiation can be increased by placing containers of water and of heavy foods, or bags of earth, so as to partially block the openings. This would still permit adequate air to be pumped through the shelter, except in very hot weather.
23. For seats, place water and food containers bedding, etc. along the side of the trench that is farther from the off-center entry trenches. If the trench floor is damp, covering it with a waterproof material, tree limbs, or brush will help.
24. Fill all available water containers, including pits which have been dug and lined with plastic, then roofed with available materials. If possible, disinfect all water stored in expedient containers, using one scant teaspoon of a chlorine bleach, such as Clorox, for each 10 gallons of water. Even if only muddy water is available, store it. If you do not have a disinfectant, it may be possible to boil water when needed.
25. Put at least your most useful emergency tools inside your shelter.
26. As time and materials permit, continue to improve your chances of surviving by doing as many of the following things as possible:
    (1) Make a homemade fallout meter, and expedient lights. (Prudent people will have made these extremely useful items well ahead of time.)

(2) Install screens or mosquito netting over the two openings, if mosquitoes or flies are a problem. Remember, however, that screen or netting reduces the air flow through a shelter -- even when the air is pumped through with a KAP.

(3) Dig a stand-up hole near the far end of the shelter. Make the hole about 15 in. in diameter and deep enough to permit the tallest of the shelter occupants to stand erect occasionally.

POLE-COVERED TRENCH SHELTER

Protection Provided

Against fallout radiation: Protection Factor 300 (PF 300) a person in the open outside this shelter would receive 300 times more fallout radiation than he would if he were inside.

Against blast: Quite good protection if built in stable earth. Blast tests have indicated that this shelter, if built in stable earth, would not be seriously damaged by blast effects of large explosions at least up to the 7-psi overpressure range. (At 7 psi, most buildings would be demolished.) Without blast doors, occupants of the shelter could be injured, although probably not fatally at this overpressure.

Against fire: Excellent, if sufficiently distant from fires producing carbon monoxide and toxic smoke.

Where Practical

In wooded areas with small trees, for builders who have an ax or a bow saw, crosscut or chain saw, and digging tools. Or in any location where the necessary poles may be obtained. In stable earth, where the water table or rock is more than 4-1/2 ft below the surface.

For Whom Practical

For a typical family or other group with two or more members able to work hard for most of 48 hours. (Stronger-than-average families with almost all members able to work hard have completed this type of shelter is about 24 hours after receiving step-by-step, well illustrated instructions, before traveling to the wooded building site and beginning to cut trees and haul poles.)

Capacity

The shelter illustrated is the minimum length recommended for 4 persons. For each additional person, add at least 2-3/4 ft to the length of the shelter room. If more than about 10 persons are to be sheltered, build 2 or more separate shelters.

Building Instructions

1. Before beginning work, study the drawings and read ALL of the following instructions. Divide the work so that some people will be digging while others are cutting and hauling poles. CHECK OFF EACH STEP WHEN COMPLETED.
2. By the time the shelter is finished, plan to have completed: (1) a ventilating pump, and (2) the storage of at least 15 gallons of drinking water per occupan.
3. Start to assemble materials and tools. Those listed are for the illustrated 4-person shelter with a room 11 ft long.

Essential Materials and Tools

- ° Saw (bow saw or crosscut preferred) and or ax for cutting poles to the lengths and diameters illustrated.
- ° Shovels (one for each two workers).
- ° Pick (if the ground is hard).
- ° Rainproof roof materials (very important in rainy, cold weather). At least 2 square yards of such material per person would be required; 3 square yards per person would be better. Shower curtains, plastic tablecloths, plastic mattress covers, canvas, and the like can be used. Also needed are 2 pieces of plastic or tightly woven cloth, each about 6 $2 X 61.2 ft, to make canopies over the two shelter openings.
- ° Materials and tools for building a simple shelter-ventilating pump, a KAP 22 in. wide and 36 in. long. Only in cold or

continuously breezy, cool weather can tolerable temperatures and humidities be maintained for days in a crowded underground shelter that lacks an air pump.

- Containers for storing adequate water.

Useful Materials and Tools

- Large cans, buckets, and / or pots with bail handles in which to carry earth and later to store drinking water and human wastes.
- Two bedsheets and two pillowcases per person for covering cracks between roofing logs, making "sandbags," and improvising bedsheet-hammocks and bedsheet-chairs.
- A file.
- A measuring tape, yardstick, or ruler.
- Rope, or strong wire (100 ft) to make earth-retaining pole walls close to the shelter openings (as explained in step 19) and for hammock supports, etc.
- Chain saw, pick-mattock, hammer, hatchet, pliers.
- Kerosene, turpentine, or oil to keep hand saws from sticking in gummy wood.
- Expedient life-support items recommended in this book.
- Mosquito netting or window screen to cover the openings, if mosquitoes or flies are likely to be a problem.

4. To save time and work, SHARPEN ALL TOOLS AND KEEP THEM SHARP.
5. Wear gloves from the start even tough hands can blister after hours of chopping and digging, and become painful and infected.
6. If possible, select a location for the shelter that is in the open and at least 50 ft from a building 9r woods. Remember that on a clear day the thermal pulse (flash of heat rays) from a very large nuclear explosion may cause fires as far away as 25 miles.

7. If the site chosen is on a steep slope, locate the shelter with its length crosswise to the direction of the slope.
8. Stake out the outlines of the trench, driving stakes. If more than 4 persons are to be sheltered, increase the length of the shelter room by 2 ft 9 in. for each additional person.
9. Clear the ground of saplings and tall grass within 10 ft of the staked outlines so that later the excavated earth can be easily shoveled back onto the completed shelter roof.
10. Start digging, throwing the first earth about 10 ft beyond the staked outlines of the trench. Less able members of the family should do the easier digging, near the surface. Those members who can use an ax and saw should cut and haul poles.
11. Pile all excavated earth at least 2 ft beyond the edges of the trench, so roofing poles can be laid directly on the ground. To make sure that the trenches are dug to the specified full widths at the bottoms, cut and use two sticks one 42 in. long and the other 22 in. long to check trench widths repeatedly.
12. At the far end of-the shelter dig the ventilation trench-emergency exit, making it 22 in. wide and 40 in. deep. This will help provide essential ventilation and cooling. In cold weather or when fallout is descending, canvas or plastic curtains should be hung in the two openings to control the air flow.
13. Make and install threshold boards, to keep the edges of earth steps and earth ledges from being broken off. (In damp earth, it is best to install threshold boards before roofing the shelter.) If boards are lacking, use small poles.
14. Unless the weather is cold, build a shelter- ventilating pump a KAP 20 in. wide X 36 in. high. (If the weather is cold, building a KAP can be safely delayed until after the shelter is completed.) A KAP should be made before a crisis, or, if possible, before leaving home.

15. Obtain fresh-cut green poles, or, as a second choice, sound, dry, untreated poles. Use no poles smaller in diameter than those specified in the accompanying drawings. For ease in hauling, select poles no more than 50% larger in diameter than those specified.
16. Lay the poles side by side over the trench. Alternate the large and small ends to keep the poles straight across the trench. If roof poles 9 ft long are being used to roof a 5-ft-wide trench, be sure to place the roof poles so that their ends extend 2 ft farther beyond one side of the trench than beyond the other side. This will enable shelter occupants, after the stoop-in shelter is completed, to widen the shelter room 2 ft on one side. First, it can be widened to provide a 2-ft- wide sleeping ledge. Later, it can be further deepened to make space for additional expedient hammocks or for double-bunk beds of poles or boards built on each side of the shelter.
17. For ease and safety later when hanging expedient bedsheet-hammocks and bed sheet-chairs in the completed shelter, place loose loops around roof poles in the approximate locations given by the diagram on the second shelter drawing. Make these loose loops of rope, or strong wire, or 16-in-wide strips of strong cloth, such as 50cv polyester bedsheet rolled up to form a "rope".
18. Cover the cracks between the logs with cloth, leaves, clay, or any other material that will keep dirt from falling down between the cracks.

    CAUTION: DO NOT try to rainproof this flat roof, and then simply cover it with earth. Water will seep through the loose earth cover, puddle on the flat roofing material, and leak through the joints between pieces of roofing material or through small holes.
19. Place 6-ft-long poles, one on top of the other, next to the entrances. This will keep earth to be placed on top of the

entryway trenches from falling into the openings. Secure these poles with wire or rope. If wire or rope is not available, make earth-filled "rolls" to hold the earth nearly vertical on the trench roof next to each opening.

20. Mound earth to a center depth of about 18 in. over the shelter roof to form the surface of the future "buried roof." Be sure to slope both sides of the mound. Then smooth its surface and remove sharp roots and stones that might puncture thin rain proofing materials to be placed upon it.
21. Place the waterproofing material on the "buried roof." If small pieces must be used, lay them in shingle-like fashion, starting at the lower sides of the mounded earth.
22. Cover the buried roof with another 18 in. of mounded earth, and smooth this final earth surface.
23. Finish the entrances by placing some shorter poles between the two longer poles next to each entryway. Bank and pack earth at least 6 in. deep around the sides of the entrances, so that .rainwater on the ground cannot run into the shelter entrances.
24. Dig surface drainage ditches around the outside of the mounded earth and around .the entrances.
25. Place a piece of water-shedding material over each of the entrances, forming an open-ended canopy to keep fallout and rain from the shelter openings. Almost all fallout would settle on these suspended canopies, rather than falling into shelter openings or would fall off their edges and onto the ground like sand.
26. Hang the KAP from the roof of the trench opening into which outdoor air can be felt flowing, so that air will be pumped in the direction of the natural flow of air. (If you have no KAP, make and use a small Directional Fan.)
27. Fill all available water containers, including pits which have been dug and lined with plastic, then roofed with available materials. If possible, disinfect all water stored in expedient

containers, using one scant teaspoon of a chlorine bleach, such as Clorox, for each 10 gallons of water. Even if only muddy water is available, store it. If you do not have a disinfectant, it may be possible to boil water when needed.

28. Put all of your emergency tools inside your shelter.
29. As time and materials permit, continue to improve your chances of surviving by doing as many of the following things as possible:
    (1) Make a homemade fallout meter, and expedient lights. (Prudent people will have made these extremely useful items well ahead of time.)
    (2) Make and hang expedient bedsheet-hammocks and bedsheet-chairs, following the installation.
    (3) Install screens or mosquito netting over the two openings, if mosquitoes or flies are a problem. Remember, however, that screen or netting reduces the air flow through a shelter even when the air is pumped through with a KAP.
    (4) Dig a stand-up hole near the far end of the shelter. Make the hole about 15 in. in diameter and deep enough to permit the tallest of the shelter occupants to stand erect occasionally.

SMALL-POLE SHELTER

Protection Provided

Against fallout radiation: Protection Factor 1000 (PF 1000), if the shelter is covered with at least 3 ft of earth. That is, a person in the open outside this shelter will receive a gamma ray dose 1000 times greater than he will receive inside the shelter.

Against blast: This shelter is excellent for preventing fatalities if it is built with strong expedient blast doors; it is still quite good if built without them. (These instructions are for fallout shelters. The instructions for making blast doors and other essentials for adequate blast protection. Without blast doors, occupants are likely to suffer serious injuries above 7 psi.) Against fire: Excellent, if sufficiently distant from fires that produce carbon monoxide and toxic smoke.

Where Practical

In wooded areas with small trees, for builders who have a saw (bow saw, crosscut, or chain saw) and digging tools. Any location is suitable if the necessary poles may be obtained there. Try to avoid roots. For belowground, semiburied, or aboveground construction. (However, aboveground construction requires the excavation and movement of so much earth that it is not practical for 2-day construction by families with only hand tools.)

For Whom Practical

For families or other groups with most members able to work hard 12 hours a day for 2 days. (Most people do not realize how hard and long they can work if given a strong incentive.)

Capacity

The drawings and lists of materials given in these instructions are for a 12-person shelter. For each additional occupant beyond 12, add 1 ft to the length of the shelter room. This shelter requires less work and materials per occupant if its room is sized for about 24 persons, because the entrances are the same regardless of the length of the room. (To make the shelter room twice as long, each of the horizontal, ladder-like braces on the floor and near the ceiling of the room can be made with two poles on a side, rather than one long pole on a side.)

If the room is sized for more than 24 people, management and hygiene problems become more difficult when it is occupied.

For 12 people to live for many days in this shelter without serious hardship, the benches and bunks must be built with the dimensions and spacings given in the illustration. Or, materials must be available for making and suspending 12 expedient bedsheet hammocks that can be converted each day into 12 bedsheet-chairs.

Building Instructions

1. Study both of the two drawings and read all of these instructions before beginning work. CHECK OFF EACH STEP WHEN COMPLETED.
2. By the time the shelter is finished, plan to have completed (1) a ventilating pump (a KAP 24 in wide and 36 in. high), essential except in cold weather, and (2) the storage of at least 15 gallons of water per occupant.
3. Start to assemble the required materials. For building a 12-person Small-Pole Shelter, the materials are:
   - Green poles. No pole should have a small end of less diameter than the minimum diameter specified for its use. The table below lists the number and sizes of poles needed to build a 12-person Small-Pole Shelter.
   - Rainproofing materials: Preferably one 100-ft roll, 12 ft wide, of 6-mil polyethylene. The minimum amount needed is 200 sq. ft. of 4-mil polyethylene, or 200 sq. ft of other waterproof plastic such as tablecloths, shower curtains, and or vinyl floor covering. Also include 100 ft. of sticks for use in drainage ditch drains (1/2-in. diameter, any lengths).
   - Nails, wire, and; or cord: Ten pounds of 40-penny nails plus 4 pounds of 16-penny nails are ideal. However, 7 pounds of 16-penny nails can serve.
   - Boards for benches and overhead bunks, if bedsheet-hammocks are not to be used. (Boards are desirable, but not essential; small poles can be used instead.) 2 X 4-in. boards 70 feet for frames (or use 3-in.-diameter poles). 1 X 8-in. boards 100 feet (or use 1-to 2-in-diameter poles).
   - Materials to build a homemade ventilating pump a KAP 24 in. wide and 36 in. high and to store at least 15 gallons of water per occupant.

4. Desirable muscle-powered tools for building a 12-person, Small-Pole Shelter are listed below. (Most builders have succeeded without having this many tools. A backhoe, chain saws, and other mechanized equipment would be helpful, but not essential.)

Tools	Quantity
Ax, long-handle	2
Bow-saw, 28-in.	2
(or 2-man crosscut saw)	1
Pick	2
Shovel, long-handle	3
Claw hammer	2
File, 10-in.	1
Steel tape, 10-ft	1

(Also useful: a 50-ft steel tape and 2 hatchets)

5. To help drain the floor, locate the shelter so that the original ground level at the entrance is about 12 inches lower than the original ground level at the far end of the shelter unless the location is in a very flat area.
6. Stake out the trench for the entire shelter. Even in very firm ground, if the illustrated 12-person shelter is being built, make the excavation at the surface 9 ft 8 in. wide and 18 ft long (3 ft longer than the entire length of the wooden shelter). The sloping sides of the excavation are necessary, even in very firm earth, to provide adequate space for backfilling and tamping.
7. Check the squareness of the staked trench outline by making its diagonals equal.
8. Clear all brush, tall grass, and the like from the ground, to a distance of 10 ft all around the staked location so that later you can easily shovel loose earth back onto the roof.

9. If the ground is unstable, excavate with sides that are appropriately less steep.
10. When digging the trench for the shelter, use a measuring stick 7 ft 8 in. long (the minimum bottom width) to repeatedly check the excavation width.
11. When digging with a shovel, pile the earth dug from near ground level about 10 ft. away from the edges of the excavation. Earth dug from 5 or 6 ft below ground level then can easily be piled on the surface only 1 to 5 ft from the edge of the excavation.
12. Finish the bottom of the excavation so that it slopes vertically 1/2 in. per foot of length toward the entrance, and also slopes toward the central drain ditch. (Later, sticks covered with porous fabric should be placed in the ditches, to serve like a crushed-rock drain leading to a sump.)
13. While some persons are excavating, others should be cutting green poles and hauling them to the site. Cut poles that have tops no smaller than the specified diameters for each type of pole (not including the bark).
14. For ease in handling poles, select wall and roof poles with top diameters no more than 50% larger than the specified minimum diameters.
15. Sort the poles by size and lay all poles of the same size together, near the excavation.
16. Before the excavation is completed, start building the ladder-like, horizontal braces of the shelter frame. Construct these braces on smooth ground near the excavation. Place two straight poles, each 10 ft 6 in. long (with small-end diameters of 4 in.), on smooth ground, parallel and 6 ft 2 in. apart. Hold these poles securely so that their outer sides are exactly 6 ft 2 in. apart, by driving two pairs of stakes into the ground so that they just touch the outsides of the two long poles. Each of the four stakes should be located about one foot from the end of a pole. To keep the 10 ft 6 in. poles from

being rotated during the next step, nail two boards or small poles across them perpendicularly as temporary' braces, about 4 ft apart.

Then with an ax or hatchet, slightly flatten the inner sides of the two poles at the spots where the ends of the 6 cross-brace poles will be nailed. Next, saw each cross-brace pole to the length required to fit snugly into its place. Finally, toenail each cross-brace pole in place, preferably with two 40-penny nails in each end.

17. Place the lower, ladder-like horizontal brace of the main room on the floor of the completed excavation.
18. Build the frame of the main room. Near the four corners of the room, secure four of its wall poles in their final vertical positions by nailing, wiring, or tying temporary brace-poles to the inner sides of these 4 wall poles and to the inner sides of the two long poles of the ladder-like horizontal brace on the bottom of the excavation. To keep the two pairs of vertical wall poles exactly 6 ft 2 in. apart until the upper ladder-like horizontal brace is secured in its place, nail a temporary horizontal brace across each pair of vertical poles, about 1 ft below their tops.
19. To support the upper ladder-like horizontal brace, nail blocks to the inner sides of the four vertical wall poles, as shown in the lower right- hand corner of the pictorial view. If you have large nails, use a block about 3 in. thick and 6 in. long, preferably cut from a green, 4-in.- diameter pole.
20. In the finished shelter, DO NOT leave any vertical support poles under the long poles of the upper ladder-like horizontal brace; to do so would seriously reduce the usable space along the walls for benches, bunks, and occupants.
21. While some workers are building the frame of the main room, other workers should make the four ladder-like horizontal braces for the two entrances, then make the complete entrances. To keep the ladder-like horizontal braces

square during construction and back-filling, nail a temporary diagonal brace across each one.

22. When the four wall poles and the two ladder-like horizontal braces of the main room are in place, put the remaining vertical wall poles in place, touching each other, until all walls are completed. When placing the wall poles, keep them vertical by alternately putting a butt and a top end uppermost. Wall poles can be held in position by backfilling and tamping about a foot of earth against their lower ends, or they can be wired in position until backfilled.
23. Be sure to use the two 5-in.-diameter poles (6 ft 2 in. long) by placing one next to the top and the other next to the bottom of each of the main doorways to the room. Study the drawings. Use braces, each 2 ft 3 in. long, to hold apart the top and bottom of each doorway thus making sure that a 24-in.-wide air pump can swing in either doorway.
24. To prevent earth from coming through the cracks between wall poles, cover the walls with cloth, plastic, rugs, roofing, or even cardboard. If none of these are available, use sticks, twigs, or grass to cover the wider cracks.
25. After all horizontal bracing and vertical wall poles are in place, begin backfilling, putting earth between the walls and trench sides. Pay particular attention to the order of filling. The earth fill behind all the walls must be brought up quite evenly, so that the earth fill behind one side is no more than 12 in. higher at any one time than the earth on the opposite side. Lightly tamp the earth fill in 6-in. layers. A pole makes a good tamper; do not use a mechanical tamper.
26. Next, lay the roof poles side by side, touching each other on top of the wall poles. Cover at least the larger cracks with plastic, roofing, boards, or sticks to keep earth from falling through. If the earth is sandy, cover the whole roof with some material such as bedsheets or plastic to keep sand from running through the cracks.

CAUTION: Donot try to rainproof this flat roof and simply cover it with earth. If you do, water will seep straight through the loose earth cover, puddle on the flat roofing material, and leak through the joints between pieces of roofing material or through small holes.

27. Mound earth over the shelter, piling it about 15 in. deep along the centerline of the roof and sloping it toward the sides of the roof, so that the earth is only about 2 in. deep over the ends of the roof poles. (Preparatory to mounding earth onto the roof, place grade stakes in position so you will be able to know the locations and depths of roof poles as you cover them.) Continue these slopes to two side drainage ditches. Smooth this mounded earth with a rake or stick and remove any sticks or rocks likely to puncture the rainproof roofing material to be laid on it.
28. Place rainproofing material on top of the smooth, mounded earth as shown in sections of the drawings to make a "buried roof." Plastic film, such as 4-mil polyethylene, is preferable. Roofing material, plastic shower curtains and tablecloths, or canvas can also be used. Be sure to overlap adjoining pieces.
29. Place the rest of the earth cover over the shelter, being sure that the corners of the shelter have at least 2-1/2 ft of earth over them. Mound the dirt, smoothing its surface so that water will tend to run off to the surface drainage ditches which should be dug all around the edges of the mounded earth..
30. Build the benches and overhead bunks. If boards are available, use them; if not, use small, straight poles. On each side, build a row of benches and bunks 9 ft long, centered in the shelter. In order to use the shelter space to the greatest advantage, make the heights and widths of the benches and bunks the same as the thoroughly tested heights (14 in. and 4 ft 5 in.) and widths (16 in. and 24 in.). Also be sure to space their vertical supports 3 ft apart so two adults can sit between each pair of vertical bunk supports.

31. Narrow the ends of the overhead bunks so that the aisle between them is about 28 in. wide for a distance of 38 in. from each doorway. This allows room for installation and operation of an expedient air pump (a KAP) for prevention of dangerous overheating in warm weather.
32. Place a canopy (open on all sides) over each entrance, to minimize the entry of sand-like fallout particles or rain.
33. To improve the floor, lay small poles between the lower brace poles, so that the floor is approximately level. Or, use sticks covered with scrap boards.
34. Fill all available water containers, including pits which have been dug and lined with plastic, then roofed with available materials. If possible, disinfect all water stored in expedient containers, using one scant teaspoon of a chlorine bleach, such as Clorox, for each 10 gallons of water. Even if only muddy water is available, store it. If you do not have a disinfectant, it may be possible to boil water when needed.
35. Put all of your emergency tools inside your shelter.
36. As time and materials permit, continue to improve your chances of surviving by doing as many of the following things as possible:
    (1) Make a homemade fallout meter, and expedient lights. (Prudent people will have made these extremely useful items well ahead of time.)
    (2) Install screens or mosquito netting over the two openings, if mosquitoes or flies are a problem. Remember, however, that screen or netting reduces the air flow through a shelter -- even when the air is pumped through with a KAP.

EXPEDIENT VENTILATION AND COOLING

(Those workers who are to work only on the shelter itself, if pushed for time, need not read this section before beginning their work.)

Install a KAP (one that is 24 in. wide and 36 in. high) near the top of the doorway through which you can feel air naturally flowing into the shelter room at that time. (If the direction of the natural air flow changes, move the KAP to the other opening.) To enable the KAP to efficiently pump fresh air from the outdoors all the way through the shelter, block the lower half of the doorway in which the KAP is installed with a quickly removable covering, such as a plastic-covered frame made of sticks. Be sure to connect the KAP's pullcord only 11 in. below its hinge line. This prevents excessive arm motions which would cause unnecessary fatigue.

In windy or cold weather, control the natural flow of air through the shelter by hanging adjustable curtains in the doorways at both ends, and or by making and using trapdoors on the tops of the vertical entryways. For adjustable curtains, use pieces of plastic, each with a supporting stick attached to its upper edge. This allows for different sized openings in the doorways: (1) an opening under the lower edge of the adjustable curtain at the air intake end of the room, and (2) an opening over the top of the curtain at the air-exhaust end of the room. In cold weather, this arrangement usually will provide adequate chimney-type ventilation for the shelter without using an air pump.

ABOVEGROUND, DOOR-COVERED SHELTER

Protection Provided

Against fallout radiation: Protection Factor about 200 (PF 200) if covered with 30 in. of earth. (A person in the open outside this shelter would receive about 200 times more fallout radiation than if he were inside.) The drawing at the end of Appendix A.4 shows the earth cover only 20 in. thick, resulting in a PF of about 100.

Against blast: Better protection than most homes. Blast tests have indicated that this shelter would be undamaged at least up to the 5-psi overpressure range from large explosions. Without blast doors the shelter's occupants could be injured at this overpressure range, although probably not fatally.

Against fire: Fair, if the cloth in the entries is covered with mud and if the shelter is sufficiently distant from fires producing carbon monoxide and toxic smoke.

Where Practical

In a location where at least one hollow-core door per occupant is available, where a dry trench at least 14 inches deep can be dug without difficulty, but the water table or rock is too close to the surface for a covered-trench shelter to be practical. (A family evacuating in a pickup truck or large station wagon can carry enough doors, with doorknobs removed. Strong boards at least 6 feet long and at least one full inch thick, or plywood at least 3/4-inch thick, also can be used to roof this shelter and to support its overhead earth shielding.

Warning: Some doors with single-thickness panels if loaded with earth will break before they bend enough to result in protective earth arching.

For Whom Practical

For a typical family or other group with two or more members able to work hard for most of 36 hours. Very little building skill is needed. (An urban family of six, with 14- and 12-year-old sons and 13- and 9-year-old daughters, completed this shelter, sized for six persons, in one long working day: 13 hours and 43 minutes after receiving the step-by-step, will illustrated instructions at their Florida home 10 miles from the rural building site. This family used its pickup truck to carry them, the interior doors, and other survival items.)

Capacity

For each additional person, add another door. (If more than about 7 persons are to be sheltered, build 2 or more separate shelters.)

Building Instructions

1. Before beginning work, study the drawing and read ALL of the following instructions. Divide the work so that some will

be digging while others are building an air pump, storing water, etc. CHECK OFF EACH STEP WHEN COMPLETED.

2. By the time the shelter is finished, plan to have completed a ventilating pump (a 16-in.-wide by 24- in.-high KAP essential except in cold weather) and the storage of 15 gallons of water per occupant.
3. Start to assemble the materials and tools needed. For the illustrated 4-person shelter, these are:

Essential Materials and Tools

- Six doors. Boards or plywood at least 5/8-in. thick can be used to replace one or more of the doors.
- At least 4 double-bed sheets for each of the first four persons, and 3 double-bed sheets for each additional person to be sheltered or enough pieces of fabric and or of plastic to cover at least as large an area as the sheets would cover. (This material is for making aboveground shelter walls, to serve as sand bags.)
- Rainproofing materials (plastic film, shower curtains, plastic tablecloths, mattress protectors, etc.) 15 square yards for the first 4 persons and 2-1/2 square yards for each additional person.
- A shovel (one shovel for each two workers is desirable). A pick or mattock if the ground is very hard.
- A knife (the only essential tool for making a small shelter-ventilating KAP) and materials for a KAP 16 in. wide and 24 in. high.
- Containers for storing water.

Useful Materials and Tools

- Two or more buckets, large cans and or large pots with bail handles to carry earth, and later to store water or wastes.
- Saw (or ax or hatchet) to cut a few boards or small poles.
- Hammer and at least 15 small nails (at least 2-1/2 in. long).

- Tape measure, yardstick, or ruler.
- Additional cloth and/ or plastic equivalent in size to 2 more double-bed sheets for each person.
- Additional waterproof material 2 more square yards per person.
- Pillowcases, or cloth or plastic bags to serve as earth-filled sand bags. The more, the better.

4. To save time and work, sharpen all tools and keep them sharp.
5. Wear gloves from the start, to help prevent blisters and infections.
6. Select a building site where there is little or no chance of the ground being covered with water, and where the water table (groundwater level) is not likely to rise closer than 18 inches to the surface.
7. To avoid the extra work of digging among roots, select a site away from trees, if practical.
8. To lessen the dangers of fire and smoke from nearby houses or trees that might catch fire, locate your shelter as far as is practical from houses and flammable vegetation.
9. Before staking out your shelter, provide one door per person to roof the main room plus one additional door for each of the two entries. Be sure the door knobs have been removed. Use the two widest doors to roof the entries.
10. To be sure that all the walls will be in the proper positions to be roofed with the available doors, lay all the doors on the ground, touching each other and in the same relative positions they will have when used to roof the shelter. When all the roof doors are on the ground, side by side, determine the exact length of the shelter room.
11. Stake out the shelter
12. Make the earth-filled "rolls" that will form the aboveground walls of your shelter. To make walls out of the rolls:

(1) Use doors as vertical forms to hold the earth-filled rolls in place until the walls are completed. (These are the same doors that you will use later to roof the shelter.)

(2) Brace the door-forms with 36-in.-long braces (boards or sticks) that press against the doors. Nail only the upper braces, using only very small nails.

(3) After the forms for the two inner sides of the shelter have been finished, put parts of the long sides of bedsheets on the ground, as illustrated. (Or use other equally wide, strong cloth or plastic material.) About a 2- ft width of cloth should be on the ground, and the rest of each sheet should be folded up out of the way, over the outsides of the door-forms. Adjacent sheets should overlap about 1 ft when making a roll than is longer than one sheet.

(4) Shovel earth onto the parts of the sheet on the ground to the height of the rolls you are making, as shown. Note that the roll to be made on one side is 2 in. higher than the roll on the other side.

(5) Shape the surface of the shoveled-on earth as illustrated, to hold the hooks" of cloth to be formed when the exposed sides of the sheets are folded down.

(6) Fold down the upper side of each sheet while pulling on it to keep it tight and without wrinkles. It should lie on the prepared earth surface, including the small narrow trench, as illustrated in the first section of this appendix.

(7) Pack earth onto the part of the folded-down sheet that is in the narrow, shallow trench. Then, as shown in the sketches at the bottom of the accompanying drawing, fold back the loose edge over this small amount of packed earth to form a "hook." (The hook keeps the weight of the earth inside a roll from pulling the cloth out of its proper position.)

(8) Make a roll first on one side of the shelter, then on the other, to keep the heights of the earth on both sides of the shelter about equal. This will keep the unequal heights of earth from pushing the door-forms out of their vertical positions.

(9) Add additional earth on top of the rolls so that the height of the level earth surface, out to the full width of a roll, is the same as the height of the cloth-covered part of the roll that is against the door-form.

(10) When the roll walls have been raised to their planned heights on both sides of the shelter, remove the braces and the doorforms - being careful to keep the brace nails from damaging the doors.

(11) The door-forms of the side-walls of the shelter can be removed before building the end-walls.

13. When smoothing the earth surfaces of the final tops of the roll walls on both sides, check to see that they have the same slope as the lower sides of the roof doors will have after they are placed on the roll walls. (A slope is necessary so that rainwater reaching the waterproof covering to be placed over the doors will run off the lower side.)
14. After the side-walls have been completed (except for their ends that form the sides of an entry) and after the door-forms have been removed, use the same doors for forms to build the two 22-in.-wide entries.
15. Use earth-filled "sand bags" (made of pillowcases or sacks, and/ or the tucked-in ends of earth- filled rolls) to make the outer ends of each entryway.
16. Make the two doorway frames if lumber, nails, and a saw are available. Make each frame as high as the wall on each side of it, and slope the top board of each frame so that it will press flat against the door to be supported. (If materials for a frame are lacking, place a single 2 by 4-in. board or a pole about 6 ft. long across the top of the entry.

17. After carefully removing all the temporary braces from the door-forms and the doors themselves, improve the slopes of the tops of all supporting walls so that the doors will be supported evenly and, without being twisted, will make contact with the smooth, sloping earth or cloth upon which they will rest.
18. If more than enough waterproof plastic or similar material is available to cover all the roof doors, also cover the tops of the walls on which the roof doors will rest. This will keep the doors from absorbing water from damp earth.
19. Dig the illustrated 14-in.-deep, 36-in.-wide trench inside the shelter. (If the water table is too high to dig down 14 in.., in some locations the walls can be raised to a height of 38 in. by cutting turf sods and laying them on top of the walls. Another way the wall height can be increased is by making additional rolls.)
20. Place the roof doors in their final positions, and cover them with waterproof material (if available). Be sure the waterproof material is folded under the higher edges of the doors to keep the material from slipping downward on the sloping doors as earth is shoveled onto the roof.
21. Extend the waterproof material on top of the doors a couple of feet beyond the lower ends of the doors if enough material is available to cover all of the roof doors.
22. When shoveling the first layer of earth onto the rainproof material protecting the doors, avoid hitting and possibly puncturing it with rocks or sharp pointed roots in the earth.
23. To make earth arching more effective in supporting most of the earth to be placed on the roof doors, first mound earth on and near the ends of the doors.
24. Cover the roof with at least 20 in. of earth. Make sure that there also is a thickness of at least 20 in. of earth at the corners of both the room and entries.
25. To prevent surface water from running into the shelter if it rains hard, mound packed earth about 5 in. high just inside

the two entries. Rain can be kept out by a small canopy or awning that extends 2 or 3 ft in front of the outermost edge of a doorway that roofs an entry.

26. If any waterproof material remains, use it to cover the floor of the shelter.
27. If the weather is warm or hot, install a 16-in.-wide by 24-in.-high air pump (a KAP). Attach its hinges to the board across the roof of the entry into which outside air is moving naturally at the time. (If short of time or materials for a KAP, make a small Directional Fan.)
28. Cover all exposed combustible material with mud, earth, or other fireproof material, to reduce the chance of exposed cloth being ignited from a nuclear explosion or heat from a nearby fire.
29. Fill all available water containers, including pits which have been dug and lined with plastic, then roofed with available materials. If possible, disinfect all water stored in expedient containers, using one scant teaspoon of a chlorine bleach, such as Clorox, for each 10 gallons of water. Even if only muddy water is available, store it. If you do not have a disinfectant, it may be possible to boil water when needed.
30. Put at least your most useful emergency tools inside your shelter.
31. As time and materials permit, continue to improve your chances of surviving by doing as many of the following things as possible:
    (1) Make a homemade fallout meter, and expedient lights. (Prudent people will have made these extremely useful items well ahead of time.)
    (2) Install screens or mosquito netting over the two openings, if mosquitoes or flies are a problem. Remember, however, that screen or netting reduces the air flow through a shelter even when the air is pumped through with a KAP.

6

Ration and Equipments Supply

Painful thirst has been experienced by very few Americans. We take for granted that we will always have enough water to drink. Most of us think of "food and water" in that order, when we think of survival essentials that should be stored. But if unprepared citizens were confined in a shelter by heavy fallout, they soon would realize that they should have given first priority to storing adequate water.

For the kidneys to eliminate waste products effectively, the average person needs to drink enough water so that he urinates at least one pint each day. (When water is not limited, most people drink enough to urinate 2 pints. Additional water is lost in perspiration, exhaled breath, and excrement.) Under cool conditions, a person could survive for weeks on 3 pints of water a day if he eats but little food and if that food is low in protein. Cool conditions, however, would be the exception in crowded belowground shelters occupied for many days. Under such circumstances four or five quarts of drinking water per day are essential in very hot weather, with none allowed for washing. For a two-week shelter stay, 15 gallons per person should be stored in or close to a shelter. This amount usually would provide for some water remaining after two weeks, to prevent thirst in case fallout dangers were to continue.

In a 1962 Navy shelter occupancy test lasting two weeks, 99 sailors each consumed an average of 2.4 quarts (2.3 liters) of water per day. The test was conducted in August near Washington, D.C.;

the weather was unseasonably cool. The shelter was not air-conditioned except during the last two days of the test.

When one is sweating heavily and not eating salty food, salt deficiency symptoms especially cramping are likely to develop within a few days. To prevent this, 6 or 8 grams of salt (about 1/4 oz, or 1/2 tablespoon) should be consumed daily in food and drink. If little or no food is eaten, this small daily salt ration should be added to drinking water. Under hot conditions, a little salt makes water taste better.

CARRYING WATER

Most families have only a few large containers that could be used for carrying water to a shelter and storing it in adequate amounts for several weeks. Polyethylene trash bags make practical expedient water containers when used as waterproof liners inside smaller fabric bags or pillowcases. (Plastic bags labeled a& being treated with insecticides or odor-controlling chemicals should not be used.) To close a plastic bag of water so that hardly any will leak out, first spread the top of the bag until the two inner sides of the opening are together. Then fold in the center so that the folded opening is 4 thicknesses, and smooth. Continue smoothly folding in the middle until the whole folded-up opening is only about 1-1/2 inches wide. Then fold the top of the bag over on itself so the folded-up opening points down. With a strip of cloth or a soft cord, bind and tie the folded-over part with a bow knot, as illustrated.

For long hikes, it is best to tie the water-holding plastic bags so that the openings 'are higher than the water levels inside.

To transport this type of expedient water bag in a vehicle, tie a rope around the fabric outer bag near its opening, so that the rope also encircles and holds the plastic liner-bags just below their tied-shut openings. The other end of this rope should then be tied to some support, to keep the openings higher than the water level.

A small pebble, a lump of earth, or a similar object should be tied inside the opening of each bag before the two are tied together, to hold them securely. The bag that is to be carried in front should have the pebble tied about 4 inches further down from the edge of its opening than the pebble tied in the bag to be carried in back. This keeps the pebbles from being pressed against the carrier's shoulder by a heavy load.

A pair of trousers with both legs tied shut at the bottoms can be used to carry a balanced load if pillowcases or other fabric bags are not at hand. Such a balanced load can be slung over the shoulder with the body erect and less strained than if the same weight were carried in a single bag-like pack on the back. However, trouser legs are quite narrow and do not provide room to carry more than a few gallons.

To prevent water from slowly leaking through the tied-shut openings ofplastic bags, the water levels inside should be kept below the openings.

STORING WATER

When storing expedient water bags in a shelter, the water levels inside should be kept below the openings.

Not many expedient shelters would be large enough to store an adequate volume of water for an occupancy lasting two or more weeks. Plastic-lined storage pits, dug in the earth close to the shelter, are dependable for storing large volumes of water using cheap, compact materials.

Large volumes of water can be stored in plastic lined rectangular pits. In order to roof them with widely available materials such as ordinary))-inch plywood or small poles, the pits should be dug no wider than 3 feet. The edges of this plastic sheet were held in place by placing them in shallow trenches dug near the sides of the pit and covering them with earth.

Earth was mounded over the plywood roof to a depth of about 30 inches, with a "buried roof" of polyethylene. The earth cover and its "buried roof" were similar to the pit covering. This rectangular pit contained about 200 gallons of water. No water leaked out after the pit had been subjected to blast effects severe enough to have flattened most substantial buildings. However, rectangular pits at higher overpressures failed, due to sidewall caving that caused leaks.

In a subsequent blast test by Boeing Aerospace Company, a plastic-lined water pit was undamaged at the 200-psi overpressure range. First a rectangular pit 4 ft. wide, 12 ft. long, and 2 ft. deep was dug. Then inside this pit a 2 x l0 x 2-ft. water-storage pit was dug, and lined with plastic film. After being filled full of water, the storage pit was covered with plywood, on which was shoveled 2 ft. of earth.

Plastic garbage cans are usually watertight; most used metal garbage cans are not. If thoroughly cleaned and disinfected with a strong chlorine bleach solution, watertight garbage cans can serve for emergency water storage, as can some wastebaskets. If new plastic film is available, it can be used as a lining to waterproof any strong box. To lessen the chances of the plastic being punctured, rough containers first should be lined with fabric.

If shelter is to be taken in or near a building, water trapped in hot water heaters and toilet flush tanks or stored in tubs might be available after an attack.

Siphoning

Pouring water out of a heavy water-storage bag is inconvenient and often results in spillage. Dipping it out can result in contamination. If a tube or piece of flexible garden hose is available, siphoning is the best way. A field-tested method is described below. To prevent the suction end of the tube from being obstructed by contact with the plastic liner of the bag, tape or tie a wire "protector" to the end, as pictured later in this section.

To start siphoning,' suck on the tube until water reaches your mouth. Next fold over the tube near its end, to keep the tube full.

To cut off the water, fold over the tube and secure it shut with a rubber band or string.

Water can be siphoned from a covered water storage pit into a belowground shelter so that the siphon will deliver running water for weeks, if necessary. The Utah family mentioned earlier siphoned all they needed of the 120 gallons of water stored in a nearby lined pit. A field-tested method of siphoning follows:

1. Dig the water storage pit far enough away from the shelter so that the covering mounds will not interfere with drainage ditches.
2. Use a flexible tube or hose which is no more than 25 feet long. For a single family, a flexible rubber tube with an inside diameter of inch (such as surgical tubing) would be best. A flexible 2-inch hose of the type used with mobile homes and boats serves well.
3. Make sure that the end in the water pit will not press against plastic and block the flow of water. This can be avoided by (1) making and attaching a wire "protector" to the end of the tube, or (2) taping or tying the end to a rock or other object, to keep the end in the desired position.
4. Protect the tube by placing it in a trench about 4 inches deep. This small trench is best dug before roofing either the storage pit or the shelter. Be sure a roof pole or board does not crush the tube. Cover the tube with earth and tie it so that the end in the storage pit cannot be accidentally pulled out of position.
5. To start the flow of water into the shelter, hold the free end of the tube at about the height of the surface of the water in the storage pit, while pulling gently on the tube so that the part in the shelter is practically straight. Exhale as much breath as you can, then place the end of the tube in your mouth, and suck hard and long. (The longer the tube or hose and the larger its diameter, the more times you will have to suck to start the flow of water.)
6. Without taking the tube out of your mouth, shut it off airtight by bending it double near the end.
7. Exhale, straighten the tube, and suck again, repeating until you feel a good flow of water into your mouth while still

sucking. Shut off the flow by bending the tube double before taking it out of your mouth.

8. Quickly lower the end of the tube (which is now full of water) and place the closed end in a container on the shelter floor. Finally, open the end to start the siphoned flow.
9. When you have siphoned enough water, stop the flow by bending the tube double. Keep it closed in the doubled-over, air-tight position with a strong rubber band or string. To prevent loss of water by accidental siphoning, suspend the end of the tube a couple of inches higher than the surface of the water in the storage pit outside and close to where the tube comes into the shelter. (Despite precautions, air may accumulate in the highest part of the tube, blocking a siphoned flow and making it necessary to re-start the siphoning by repeating the sucking.)

DISINFECTING WATER

Water-borne diseases probably would kill more survivors of a nuclear attack than would fallout- contaminated water. Before an attack, if water from a municipal source is stored in expedient containers that could be unclean, it should be disinfected. For long storage, it is best to disinfect all water, since even a few organisms may multiply rapidly and give stored water a bad taste or odor. Properly disinfected water remains safe for many years if stored in thick plastic or glass containers sealed airtight. For multi-year storage do not use thin plastic containers, such as milkjugs, which in time often develop leaks. Any household bleach solution, such as Clorox, that contains sodium hypochlorite as its only active ingredient may be used as a source of chlorine for disinfecting. The amount of sodium hypochlorite, usually 5.25%, is printed on the label. (In recent years, perhaps as a precaution against drinking undiluted chlorine bleach solution, some household bleach containers show a warning such as "Not For Personal Use."

This warning can be safely disregarded if the label states that the bleach contains only sodium hypochlorite as its active ingredient, and if only the small quantities specified in these and other instructions are used to disinfect water.) Add 1 scant teaspoonful to each 10 gallons of clear water, and stir. Add 2 scant teaspoonfuls if the water is muddy or colored. Wait at least 30 minutes before drinking, to allow enough time for the chlorine to kill all the microorganisms. Properly disinfected water should have a slight chlorine odor.

To disinfect small quantities of water, put 2 drops of household bleach containing 5.25% sodium hypochlorite in each quart of clearwater. Use 4 drops if the water is muddy or colored. If a dropper is not available, use a spoon and a square-ended strip of paper or thin cloth about 1/4 inch wide by 2 inches long. Put the strip in the spoon with an end hanging down about 2 inch beyond the end of the spoon.

Then when bleach is placed in the spoon and the spoon is carefully tipped, drops the size of those from a medicine dropper will drip off the end of the strip. As a second choice, 2% tincture of iodine can be used. Add 5 drops to each quart of clear water, and let stand 30 minutes. If the water is cloudy, add 10 drops to each quart. Commercial water purification tablets should be used as directed.

If neither safe water nor chemicals for disinfecting it are available during a crisis, store plenty of the best water at hand even muddy river water. Most mud settles to the bottom in a few days; even in a crowded shelter ways often could be found to boil water. Bringing water to a boil for one minute kills all types of disease-causing bacteria. Boiling for 10 to 20 minutes is required to kill some rarer infective organisms.

SOURCES OF WATER IN FALLOUT AREAS

Survivors of a nuclear attack should realize that neither fallout particles nor dissolved radioactive elements or compounds can be removed from water by chemical disinfection or boiling. Therefore, water should be obtained from the least radioactive sources available. Before a supply of stored drinking water has been exhausted, other sources should be located. The main water sources are given below, with the safest source listed first and the other sources listed in decreasing order of safety.

1. Water from deep wells and from water tanks and covered reservoirs into which no fallout particles or fallout-contaminated water has been introduced. (Caution: Although most spring water would be safe, some spring water is surface water that has flowed into and through underground channels without having been filtered.)
2. Water from covered seepage pits or shallow, hand-dug wells. This water is usually safe IF fallout or fallout-contaminated surface water has been prevented from entering by the use of waterproof coverings and by waterproofing the surrounding ground to keep water from running down outside the well casing. It shows a well dug to obtain safe water from a fallout contaminated source. If the earth is not sandy, gravelly, or too porous, filtration through earth is very effective.
3. Contaminated water from deep lakes. Water from a deep lake would be much less contaminated by dissolved radioactive material and fallout particles than water from a shallow pond would be, if both had the same amount of fallout per square foot of surface area deposited in them. Furthermore, fallout particles settle to the bottom more rapidly in deep lakes than in shallow ponds, which are agitated more by wind.
4. Contaminated water from shallow ponds and other shallow, still water.
5. Contaminated water from streams, which would be especially dangerous if the stream is muddy from the first heavy rains after fallout is deposited. The first runoff will contain most of the radioactive material that can be dissolved from fallout particles deposited on the drainage area. Runoff after the first few heavy rains following the deposit of fallout is not likely to contain much dissolved radioactive material, or fallout.

6. Water collected from fallout-contaminated roofs. This would contain more fallout particles than would the runoff from the ground.
7. Water obtained by melting snow that has fallen through air containing fallout particles, or from snow lying on the ground onto which fallout has fallen. Avoid using such water for drinking or cooking, if possible.

Water from Wells

The wells of farms and rural homes would be the best sources of water for millions of survivors. Following a massive nuclear attack, the electric pumps and the pipes in wells usually would be useless.

Electric power in most areas would be eliminated by the effects of electromagnetic pulse (EM P) from high-altitude bursts and by the effects of blast and fire on power stations, transformers, and transmission lines. However, enough people would know how to remove these pipes and pumps from wells so that bail- cans could be used to reach water and bring up enough for drinking and basic hygiene.

An ordinary large fruit-juice can will serve, if its diameter is at least 1 inch smaller than the diameter of the well-casing pipe. A hole about 1 inch in diameter should be cut in the center of the can's bottom. The hole should be cut from the inside of the can: this keeps the inside of the bottom smooth, so it will serve as a smooth seat for a practically watertight valve. To cut the hole, stand the can on a flat wood surface and press down repeatedly with the point of a sheath knife, a butcher knife, or a sharpened screwdriver.

The best material for the circular, unattached is soft rubber, smooth and thin, such as inner-tube rubber. Alternately, the lid of a can about 3/4 inch smaller in diameter than the bail- can may be used, with several thicknesses of plastic film taped to its smooth lower side. Plastic film about 4 mils thick is best. The bail (handle) of a bail-can should be made of wire, with a loop at the top to which a rope or strong cord should be attached.

Filling-time can be reduced by taping half-a pound of rocks or metal to the bottom of the bail-can.

REMOVING FALLOUT PARTICLES AND DISSOLVED RADIOACTIVE MATERIAL FROM WATER

The dangers from drinking fallout contaminated water could be greatly lessened by using expedient settling and filtration methods to remove fallout particles and most of the dissolved radioactive material. Fortunately, in areas of heavy fallout, less than 2% of the radioactivity of the fallout particles contained in the water would become dissolved in water.25 If nearly all the radioactive fallout particles could be removed by filtering or settling methods, few casualties would be likely to result from drinking and cooking with most fallout- contaminated water.

Filtering

Filtering through earth removes essentially all of the fallout particles and more of the dissolved radioactive material than does boiling-water distillation, a generally impractical purification method that does not eliminate dangerous radioactive iodines. Earth filters are also more effective in removing radioactive iodines than are ordinary ion-exchange water softeners or charcoal filters. In areas of heavy fallout, about 99% of the radioactivity in water could be removed by filtering it through ordinary earth.

To make the simple, effective filter the only materials needed are those found in and around the home. This expedient filter can be built easily by proceeding as follows:

1. Perforate the bottom of a 5-gallon can, a large bucket, a watertight wastebasket, or a similar container with about a dozen nail holes. Punch the holes from the bottom upward, staying within about 2 inches of the center.
2. Place a layer about 1 inches thick of washed pebbles or small stones on the bottom of the can. If pebbles are not available, twisted coat-hanger wires or small sticks can be used.

3. Cover the pebbles with one thickness of terrycloth towel, burlap sackcloth, or other quite porous cloth. Cut the cloth in a roughly circular shape about 3 inches larger than the diameter of the can.
4. Take soil containing some clay almost any soil will do from at least 4 inches below the surface of the ground. (Nearly all fallout particles remain near the surface except after deposition on sand or gravel.)
5. Pulverize the soil, then gently press it in layers over the cloth that covers the pebbles, so that the cloth is held snugly against the sides of the can. Do not use pure clay (not porous enough) or sand (too porous). The soil in the can should be 6 to 7 inches thick.
6. Completely cover the surface of the soil layer with one thickness of fabric as porous as a bath towel. This is to keep the soil from being eroded as water is poured into the filtering can. The cloth also will remove some of the particles from the water. A dozen small stones placed on the cloth near its edges will secure it adequately.
7. Support the filter can on rods or sticks placed across the top of a container that is larger in diameter than the filter can. (A dishpan will do.)

The contaminated water should be poured into the filter can, preferably after allowing it to settle as described below. The filtered water should be disinfected by one of the previously described methods.

If the 6 or 7 inches of filtering soil is a sandy clay loam, the filter initially will deliver about 6 quarts of clear water per hour. (If the filtration rate is faster than about 1 quart in 10 minutes, remove the upper fabric and recompress the soil.) After several hours, the rate will be reduced to about 2 quarts per hour.

When the filtering rate becomes too slow, it can be increased by removing and rinsing the surface fabric, removing about 1 inch of soil, and then replacing the fabric. The life of a filter is extended and its efficiency increased if muddy water is first allowed to settle for several hours in a separate container, as described below. After about 50 quarts have been filtered, rebuild the filter by replacing the used soil with fresh soil.

Settling

Settling is one of the easiest methods to remove most fallout particles from water. Furthermore, if the water to be used is muddy or murky, settling it before filtering will extend the life of the filter. The procedure is as follows:

1. Fill a bucket or other deep container three quarters full of the contaminated water.
2. Dig pulverized clay or clayey soil from a depth of four or more inches below ground surface, and stir it into the water. Use about a 1-inch depth of dry clay or dry clayey soil for every 4-inch depth of water. Stir until practically all the clay particles are suspended in the water.
3. Let the clay settle for at least 6 hours. The settling clay particles will carry most of the suspended fallout particles to the bottom and cover them.
4. Carefully dip out or siphon the clear water, and disinfect it.

Settling and Filtering

Although dissolved radioactive material usually is only a minor danger in fallout-contaminated water, it is safest to filter even the clear water produced by settling, if an earth filter is available. Finally as always the water should be disinfected.

POST-FALLOUT REPLENISHMENT OF STORED WATER

When fallout decays enough to permit shelter occupants to go out of their shelters for short periods, they should try to replenish their stored water. An enemy may make scattered nuclear strikes for weeks after an initial massive attack. Some survivors may be forced back into their shelters by the resultant fallout. Therefore, all available water containers should be used to store the least contaminated water within reach. Even without filtering, water collected and stored shortly after the occurrence of fallout will become increasingly safer with time, due particularly to the rapid decay of radioactive iodines. These would be the most dangerous contaminants of water during the first few weeks after an attack.

FOOD

Minimum Needs

The average American is accustomed to eating regularly and abundantly. He may not realize that for most people food would not be essential for survival during the first two or three weeks following a nuclear attack. Exceptions would be infants, small children, and the aged and sick, some of whom might die within a week without proper nourishment. Other things are more important for short-term survival: adequate shelter against the dangers from blast and fallout, an adequate supply of air, and enough water.

The average American also may not realize that small daily amounts of a few unprocessed staple foods would enable him to survive for many months, or even for years. A healthy person if he is determined to live and if he learns how to prepare and use whole-grain wheat or corn can maintain his health for several months. If beans are also available and are substituted for some of the grain, the ration would be improved and could maintain health for many months.

The nutritional information given in this chapter is taken from a July, 1979 publication, Maintaining Nutritional Adequacy During a Prolonged Food Crisis. This book brings together from worldwide sources the nutritional facts needed to help unprepared people use unaccustomed foods advantageously during the prolonged crisis that would follow a heavy nuclear attack. The practical know-how which will be given in this chapter regarding the expedient processing and cooking of basic grains and beans is based on old ways which are mostly unknown to modern Americans. These methods have been improved and field-tested by civil defense researchers at Oak Ridge National Laboratory.

Loss of High-protein Animal Foods

A massive nuclear attack would eliminate the luxurious, complicated American system of food production, processing, and distribution. Extensive, heavy fallout and the inability of farmers to feed their animals would kill most of the cattle, hogs, and chickens that are the basis of our high-protein diet. The livestock most likely to survive despite their owners' inability to care for them would be cattle on pasture. However, these grazing animals would swallow large numbers of fallout particles along with grass, and many would drink contaminated water. Their digestive tracts would suffer severe radiation damage. Also, they would suffer radiation burns from fallout particles. Thus in an outdoor area where the total dose from gamma radiation emitted within a few days from fallout particles on the ground might be only 150 R, most grazing animals probably would be killed by the combined effects of external gamma- ray radiation, beta burns, and internal radiation.

Precautions When Eating Meat

In areas where the fallout would not be enough to sicken animals, their meat would be safe food. In fallout areas, however, animals that have eaten or drunk fallout-contaminated food or water will have concentrated radioactive atoms and molecules in their internal organs. The thyroid gland, kidneys, and liver especially should not be eaten. If an animal appears to be sick, it should not be eaten. The animal might be suffering from a sickening or fatal radiation dose and might have developed a bacterial infection as a result of this dose. Meat contaminated with the toxins produced by some kinds of bacteria could cause severe illness or death if eaten, even if thoroughly cooked.

Under crisis conditions, all meat should be cooked until it is extremely well done - cooked long past the time when it loses the last of its pink color. To be sure that the center of each piece of meat is raised to boiling temperature, the meat should be cut into pieces that are less than 1/2-inch thick before cooking. This precaution also reduces cooking time and saves fuel.

Survival of Breeding Stock

Extensive areas of the United States would not receive fallout heavy enough to kill grazing animals. The millions of surviving animals would provide some food and the fertile breeding stock needed for national recovery. The loss of fertility caused by severe radiation doses is rarely permanent. Extensive experiments with animals have shown that the offspring of severely irradiated animals are healthy and fertile.

Living on Basic Plant Foods

Even if almost all food-producing animals were lost, most surviving Americans should be able to live on the foods that enable most of the world's population to live and multiply: grains, beans, and vegetables. And because of the remarkable productivity of American agriculture, there usually would be enough grain and beans in storage to supply surviving Americans with sufficient food for at least a year following a heavy nuclear attack. The problem would be to get the unprocessed foods, which are stored in food-producing regions, to the majority of survivors who would be outside these regions. Surprisingly little transportation would be needed to carry adequate quantities of these unprocessed foods to survivors in famine areas. A single large trailer truck can haul 40,000 pounds of wheat enough to keep 40,000 people from feeling hunger pains for a day. More than enough such trucks and the fuel needed to carry basic foods to food-short areas would survive a massive nuclear attack. It is likely that reasonably strong American leadership and morale would prevail so that, after the first few weeks, millions of the survivors in starving areas should receive basic unprocessed foods.

Eating food produced in the years after a large attack would cause an increase in the cancer rate, due primarily to its content of radioactive strontium and cesium from fallout-contaminated soil. Over the first 30 years following an attack, this increase would be a small fraction of the number of additional cancer deaths that would result from external radiation. Cancer deaths would be one of the tragic, delayed costs of a nuclear war, but all together would not be numerous enough to endanger the long-term survival of the population.

Live Off the Land?

Very few survivors of a heavy attack would be in areas where they could live off the land like primitive hunters and gatherers. In extensive areas where fallout would not be heavy enough to kill human beings, wild creatures would die from the combined effects 'of external gamma radiation, swallowed fallout particles, and beta burns on their bodies. Survival plans should not include dependence on hunting, fishing, or gathering wild plants.

Food for Shelter Occupants

Most people would need very little food to live several weeks; however, the time when survivors of blast and fallout would leave their shelters would mark the beginning of a much longer period of privation and hard manual labor. Therefore, to maintain physical strength and morale, persons in shelters ideally should have enough healthful food to provide well-balanced, adequate meals for many weeks.

In most American homes there are only enough ready-to-eat, concentrated foods to last a few days. Obviously, it would be an important survival advantage to keep on hand a two-week supply of easily transportable foods. In any case, occupants of shelters would be uncertain about when they could get more food and would have to make hard decisions about how much to eat each day. During the first few weeks of a food crisis, lack of vitamins and other essentials of a well-balanced diet would not be of primary importance to previously well-nourished people. Healthful foods with enough calories to provide adequate energy would meet short-term needs.

If water is in short supply, high-protein foods such as meat are best eaten only in moderation, since a person eating high-protein foods requires more water than is needed when consuming an equal number of calories from foods high in carbohydrates.

Expedient Processing of Grainsa ND Soybeans

Whole-kernel grains or soybeans cannot be eaten in sufficient quantities to maintain vigor and health if merely boiled or parched. A little boiled whole-kernel wheat is a pleasantly chewy breakfast cereal, but experimenters at Oak Ridge got sore tongues and very loose bowels when they tried to eat enough boiled whole-kernel wheat to supply even half of their daily energy needs. Some pioneers, however, ate large quantities of whole-kernel wheat without harmful results after boiling and simmering it for many hours. Even the most primitive peoples who subsist primarily on grains grind or pound them into a meal or paste before cooking. (Rice is the only important exception.) Few Americans know how to process whole-kernel grains and soybeans (our largest food reserves) into meal. This ignorance could be fatal to survivors of a nuclear attack.

Making an expedient metate, the hollowed-out grinding stone of Mexican Indians, proved impractical under simulated post-attack conditions. Pounding grain into meal with a rock or a capped, solid-ended piece of pipe is extremely slow work. The best expedient means developed and field-tested for pounding grain or beans into meal and flour is an improvised 3-pipe grain mill. Instructions for making and using this effective grain-pounding device follow.

Improvised Grain Mill

The grain mill described can efficiently pound whole-grain wheat, corn, etc., into meal and flour thereby greatly improving digestibility and avoiding the diarrhea and sore mouths that would result from eating large quantities of unground grain.

To Build:

(1) Cut 3 lengths of pipe, each 30 inches long; 3/4-inch-diameter steel pipe (such as ordinary water pipe) is best.

(2) Cut the working ends of the pipe off squarely. Remove all roughness, leaving the full-wall thickness. Each working end should have the full diameter of the pipe.

(3) In preparation for binding the three pieces of pipe together into a firm bundle, encircle each piece of pipe with cushioning, slip-preventing tape, string or cloth in the locations illustrated.

(4) Tape or otherwise bind the 3 pipes into a secure bundle so that their working ends are as even as possible and are in the same plane resting evenly on a flat surface.

(5) Cut the top smoothly out of a large can. A 4-inch-diameter, 7-inch-high fruit-juice can is ideal. If you do not have a can, improvise something to keep grain together while pounding it.

To Make Meal And Flour:

(1) Put clean, dry grain ONE INCH DEEP in the can.

(2) To prevent blistering your hands, wear gloves, or wrap cloth around the upper part of the bundle of pipes.

(3) Place the can (or open-ended cylinder) on a hard, smooth, solid surface, such as concrete.

(4) To pound the grain, sit with the can held between your feet. Move the bundle of pipes straight up and down about 3 inches, with a rapid stroke.

(5) If the can is 4 inches in diameter, in 4 minutes you should be able to pound 1-1/2 lb. (one cup) of whole-kernel wheat into 1/5 lb. of fine meal and flour, and 3/10 lb. of coarse meal and fine-cracked wheat.

(6) To separate the pounded grain into fine meal, flour, coarse meal, and fine-cracked wheat, use a sieve made of window screen.

(7) To separate flour for feeding small children, place some pounded grain in an 18 X 18-inch piece of fine nylon net, gather the edges of the net together so as to hold the grain, and shake this bag-like container.

(8) To make flour fine enough for babies, pound fine meal and coarse flour still finer, and sieve it through a piece of cheesecloth or similar material.

As soon as fallout decay permits travel, the grain-grinding machines on tens of thousands of hog and cattle farms should be used for milling grain for survivors. It is vitally important to national recovery and individual survival to get back as soon as possible to labor-saving, mechanized ways of doing essential work. In an ORNL experiment, a farmer used a John Deere Grinder-Mixer powered by a 100-hp tractor to grind large samples of wheat and barley. When it is used to grind rather coarse meal for hogs, this machine is rated at 12 tons per hour. Set to grind a finer meal-flour mixture for human consumption, it ground both hard wheat and feed barley at a rate of about 9 tons per hour. This is 2400 times as fast as using muscle power to operate even the best expedient grain mill. With its finest screen installed, this large machine can produce about 3 tons of whole wheat flour per hour.

Unlike wheat and corn, the kernels of barley, grain sorghums, and oats have rough, fibrous hulls that must be removed from the digestible parts to produce an acceptable food. Moistening the grain will toughen such hulls and make them easier to remove. If the grain is promptly pounded or ground into meal, the toughened hulls will break into larger pieces than will the hulls of undampened grain. A small amount of water, weighing about 2% of the weight of the grain, should be used to dampen the grain. For 3 pounds of grain (about 6 cups), sprinkle with about one ounce (28 grams, or about 2 tablespoons) of water, while stirring constantly to moisten all the kernels. After about 5 minutes of stirring, the grain will appear dry. The small amount of water will have dampened and toughened the hulls, but the edible parts- inside will have remained dry. Larger pieces of hull are easier to remove after grinding than smaller pieces.

One way to remove ground-up hulls from meal is by flotation. Put some of the meal-hulls mixture about 1 inch deep in a pan or pot, cover the mixture with water, and stir. Skim off the floating hulls, then pour off the water and more hulls. Sunken pieces of hulls that settle on top of the heavier meal can be removed with one's fingers as the last of the water is poured off. To produce a barley meal good for very small children, the small pieces of hulls must again be separated by flotation.

To lessen their laxative effects, all grains should be ground as finely as possible, an i ... e hulls should be removed. Grains also will be digested more ...sily if they are finely ground. The occupants of crowded shelters should be especially careful to avoid foods that cause diarrhea.

Cooking With Minimum Fuel

In areas of heavy fallout, people would have to remain continuously in crowded shelters for many days. Then they would have to stay in the shelters most of each 24 hours for weeks. Most shelter occupants soon would consume all of their ready-to-eat foods; therefore, they should have portable, efficient cook stoves. A cook stove is important for another reason: to help maintain morale. Even in warm weather, people need some hot food and drink for the comforting effect and to promote a sense of well-being. This is particularly true when people are under stress. The Bucket Stove pictured on the following pages was the most satisfactory of several models of expedient stoves developed at Oak Ridge and later field-tested.

Bucket Stove

If operated properly, this stove burns only about 1/2 pound of dry wood or newspaper to heat 3 quarts of water from 600 F to boiling.

Materials required for the stove:

* A metal bucket or can, 12- to 16-quart sizes preferred. The illustrations show a 14-quart bucket and a 6-quart pot.
* Nine all-metal coat hangers for the parts made of wire. (To secure the separate parts of the movable coat-hanger wire grate, 2 feet of finer wire is helpful.)

* A 6 X 10-inch piece of a large fruit-juice can, for a damper.

Construction:

With a chisel (or a sharpened screw driver) and a hammer, cut a 4-1/2 X 4-1/2-inch hole in the side of the bucket about 1-1/2 inches above its bottom. To avoid denting the side of the bucket when chiseling out the hole, place the bucket over the end of a log or similar solid object.

To make the damper, cut a 6-inch-wide by 10-inch-high piece out of a large fruit-juice can or from similar light metal. Then make the two coathanger-wire springs illustrated, and attach them to the piece of metal by bending and hammering the outer 1 inch of the two 6-inch-long sides over and around the two spring wires. This damper can be slid up and down, to open and close the hole in the bucket. The springs hold it in any desired position. (If materials for making this damper are not available, the air supply can be regulated fairly well by placing a brick, rock, or piece of metal so that it will block off part of the hole in the side of the bucket.)

To make a support for the pot, punch 4 holes in the sides of the bucket, equally spaced around it and about 3-1/2 inches below the bucket's top. Then run a coat-hanger wire through each of the two pairs of holes on opposite sides of the bucket.

Bend these two wires over the top of the bucket, as illustrated, so that their four ends form free-ended springs to hold the cooking pot centered in the bucket. Pressure on the pot from these four free-ended, sliding springs does not hinder putting it into the stove or taking it out.

To lessen heat losses through the sides and bottom of the bucket, cover the bottom with about 1 inch of dry sand or earth. Then line part of the inside and bottom with two thicknesses of heavy-duty aluminum foil, if available.

To make it easier to place the pot in the stove or take it out without spilling its contents, replace the original bucket handle with a longer piece of strong wire.

Operation:

The Bucket Stove owes its efficiency to: (1) the adjustable air supply that flows up through the burning fuel, (2) the movable grate that lets the operator keep the maximum amount of flame in contact with the bottom of the cooking pot, and (3) the space between the sides of the pot and the inside of the bucket that keeps the rising hot gases in close contact with the sides of the pot.

In a shelter, a Bucket Stove should be placed as near as practical to an air exhaust opening before a fire is started in it.

If wood is to be burned, cut and split dry wood into small pieces approximately 1/2 inch square and 6 inches long. Start the fire with paper and small slivers of wood, placing some under the wire grate. To keep fuel from getting damp in a humid shelter, keep it in a large plastic bag.

If newspaper is to be burned, use half-pages folded and twisted into 5-inch-long "sticks," as illustrated. Using the wire tongs, feed a paper "stick" into the fire about every half-minute.

Add fuel and adjust the damper to keep the flame high enough to reach the bottom of the pot, but not so high as to go up the sides of the pot.

To use the Bucket Stove for heating in very cold weather, remove the pot and any insulation around the sides of the bucket; burn somewhat more fuel per minute.

If used with the Fireless Cooker described on the following pages, a Bucket Stove can be used to thoroughly cook beans, grain, or tough meat in water. Three quarts of such food can be cooked with less fuel than is required to soft-boil an egg over a small campfire.

Fireless Cooker

A Fireless Cooker cooks by keeping a lidded pot of boiling-hot food so well insulated all around that it loses heat very slowly. One of these simple fuel-saving devices made from a bushel basket filled with insulating newspapers, with a towel-lined cavity in the center. The Cavity is the size of the 6-quart pot. A towel in this cavity goes all around the pot and will be placed over it to restrict air circulation. If the boiling-hot pot of food is then covered with newspapers about 4 inches thick, the temperature will remain for hours so near boiling that in 4 or 5 hours even slow-cooking food will be ready to eat.

The essential materials for making an effective Fireless Cooker are enough of any good insulating materials (blankets, coats, paper, hay that is dry and pliable) to cover the boiling-hot pot all over with at least 3 or 4 inches of insulation. A container to keep the insulating materials in place around the pot is useful.

Wheat, other grains, and small pieces of tough meat can be thoroughly cooked by boiling them briskly for only about 5 minutes, then insulating the pot in a Fireless Cooker for 4 or 5 hours, or overnight. Whole beans should be boiled for 10 to 15 minutes before they are placed in a Fireless Cooker.

COOKING GRAIN AND BEANS WHEN SHORT OF FUEL OR POTS

Cooking Grain Alone

When whole grains are pounded or ground by expedient means, the result usually is a mixture of coarse meal, fine meal, and a little flour. Under shelter conditions, the best way to cook such meal is first to bring the water to a boil (3 parts of water for 1 part of meal). Add 1 teaspoon (5 grams) of salt per pound of dry meal.

Remove the pot from the fire (or stop adding fuel to a Bucket Stove) and quickly stir the meal into the hot water. (If the meal is stirred into briskly boiling water, lumping becomes a worse problem.) Then, while stirring constantly, again bring the pot to a rolling boil. Since the meal is just beginning to swell, more unabsorbed water remains, so there is less sticking and scorching than if the meal were added to cold water and then brought to a boil.

If any type of Fireless Cooker is available, the hot cereal only has to be boiled and stirred long enough so that no thin, watery part remains. This usually takes about 5 minutes. Continue to cook, either in the Fireless Cooker for at least 4 or 5 hours, or by boiling for an additional 15 or 20 minutes.

When it is necessary to boil grain meal for many minutes, minimize sticking and scorching by cooking 1 part of dry meal with at least 4 parts of water. However, cooking a thinner hot cereal has a disadvantage during a food crisis: an increased volume of food must be eaten to satisfy one's energy needs.

If grain were the only food available, few Americans doing physical work could eat enough of it to maintain their weight at first, until their digestive tracts enlarged from eating the very bulky foods. This adaptation could take a few months. Small children could not adjust adequately to an all-grain diet: for them, concentrated foods such as fats also are needed to provide enough calories to maintain growth and health.

Cooking Grain and Beans Together

When soybeans are being used to supplement the lower quality proteins of grain and when fuel or pots are in short supply, first grind or pound the beans into a fine meal. To further reduce cooking time, soak the bean meal for a couple of hours, keeping it covered with water as it swells. Next put the soaked bean meal into a pot containing about 3 times as much water as the combined volume of a mixture of 1 part of dry bean meal and 3 or 4 parts of dry grain meal. Gently boil the bean meal for about 15 minutes, stirring frequently, before adding the grain meal and completing the cooking.

Stop boiling and add the grain meal while stirring constantly. Again bring the pot to a boil, stirring to prevent sticking and scorching, and boil until the meal has swelled enough to have absorbed all the water. After salting, boil the grain-bean mush for another 15 minutes or more before eating, or put it in a fireless cooker for at least 4 or 5 hours.

Soybeans boiled alone have a taste that most people find objectionable. Also, whole soybeans must be boiled for a couple of hours to soften them sufficiently.

But if soybeans are pounded or ground into a fine meal, and then 1 part of the soybean meal is boiled with 4 parts of meal made from corn or another grain, the soybeans give a pleasant sweetish taste to the resulting mush. The unpleasant soybean taste is eliminated. If cooked as described above, soybeans and other beans or dried peas can be made digestible and palatable with minimum cooking.

100% Grain and 100% Bean Diets

A diet consisting solely of wheat, corn, or rice, and salt has most of the essential nutrients. The critical deficiencies would be vitamins A, C, and D. Such a grain-based diet can serve adults and older children as their '"staff of life" for months. Table 9.1 shows how less than 1-3/4pounds of whole wheat or dry yellow corn satisfies most of the essential nutritional requirements of a long-term emergency ration. [The nutritional values that are deficient are printed in bold type, to make an easier comparison with the Emergency Recommendations, also printed in bold type. Food energy is given in kilocalories (kcal), commonly called calories (Cal).] Expedient ways of supplying the nutrients missing from these rations are described in a following section of this chapter.

Other common whole grains would serve about as well as wheat and yellow corn. At least 1/6 oz of salt per day (about 5 grams) is essential for any ration that is to be eaten for more than a few' days, but 1/3 oz. (about 10 g or 3/4 tablespoon) should be available to allow for increased salt needs and to make grain and beans more palatable. This additional salt would be consumed as needed.

To repeat: few Americans at first would be able to eat the 3 or 4 quarts of thick mush that would be necessary with a ration consisting solely of whole-kernel wheat or corn.

Only healthy Americans determined to survive would be likely to fare well for months on such unaccustomed and monotonous food as an all-grain diet. Eating two or more different kinds of grain and cooking in different ways would make an all-grain diet both more acceptable and more nourishing.

Not many people would be able to eat 27 oz (dry weight before cooking) of beans in a day, and fewer yet could eat a daily ration of almost 23 oz of soybeans. Beans as single-food diets are not recommended because their large protein content requires the drinking of more fluids. Roasted peanuts would provide a better single-food ration.

Grain Supplemented with Beans

People who live on essentially vegetarian diets eat a little of their higher-quality protein food at every meal, along with the grain that is their main source of nutrition.

Thus Mexicans eat some beans along with their corn tortillas, and Chinese eat a little fermented soybean food or a bit of meat or fish with a bowl of rice.

a) Salt (1/3oz., or 10 g., or 3/4 tablespoon) should be available. This would be consumed as needed.

b) White corn supplies no Vitamin A, whereas yellow corn supplies 49 RE (retinol equivalent, a measure of Vitamin A value) per 100 g dry weight. Most corn in the United States is yellow corn.

c) If a diet contains some animal protein such as meat, eggs, or milk, the recommended protein would be less than 55 g per day. If most of the protein is from milk or eggs, only 41 g per day is recommended.

d) The niacin in corn is not fully available unless the corn is treated with an alkali, such as the lime or ashes Mexicans (and many Americans) add to the water in which corn kernels are soaked or boiled.

e) Infants, children, and pregnant and lactating women should receive 10 g (10 micrograms, or 400 IU) of vitamin D. For others, the current recommended daily allowance (RDA) for vitamin D is 200 IU (5 g).

Nutritionists have found that grains are low in some of the essential amino acids that the human body needs to build its proteins.

For long-term good health, the essential amino acids must be supplied in the right proportions with each meal by eating some foods with more complete proteins than grains have. Therefore, in a prolonged food crisis one should strive to eat at every meal at least a little of any higher-quality protein foods that are available. These include ordinary beans, soybeans, milk powder, meat, and eggs.

By adding 7.0 oz (200 g) of red beans (or other common dried beans) to 21.1 oz (600 g) of either whole wheat or yellow corn, with salt added, you can produce rations that contain adequate amounts of all the important nutrients except vitamin C, vitamin A, vitamin D, and fat.

If 5.3 oz (150 g) of soybeans are substituted for the red beans, the fat requirement is satisfied. The 600 g of yellow corn contains enough carotene to enable the body to produce more than half the emergency recommendation of vitamin A. The small deficiencies in riboflavin would not cause sickness.

Other abundant grains, such as grain sorghums or barley, may be used instead of the wheat or corn shown in Table 9.2 to produce fairly well-balanced rations. Other legumes would serve to supplement grain about as well as red beans. (Peanuts are the exception: although higher in energy (fat) than any other unprocessed food, the quality of their protein is not as high as that of other legumes.)

EXPEDIENT WAYS TO SUPPLY DEFICIENT ESSENTIAL NUTRIENTS

Vitamin C

A deficiency of vitamin C (ascorbic acid) causes scurvy. This deadly scourge would be the first nutritional disease to afflict people having only grain and/or beans and lacking the know-how needed to sprout them and produce enough vitamin C. Within only 4 to 6 weeks of eating a ration containing no vitamin C, the first symptom of scurvy would appear: swollen and bleeding gums. This would be followed by weakness, then large bruises, hemorrhages, and wounds that would not heal. Finally, death from hemorrhages and heart failure would result. The simplest and least expensive way to make sure that you, your family and neighbors do not suffer or die post-attack from scurvy is to buy one kilogram (1,000,000 milligrams) of pure vitamin C, which is the crystalline "ascorbic acid" form. Unlike vitamin C tablets, pure vitamin C crystals do not deteriorate. An inexpensive mail-order source is Bronson Pharmaceutical, 4526 Rinetti Lane, La Canada, California 91011; in 1988 I bought one kilogram for $18.75, postage paid. An ample daily dose is 25 milligrams, about 0.0009 ounce. Ten grams (about one third ounce) is enough for a whole year for one person who is eating only unsprouted grain and/or other foods providing no vitamin C.

One gram (1,000 mg) of crystalline ascorbic acid is 1/4 teaspoonful. If you do not have a 1/4 teaspoon, put one level teaspoonful of the crystals on a piece of paper, and divide the little pile into 4 equal parts; each will be approximately 1,000 mg. One of these 1,000 mg piles can easily be divided into 4 tiny piles, each 250 mg. A 250 mg pile provides 10 ample daily doses of 25 mg each. If your family has a 1,000,000 mg supply, taking a 50 mg daily dose of pure crystalline ascorbic acid may be preferred, either sprinkled on food or dissolved in water.

Daily rations of whole wheat or yellow corn supplemented with soybeans or red beans. Recommended daily salt ration, including salt in food: 3/4 tablespoon (1/3 0z, or ID g).

a) White corn supplies no vitamin A, whereas yellow corn supplies 49RE (retinol equivalent, a measure of vitamin A value) per 100g dry weight. Most corn in the United States is yellow corn.

b) If a diet contains animal protein such as meat, eggs or milk, the recommended protein would be less than 55g per day. If all the protein is from milk or eggs, only 41g per day is required.

c) The niacin in corn is not fully available unless corn is treated with an alkali, such as the lime or ashes added by Mexicans and Americans in the South and Southwest to the water in which they soak or boil corn kernels.

d) Infants, children, and pregnant and lactating women should receive 10 g (10 micrograms, or 400 IU) of vitamin D. For others, the Current recommended daily allowance (RDA) for vitamin D is 200 IU (5 g).

One good expedient way to prevent or cure scurvy is to eat sprouted seeds not just the sprouts. Sprouted beans prevented scurvy during a famine in India. Captain James Cook was able to keep his sailors from developing scurvy during a three-year voyage by having them drink an unfermented beer made from dried, sprouted barley. For centuries the Chinese have prevented scurvy during the long winters of northern China by consuming sprouted beans.

Only 10 mg of vitamin C taken each day (1/5 of the smallest vitamin C tablet) is enough to prevent scurvy. If a little over an ounce (about 30 grams) of dry beans or dry wheat is sprouted until the sprouts are a little longer than the seeds, the sprouted seeds will supply 10 to 15 mg of vitamin C. Such sprouting, if done at normal room temperature, requires about 48 hours. To prevent sickness and to make sprouted beans more digestible, the sprouted seeds should be boiled in water for not longer than 2 minutes. Longer cooking will destroy too much vitamin C.

Usual sprouting methods produce longer sprouts than are necessary when production of enough vitamin C is the objective. These methods involve rinsing the sprouting seeds several times a day in safe water. Since even survivors not confined to shelters are likely to be short of water should be used. First the seeds to be sprouted are picked clean of trash and broken seeds. Then the seeds are covered with water and soaked for about 12 hours. Next, the water is drained off and the soaked, swollen seeds are placed on the inside of a plastic bag or ajar, in a layer no more than an inch deep. If a plastic bag is used, you should make two loose rolls of paper, crumple them a little, dampen them, and place them inside the bag, along its sides. These two dampened paper rolls keep the plastic from resting on the seeds and form an air passage down the center of the bag. Wet paper should be placed in the mouth of the bag or jar so as to leave an air opening of only about 1 square inch.

If this paper is kept moist, the seeds will remain sufficiently damp while receiving enough circulating air to prevent molding. They will sprout sufficiently after about 48 hours at normal room temperature.

Sprouting seeds also increases their content of riboflavin, niacin, and folic acid. Sprouted beans are more digestible than raw, unsprouted beans, but not as easily digested or nourishing as are sprouted beans that have been boiled or sauteed for a couple of minutes. Sprouting is not a substitute for cooking. Contrary to the claims of some health food publications, sprouting does not increase the protein content of seeds, nor does it improve protein quality. Furthermore, sprouting reduces the caloric value of seeds. The warmth generated by germinating seeds reduces their energy value somewhat, as compared to unsprouted seeds.

Vitamin A

Well-nourished adults have enough vitamin A stored in their livers to prevent vitamin A deficiency problems for several months, even if their diet during that time contains none of this essential vitamin. Children would be affected by deficiencies sooner than adults. The first symptom is an inability to see well in dim light. Continuing deficiency causes changes in body tissues. In infants and children, lack of vitamin A can result in stunted growth and serious eye problems even blindness. Therefore, a survival diet should be balanced with respect to vitamin A as soon as possible, with children having priority.

Milk, butter, and margarine are common vitamin A sources that would not be available to most survivors. If these were no longer available, yellow corn, carrots, and green, leafy vegetables (including dandelion greens) would be the best sources. If these foods were not obtainable, the next best source would be sprouted whole-kernel wheat or other grains if seeds could be sprouted for three days in the light, so that the sprouts are green. Although better than no source, sprouting is not a very satisfactory way to meet vitamin A requirements. The development of fibrous roots makes 3-day sprouted wheat kernels difficult to eat. And one must eat a large amount of seeds with green sprouts and roots to satisfy the recommended daily emergency requirements up to 51-1/2 cups of 5-day sprouted alfalfa seeds. Survivors of a nuclear attack would wish they had kept an emergency store of multivitamin pills.

Vitamin D

Without vitamin D, calcium is not adequately absorbed. As a result, infants and children would develop rickets (a disease of defective bone mineralization). A massive nuclear attack would cut off the vast majority of Americans from their main source of vitamin D, fortified milk.

Vitamin D can be formed in the body if the skin is exposed to the ultraviolet rays of the sun. Infants should be exposed to sunlight Very cautiously, initially for only a few minutes especially after a massive nuclear attack. Such an attack possibly could cause atmospheric changes that would permit more ultraviolet light to reach the earth's surface, causing sunburn in the U.S. as severe as on the equator today. In cold weather, maximum exposure of skin to sunlight is best done in a shallow pit shielded from the wind. Exposure in a shallow pit would give about 90 percent protection from gamma radiation from fallout particles on the surrounding ground.

Niacin and Calcium

Niacin deficiency causes pellagra, a disease that results in weakness, a rash on skin exposed to the sun, severe diarrhea, and mental deterioration. If a typical modern American had a diet primarily of corn and lacked the foods that normally supply niacin, symptoms of pellagra would first appear in about 6 months. Since corn is by far our largest crop the U.S. production in 1985 was about 425 billion pounds the skillful treatment of corn would be important to post-attack survival and recovery.

During the first part of this century, pellagra killed thousands of Americans inthe South each year. These people had corn for their principal staple and ate few animal protein foods or beans. Yet

Mexicans, who eat even more corn than did those Southerners- and have even fewer foods of animal origin -- do not suffer from pellagra. The Mexicans' freedom from pellagra is mainly due to their traditional method of soaking and boiling their dried corn in a lime-water solution. They use either dry, unslaked lime (calcium oxide, a dangerously corrosive substance made by roasting limestone) or dry, slaked lime (calcium hydroxide, made by adding water to unslaked lime). Dry lime weighing about 1% as much as the dry corn is added to the soak water, producing an alkaline solution. Wood ashes also can be used instead of lime to make an alkali solution. The alkali treatment of corn makes the niacin available to the human body. However, the niacin in dried corn is not readily available to the body unless the corn has received an alkali treatment. Treating corn with lime has another nutritional advantage: the low calcium content of corn is significantly increased.

Fat

The emergency recommendation for fat is slightly over 1 ounce per day (30 g) of fat or cooking oil. This amount of fat provides only 10% of the calories in the emergency diet, which does not specify a greater amount because fats would be in very short supply after a nuclear attack. This amount is very low when compared to the average diet eaten in this country, in which fat provides about 40% of the calories. It would be difficult for many Americans to consume sufficient calories to maintain normal weight and morale without a higher fat intake; more fat should be made available as soon as possible. Increased fat intake is especially important for young children, to provide calories needed for normal growth and development. Oak Ridge National Laboratory field tests have shown that toddlers and old people, especially, prefer considerably more oil added to grain mush than the emergency recommendation of 10%.

Vitamin B-12 and Animal Protein

Vitamin B-12 is the only essential nutrient that is available in nature solely from animal sources. Since a normal person has a 2 to 4-year supply of vitamin B-12 stored in his liver, a deficiency should not develop before enough food of animal origin would again be available.

Many adults who are strict vegetarians keep in good health for years without any animal sources of food by using grains and beans together. It is more difficult to maintain normal growth and development in young children on vegetarian diets. When sufficient animal sources of food are available, enough should be provided to supply 7 grams of animal protein daily. This could be provided by about 1.4 ounces (38 g) of lean meat, 0.7 ounce (20 g) of nonfat dry milk, or one medium-sized egg. When supplies are limited, young children should be given priority. Again: a little of these high-grade supplementary protein foods should be eaten with every meal.

Iron

Most people live out their lives without benefit of an iron supplement. However, many pregnant and nursing women and some children need supplemental iron to prevent anemia. One tested expedient way to make more iron available is to use iron pots and pans, especially for cooking acid foods such as tomatoes. Another is to place plain iron nails (not galvanized nails) in vinegar until small amounts of iron begin to float to the surface. This usually takes 2 to 4 weeks. Then a teaspoon of iron-vinegar solution will contain about 30 to 60 mg of iron, enough for a daily supplement. The emergency recommendation is 10 mg per day. A teaspoon of the iron-vinegar solution is best taken in a glass of water. The iron content of fruit, such as an apple, can be increased by placing iron nails in it for a few days.

Food Reserves

Russia, China, and other countries that make serious preparations to survive disasters store large quantities of food primarily grain--both in farming areas and near population centers. In contrast, the usually large U.S. stocks of grain and soybeans are an unplanned survival resource resulting from the production of more food than

Americans can eat or sell abroad. The high productivity of U.S. agriculture is another unplanned survival asset. Providing enough calories and other essential nutrients for 100 million surviving Americans would necessitate the annual raising of only about 12% of our 1985 crop of corn, wheat, grain sorghum, and soybeans - if nothing else were produced.

In 1985, the U.S. production of corn, wheat, soybeans, and grain sorghum totaled about 625 billion pounds - about 7 pounds per day for one year for every American. A total of 2 pounds per person per day of these basic staples, would be sufficient to provide the essentials of an adequate vegetarian diet weighing about 27 ounces. The remaining 5 ounces of the 2 pounds would feed enough chickens to meet a survivor's minimum long-term requirement for animal protein.

If corn, wheat, grain sorghum, and soybeans were the only crops raised, the annual production would need to be only 730 pounds per person. Our 1985 annual production would have supplied every adult, child, and infant in a population of 100 million with 6250 pounds of these four staples. This is more than 8 times enough to maintain good nutrition by Chinese standards.

Recovery from a massive nuclear attack would depend largely on sufficient food reserves being available to enable survivors to concentrate on restoring the essentials of mechanized farming. Enough housing would remain intact or could be built to provide adequate shelter for the first few crucial years; enough clothing and fabrics would be available. But if survivors were forced by hunger to expend their energies attempting primitive subsistence farming, many deaths from starvation would occur and the prospects for national recovery would be greatly reduced.

Americans' greatest survival asset at the end of 1985 was about 17 billion bushels (about 850 billion pounds) of wheat, corn, grain sorghums, and soybeans in storage, mostly on farms. If 200 million Americans were to survive a limited nuclear attack and if only half of this stored food reserve could be delivered to the needy, each survivor would have adequate food for over 3 years, by Chinese nutritional standards. In view of the crucial importance of large food reserves to the prospects for individual and national survival, it is to be hoped that U.S, food surpluses and large annual carry-overs will continue.

A Basic Survival Ration to Store

A ration composed of the basic foods provides about 2600 calories per day and is nutritionally balanced. It keeps better than a ration of typical American foods, requires much less space to store or transport, and is much less expensive. The author and some friends have stored enough of these basic foods to last their families several months during a crisis, and have eaten large quantities of these foods with satisfaction over the past 20 years. (A different emergency ration should be stored for infants and very small children, as will be explained in the following section.) Field tests have indicated that the majority of Americans would find these basic foods acceptable under crisis conditions. In normal times, however, no one should store this or any other emergency food supply until after he has prepared, eaten, and found its components satisfactory.

Table. A basic survival ration for multi-year storage

	Ounces per day	Grams per day	Pounds for 30 days full ration	Kilograms for 30 days full ration
Whole-kernel hard wheat	16	454	30	13.6
Beans	5	142	9.4	4.3
Nonfat milk powder	2	57	3.8	1.7
Vegetable oil	1	28	1.9	0.9
Sugar	2	57	3.8	1.7
Salt (iodized)	1/3	10	0.63	0.3
Total Weights	10	748	49.5	22.5
Multi-vitamin pills:		1 pill each day		

Unprocessed grains and beans provide adequate nourishment for many millions of the world's people who have little else to eat.

Dry grains and beans are very compact: a 5-gallon can holds about 38 pounds of hard wheat. Yet when cooked, dry whole grains become bulky and give a well-fed feeling a distinct advantage if it is necessary to go on short rations during a prolonged crisis.

This basic ration has two disadvantages: (1) it requires cooking, and (2) Americans are unaccustomed to such a diet. Cooking difficulties can be minimized by having a grain-grinding device, a bucket stove with a few pounds of dry wood or newspapers for fuel, and the know-how to make a "fireless cooker" by using available insulating materials such as extra clothing. The disadvantage of starting to eat unaccustomed foods at a stressful time can be lessened by eating more whole grains and beans in normal times thereby, incidentally, saving money and improving a typical American diet by reducing fat and increasing bulk and fiber. When storing enough of this ration to last for several months or a year, it is best to select several kinds of beans for variety and improved nutrition. If soybeans are included, take into account the differences between soybeans and common beans, as noted earlier in this chapter.

In many areas it is difficult to buy wheat and beans at prices nearly as low as the farmer receives for these commodities. However, in an increasing number of communities, at least one store sells whole-grain wheat and beans in large sacks at reasonable prices. Mormons, who store food for a range of possible personal and national disasters, are often the best sources of information about where to get basic foods in quantity, at reasonable cost. Soon after purchase, bulk foods should be removed from sacks (but not necessarily from sealed-plastic liner-bags) and sealed in metal containers or in thick-walled plastic containers for storage. Especially in the more humid parts of the United States, grain and beans should be frequently checked for moisture. If necessary, these foods should be dried out and rid of insects as described later in this chapter.

Vegetable oil stores as well in plastic bottles as in glass ones. The toughness and lightness of plastic bottles make them better than glass for carrying when evacuating or for using in a shelter. Since a pound of oil provides about 2-1/4 times as much energy as does a pound of sugar, dry grain, or milk powder, storing additional vegetable oil is an efficient way to improve a grain diet and make it more like the 40%-fat diet of typical Americans.

All multivitamin pills providing 5000 International Units (1500 mg retinol equivalent) vitamin A, 400 IU (10 mg) of vitamin D, and 50 to 100 mg of vitamin C, must meet U.S. Government standards, so the least expensive usually are quite adequate. Storage in a refrigerator greatly lengthens the time before vitamin pills must be replaced with fresh ones. Because vitamin C is so essential, yet very inexpensive and long-lasting, it is prudent to store a large bottle.

It would be wise to have on hand ready-to-eat, compact foods for use during a week or two in a shelter, in addition to those normally kept in the kitchen. It is not necessary to buy expensive "survival foods" or the special dehydrated foods carried by many backpackers.

All large food stores sell the following concentrated foods: non-fat milk powder, canned peanuts, compact ready-to-eat dry cereals such as Grape Nuts, canned meat and fish, white sugar, vegetable oil in plastic bottles, iodized salt, and daily multivitamin pills. If shelter occupants have a way to boil water, it is advisable to include rice, noodles, and an "instant" cooked cereal such as oatmeal or wheat along with coffee and tea for those who habitually drink these beverages.

Parched grain is a ready-to-eat food that has been used for thousands of years. Whole-kernel wheat, corn, and rice can be parched by the following method: Place the kernels about 1/4-inch deep in a pan, a skillet, or a tin can while shaking it over a flame, hot coals, or a red hot electric burner. The kernels will puff and brown slightly when parched. These parched grains are not difficult to chew and can be pounded to a meal more easily than can the raw kernels. Parched grain-stores well if kept dry and free of insects.

Emergency Food for Babies

Infants and very small children would be the first victims of starvation after a heavy nuclear attack, unless special preparations are made on their behalf. Our huge stocks of unprocessed foods, which could prevent the majority of unprepared survivors from dying of hunger, would not be suitable for the very young. They need foods that are more concentrated and less rough. Most American mothers do not nurse their infants, and if a family's supply of baby foods were exhausted the parents might experience the agony of seeing their baby slowly starve.

Few Americans have watched babies starving. In China, I saw anguish on starving mothers' faces as they patted and squeezed their flat breasts, trying to get a little more milk into their weak babies' mouths. I saw this unforgettable tragedy in the midst of tens of thousands of Chinese evacuating on foot before a ruthless Japanese army during World War II.

Years later, my wife and I stored several hundred pounds of milk powder while our five children were small. I believe that parents who fear the use of nuclear weapons will be glad to bear the small expense of keeping on hand the emergency baby foods. (More detailed descriptions of these and many other foods, with instructions for their use, are given in an Oak Ridge National Laboratory report, Maintaining Nutritional Adequacy During A Prolonged Food Crisis, ORNL-5352, 1979.

To make a formula adequate for a 24-hour period, the quantities of instant non-fat dry milk, vegetable cooking oil, and sugar listed in the "Per Day" should be added to 4 cups of safe water. This formula can be prepared daily in cool weather or when a refrigerator is available. In warm or hot weather, or under unsanitary conditions, it is safer to make a formula 3 times a day. To do so, add 1/3 cup plus 2 teaspoons (a little less than one ounce) of instant nonfat milk powder to 1-1/3 cups (2/3 pint) of boiled water, and stir thoroughly. Then add 1 tablespoon (about 1/3 ounce, or 9 grams) of vegetable oil and 2 teaspoons of sugar, and stir. (If regular bakers' milk powder is used, 1/4 cup is enough when making one-third of the daily formula, 3 times a day.) If baby bottles are not at hand, milk can be spoon-fed to an infant.

Especially during a war crisis, the best and most dependable food for an infant is mother's milk provided the mother is assured an adequate diet. The possibility of disaster is one more reason why a mother should nurse her baby for a full year. Storing additional high-protein foods and fats for a nursing mother usually will be better insurance against her infant getting sick or starving than keeping adequate stocks of baby foods and the equipment necessary for sanitary feeding after evacuation or an attack.

Table. Emergency food supply for one baby

Ingredients	Per Day		Per Month		Per 6 Months	Per 6 Months
	Volumes and Ounces	Grams	Pounds	Kilograms	Pounds	Kilograms
Instant non-fatdry milk	1 cup + 2 tablespoons (2-3/4 oz)	8	6	2.72	32	15
Vegetable cooking oil	3 tablespoons (1 oz)	30	2	0.9	12	55
Sugar	2 tablespoons (0.7 oz)	20	1.3	0.6	8	3.6
Standard daily multi-vitamin pills	1/3 pill		10 pills		60 pills	

To give a daily vitamin supplement to a baby, a multivitamin pill should be crushed to a fine powder between two spoons and dissolved in a small amount of fluid, so that the baby can easily swallow it. If an infant does not receive adequate amounts of vitamins A, D, and C, he will develop deficiency symptoms in 1 to 3 months, depending on the amounts stored in his body. Vitamin C deficiency, the first to appear, can be prevented by giving an infant 15 mg of vitamin C each day (about 1/3 of a 50-mg vitamin C tablet, pulverized) or customary foods containing vitamin C, such as orange juice. Lacking these sources, the juice squeezed from sprouted grains or legumes can be used. If no vitamin pills or foods rich in vitamin D are available, exposure of the baby's skin to sunlight will cause his body to produce vitamin D. It would be wise to wait about 30 days after an attack before exposing the baby to sunlight. After that, short exposures would be safe except in areas of extremely heavy fallout. As a further precaution, the baby can be placed in an open, shallow pit that will provide shielding from radiation given off by fallout particles on the ground. Initial exposure should be very short, no more than 10 minutes.

If sufficient milk is not obtainable, even infants younger than six months should be given solid food. Solid foods for babies must be pureed to a fine texture. Using a modern baby food grinder makes pureeing quick and easy work. Under crisis conditions, a grinder should be cleaned and disinfected like other baby-feeding utensils, as described later in this section.

Several expedient methods are available: the food can be pressed through a sieve, mashed with a fork or spoon, or squeezed through a porous cloth. Good sanitation must be maintained; all foods should be brought to a boil after pureeing to insure that the food is safe from bacteria.

A pureed solid baby food can be made by first boiling together 3 parts of a cereal grain and 1 part of beans until they are soft. Then the mixture should be pressed through a sieve. The sieve catches the tough hulls from the grain kernels and the skins from the beans. The grain-beans combination will provide needed calories and a well-supplemented protein. The beans also supply the additional iron that a baby needs by the time he is 6 months old. Flours made from whole grains or beans, as previously described, also can be used; however, these may contain more rough material.

Some grains are preferable to others. It is easier to sieve cooked corn kernels than cooked wheat kernels. Since wheat is the grain most likely to cause allergies, it should not be fed to an infant until he is 6 to 7 months old if other grains, such as rice or corn, are available. Small children also need more protein than can be supplied by grains alone. As a substitute for milk, some bean food should be provided at every meal. If the available diet is deficient in a concentrated energy source such as fat or sugar, a child's feedings should be increased to 4 or 5 times a day, to enable him to assimilate more. Whenever possible, a small child should have a daily diet that contains at least one ounce of fat (3 tablespoons, without scraping the spoon). This would provide more than 10% of a young child's calories in the form of fat, which would be beneficial.

If under emergency conditions it is not practical to boil infant feeding utensils, they can be sterilized with a bleach solution. Add one teaspoon of ordinary household bleach to a quart of water. (Ordinary household bleach contains 5.25% sodium hypochlorite as its only active ingredient and supplies approximately 5% available chlorine. If the strength of the bleach is unknown, add 3 teaspoons per quart.) Directions for safe feeding without boiling follow:

The Utensils

(Include at least one 1-quart and one 1-pint mason jar, for keeping prepared formula sterile until used.)

1. Immediately after feeding, wash the inside and outside of all utensils used to prepare the formula and to feed the infant.
2. Fill a covered container with clean, cold water and add the appropriate amount of chlorine bleach.
3. Totally immerse all utensils until the next feeding (3 or 4 hours). Be sure that the bottle, if used, is filled with bleach solution. Keep container covered.

At Feeding Time

1. Wash hands before preparing food.
2. Remove utensils from the disinfectant chlorine solution and drain, but do not rinse or dry.
3. Prepare formula; feed the baby.

4. Immediately after feeding, wash utensils in clean water and immerse again in the disinfectant solution.
5. Prepare fresh chlorine solution each day.

Storage of Foods

Whole grains and white sugar can be stored successfully for decades; dried beans, non-fat milk powder, and vegetable oil can be stored for several years. Some rules for good storage follow:

- Keep food dry. The most dependable way to assure continuing dryness is to store dry grain in metal containers, such as ordinary 5-gallon metal storage cans or 55-gallon metal drums with gasketed lids. Filled 5-gallon cans are light enough to be easily carried in an automobile when evacuating.

  Particularly in humid areas, grain which seems to be dry often is not dry enough to store for a long period. To be sure that grain is dry enough to store for years, use a drying agent. The best drying agent for this purpose is silica gel with color indicator. The gel is blue when it is capable of absorbing water and pink when it needs to be heated to become an effective drying agent again. Silica gel is inexpensive if bought from chemical supply firms located in most cities. By heating it in a hot oven or in a can over a fire until it turns blue again, silica gel can be used repeatedly for years.

  The best containers for the silica gel used to dry grain (or to determine its dryness) are homemade cloth envelopes large enough for a heaping cupful of the gel. A clear plastic window should be stitched in, through which color changes can be observed. Put an envelope of silica gel on top of the grain in a 5-gallon can filled to within a couple of inches of its top. Then close the can tightly. Even a rather loose-fitting lid can be sealed tightly with tape. If after a few days the silica gel is still blue, the grain is dry enough. If the silica gel has turned pink, repeat the process with fresh envelopes until it can be seen that the grain is dry.

- Keep grains and beans free of weevils, other insects, and rodents. Dry ice(carbon dioxide) is the safest means still widely available to the public for ridding grain and beans of insects. Place about 4 inches of dry ice on top of the grain in a 5-gallon metal container. Put the lid on somewhat loosely, so that air in the grain can be driven out of the can. (This will happen as the dry ice vaporizes and the heavy carbon dioxide gas sinks into the grain and displaces the air around the kernels.) After an hour or two, tighten the lid and seal it with tape. After one month, all insects in this carbon-dioxide atmosphere will have died from lack of oxygen.
- Store foods in the coolest available place, out of the light. Remember that the storage life of most foods is cut in half by an increase of 18 F (10 C) in storage temperature.30 Thus 48 months of storage at 52 degrees F is equivalent to 24 months at 70 degrees F, and to 12 months at 88 degrees F. Illustrative of the importance of cool storage are my experiences in storing nonfat milk powder in an earth-covered, cool shelter. In steel drums I stored unopened 100-pound bags of compact, non-fat milk powder that I bought from bakeries. The cost per pound was much less than I would have paid for the largest packages sold in supermarkets. After 7 years storage at temperatures of about 50 degrees F the year around, my milk powder was still good as good as it would have been if stored in a normally air-conditioned and heated home for about 3 years.
- Do not place stored metal containers directly on the floor. To avoid possible condensation of moisture and the rusting that results, place containers on spaced boards. For long term storage in damp permanent shelters or damp basements, use solid-plastic containers with thick walls.
- Rotate stored foods. Eat the oldest food of each type and replace it with fresh food. Although cooking oil and non-fat milk powder remain edible after several years of storage

at room temperature, these and most other dry foods are more nourishing and taste better if stored for no more than 2 years. Most canned foods taste better if kept no more than one year. Exceptions are whole grains and white sugar, which stay good for decades if stored properly.

- Store plenty of salt. In our modern world salt is so abundant and cheap that most Americans do not realize that in many areas soon after a major nuclear attack salt would become a hard-to-get essential nutrient. Persons working hard without salt would suffer cramps and feel exhausted within a few days. Most famine relief shipments of grain probably would not include salt. So store enough salt both to salt your family's food for months and to trade for other necessities.

Seeds

For thousands of years storing seeds has been an essential part of the survival preparations made by millions of prudent people fearing attack. Seeds are hopes for future food and the defeat of famine, that lethal follower of disastrous wars.

Among the most impressive sounds I ever heard were faint, distant rattles of small stones, heard on a quiet, black, freezing night in 1944. An air raid was expected before dawn. I was standing on one of the bare hills outside Kunming, China, trying to pinpoint the sources of lights that Japanese agents had used just before previous air raids to guide attacking bombers to blacked-out Kunming.

Puzzled by sounds of cautious digging starting at about 2:00AM, I asked my interpreter if he knew what was going on. He told me that farmers walked most of the night to make sure that no one was following them, and were burying sealed jars of seeds in secret places, far enough from homes so that probably no one would hear them digging.

My interpreter did not need to tell me that if the advancing Japanese troops succeeded in taking Kunming they would ruthlessly strip the surrounding countryside of all food they could find. Then those prudent farmers would have seeds and hope in a starving land.

If you doubt that enough of our current 'oversupply" of stored whole grains, soybeans, milk powder, etc. would reach you after a nuclear attack, you should store seeds known to grow well in your area.

When getting your supply of survival seeds, remember:

- Grains and beans are the best plant sources of energy and protein.
- Even if you have enough vitamins for several months, you may not be able to buy more until long after a nuclear war.
- The deadly curses of scurvy, vitamin A deficiencies, and pellagra can be prevented by eating the plants, seeds, and sprouted seeds described earlier in this chapter.
- Plants grown from hybrid seeds give larger yields, but do not produce as productive seeds as do plants grown from good non-hybrid seeds.
- Seeds of proven productivity in your locality may be more valuable than money after a major nuclear attack.
- You should get mostly non-hybrid and store seeds, after learning from experienced local gardeners which are best.

7

Clothing and Protective Items

Basic Principles of Cold Weather Clothing

If Americans would learn to use skillfully the ordinary clothing, towels, cloth, newspapers, and paper bags in their homes, they could keep warm enough to stay healthy even under much colder conditions than they believe endurable without specialized outdoor winter clothing. Efficient cold- weather clothing can be improvised if the following ways of conserving body heat are understood and used:

- Trap "dead" air. Covering enough of your body with a thick layer of trapped "dead" air is the basic requirement for keeping warm. Efficient body insulation works: Both the air warmed by close contact with the skin and the water vapor from evaporated perspiration flow outward into the insulating material. Any material that breaks up and separates air into spaces no more than 1/8 inch across has efficient cells of "dead" air. Air that is within 1/16 inch of any surface whether that of a filament of goose down or of a piece of paper is slowed down by "sticking" to that surface and becoming hard to move. Trapped "dead" air moves outward very slowly, carrying heat away from the body at a slow rate thus minimizing heat losses by convection.
- Use windbreaker materials. An outer windbreaker layer of clothing that is essentially air-tight, such as a brown paper bag worn over a knit wool cap, prevents the escape of warmed air and results in an insulating layer of trapped

"dead" air. A single layer of good windbreaker material also prevents cold outside air from being blown into the insulating material and displacing warmed air.

The best windbreaker materials permit very little air to pass through them, while at the same time they allow water vapor to escape. Perspiration that cannot be felt or seen on cool skin continually evaporates, forming warm water vapor close to the skin. This moisture escapes outward through good insulating and windbreaker materials; as a result, underlying body insulation remains dry and efficient. Water vapor can pass readily through many sheets of newspaper or unglazed brown paper, although not enough wind can flow through a single sheet to be felt.

° Prevent excessive heat losses by conduction. Body heat also is lost by conduction the direct flow of heat into a colder material. For example, if one sleeps in an excellent goose-down sleeping bag laid directly on cold ground, body weight will compress the down to a small fraction of an inch. This barrier to heat flow' is too thin and will cause the body to lose heat rapidly to the cold earth. Likewise, the soles of ordinary shoes are such poor insulators that standing or walking on frozen ground sometimes results in frozen feet.

Minimizing Heat Losses from Head and Neck

The head and neck of the girl are insulated almost as well as if she were wearing the hood of a skin-side-out Eskimo parka. She folded a large, fluffy bath towel and placed it over her head, neck, and the upper part of her body. A brown paper bag was worn over the towel. The edges of the face hole cut in the bag were taped to prevent tearing. A strip of cloth was tied around the part of the bag over her neck. Such a parka-like covering not only is the most efficient way to insulate the head and neck but also prevents air warmed by the body from escaping upward around the neck. The girl also is wearing a man's shirt large enough to cover and hold thick newspaper insulation around her body and arms. It is very important to prevent heat losses from the head and neck, which have many blood vessels near the skin surface. Heat losses from these vital parts cannot be sensed nearly as well as heat losses from other parts of the body. Furthermore, blood vessels near the surface in the head and neck do not automatically constrict to reduce heat losses, as they do in other parts of the body when heat is being lost faster than it can be supplied by metabolism. So when a person is in the cold particularly when inactive he should keep his hands, feet, and whole body warmer by insulating his head and neck very well. (One difficulty in following this advice is that a wellcovered head often will feel unpleasantly warm even sweaty before one's body temperature rises enough to increase the warming flow of blood to hands and feet.)

Insulating the Whole Body

Occupants of freezing-cold shelters can keep warm enough to sleep without blankets by skillfully using ordinary indoor clothing plus paper and pieces of cloth to insulate their whole bodies. The shelter's ventilation openings were adjusted so that the inside temperature remained a few degrees below freezing, to prevent frozen earth from melting into icy mud. These girls had insulated themselves well. First, they covered their cotton shirts and pants with 10 thicknesses of newspaper wrapped around their bodies and tied with strips of cloth. Then around each arm and leg they wrapped and tied 8 sheets of newspaper, thus insulating their limbs with at least 16 thicknesses.

As an outer covering over their legs, they wrapped wide strips torn from a bedsheet. Their expedient foot coverings were of the type described in a following paragraph. Their heads and necks were insulated with towels covered with brown paper bags. Old cotton raincoats allowed water vapor to pass through and helped hold in place the insulating newspapers, which extended to cover the girls' bare hands.

The girls slept on newspapers spread about an inch thick over the gravel floor of the trench. When sleeping on cold or frozen ground, it is best to place newspapers or other insulation on top of a layer of small limb-tips or brush, so that drying air can circulate under the bedding. A sheet of plastic under bedding will keep it from being dampened by a wet floor but will not prevent it from being dampened after a few days by condensed water vapor from the sleeper's body. Newspaper and other paper through which water vapor can pass are such good windbreaker materials that they can be used under any loose fitting outer garment even one through which air can pass quite readily. They also provide good insulation. Many thicknesses of newspaper covered my body and arms and extended like cuffs from my sleeves. A porous cotton bathrobe covered the newspapers and helped hold them in place. Because so little heat was lost through this clothing, plenty of warm blood continued to flow to my bare hands, ridding my body of excess heat by radiation.

Improvised Winter Footwear

Cold-weather footwear that is warmer than all but the best-insulated winter boots can be improvised readily. The trick is learning how to tie the several insulating layers securely in place, so that you could hike for miles in the snow if necessary. For use in dry snow, first tie a porous insulating layer such as two bath towels or 10 big sheets of newspaper over each shoe. If you have no low- heeled shoes, make a paper sole by folding 3 large newspaper sheets to make a sole that has 72 thicknesses of paper. Then proceed in the following manner:

1. Place your foot and the sole on 10 newspaper sheets.
2. Fold all the sheets over the top of your foot while keeping the sole in the proper place.
3. Use a strip of cloth about 3 inches wide and 5 feet long to tie the papers in front of your ankle with a single overhand knot (half of a square knot). With the same strip, tie another single overhand knot over the tendon behind the ankle. Finally, tie a bow knot in front of the ankle.
4. Cover the insulating layer with a tough fabric, such as canvas or burlap sack material; secure with a second strip of cloth and tie as described above.

If the snow is wet, place a piece of strong plastic film or coated fabric outside the insulating layer, after securing it with the first strip of cloth. The outer protective covering should be tied over the waterproofing, with the second strip of cloth securing both it and the waterproofing. (When resting or sleeping in a dry place, remove any moisture proof layer in the foot coverings, to let your feet dry.)

Persons who have not worked outdoors in icy weather seldom realize the importance of warm footwear for winter. Russian civil defense manuals direct urban citizens to take winter boots with them when they evacuate, even in summer.

Keeping Warm Without Fire

- If occupants of a cold room or shelter lack adequate clothing and bedding, all should lie close together.
- Always place some insulating material between your body and a cold floor. (Pieces of shag rug are excellent.) Plastic film should be placed under the insulating material if the ground is damp.
- Go to bed or put on all your body insulation before you begin to feel cold. Once the loss of body heat causes blood vessels in your hands and feet to constrict, it often is hard to get these vessels to return to normal dilation again.
- Do not jump up and down or wave your arms to get or to keep warm. The wind-chill factor is a measure of air movement over your skin; rapid body movements always cause some such air movement. If practical, lie down and cover up; then do muscular tension exercises by repeatedly tightening all your muscles so tight that you tremble.
- Prevent sweating and the dampening of insulation by taking off or opening up clothing as you begin to exercise, before you begin to sweat.
- If you are getting cold, don't smoke. Nicotine causes blood vessels to constrict and the flow of blood to hands and feet to be reduced.

° Don't drink an alcoholic beverage to warm yourself. Alcohol causes increased blood flow close to the skin surface, resulting in rapid loss of body heat. It is impossible for alcohol to make up for such loss for very long.

Rainwear

All that is needed to make serviceable, improvised rainwear is waterproof material and waterproof tape. Plastic film from large trash bags will do; 4-mil polyethylene is better; tough, lightweight, coated fabric is best. Fabric duct tape is the best widely available tape.

Rain chaps are separate leg coverings, each with a loop to suspend it from one's belt and usually made large enough to be pulled on and off over the shoes and trousers. Rain chaps are better than waterproof trousers for working or walking while wearing a poncho or raincoat, because body movements cause drying air to be literally pumped under the chaps. This air keeps trousers and legs dry, and therefore warmer.

In the same way, a poncho or rain cape will allow plenty of air to reach the garments under them while one is working. When exercise is stopped, clothing underneath will stay dry and warm for some time.

Sandals

Shoes are almost always in short supply for years following a disastrous war. Except in very cold weather, sandals can be made to serve quite well. The best sandal designs for hard work and serious walking have a strap around the heel and in front of the ankle, with no thong between the toes.

Such sandals also have the advantage of enabling one to wear socks and other foot insulation inside the straps.

Clothing to Protect Against Beta Burns

If fresh and very radioactive fallout particles remain for long on the skin or extremely close to the skin, beta burns result. Any clothing that keeps fallout off the skin helps greatly. The best expedient protection is given by an outer layer of easily removable clothing similar to the improvised rainwear previously described, but fully covering the hair and neck and providing plastic trousers instead of chaps. Removable shoe coverings are highly advisable. All such protective coverings should be removed before entering a shelter, or removed in the entryway before going into the shelter room.

If a person has fallout particles on clothing that he must continue to wear, he should vigorously brush his outer clothing before entering a shelter room. If fallout particles are washed off, rinsed off, or otherwise removed from the skin within a few minutes, no beta burns will result.

A few days after a nuclear explosion, fallout particles are not radioactive enough to cause beta burns. In areas of heavy fallout, the danger from external doses of gamma radiation from fallout on the ground will continue much longer than will the risk of beta burns from some of these same fallout particles. The gamma rays given off by fallout particles brought into a shelter on clothing or bodies would subject shelter occupants to gamma doses so small as to be of no significance by wartime standards.

Nor would shelter occupants be endangered by radiation from the body of a person who, before reaching shelter, had received a gamma dose large enough to kill him many times over. Except in science fiction stories, the body of such a person does not become radioactive."

Fallout Masks

For the majority of Americans in most fallout areas, means for filtering fallout particles out of the air they breathe would not be essential survival equipment.

Most fallout particles tiny enough to enter one's lungs would fall to earth so slowly that they would reach ground thousands of miles away from the explosions. By then, radioactive decay would make them much less dangerous, and their deposition would be spread out over much of the earth.

In past years American-endangering Soviet warheads typically' were between 20 and one megaton. Explosions this large would inject almost all fallout particles into the stratosphere, high above rain clouds.

Today thousands of deployed Soviet ICBM warheads are between 550 and 100 kilotons. Both surface bursts and air bursts of today's smaller warheads would inject most of their radioactive particles into the troposphere, from whence rain-outs and snow-outs would bring huge numbers of even tiny particles to earth in '"hot spots" scattered across America.

Persons living in dry, windy areas often wear dust masks and goggles to protect their noses and eyes from dust and sand particles. If fallout particles are mixed with dust and sand that is being blown into a shelter, then persons in windy areas who occupy small below-ground expedient shelters should cover their noses and mouths with several thicknesses of towels or other cloth.

Those who have dust masks should wear them, especially when working outside in dry, windy weather soon after fallout deposition. Other than whole-body exposure to gamma rays, the main danger to well informed people would be from possible beta burns caused by fresh. "hot" fallout particles that would collect in nasal passageways, and from swallowed fallout particles. (Much of the material continually eliminated from the nose and throat is swallowed.)

In some fallout "hot spots" a secondary danger would be breathing extremely small, "hot" fallout particles into one's lungs, after a rain-out of tiny fallout particles from fallout clouds produced by today's typical kiloton-range Soviet warheads. In some areas "hot" particles would be dried and blown about by the winds within hours of their deposition in rain showers.

Making a homemade dust and fallout mask is still not a high priority survival project. In normal times, it is better to buy and store good masks and goggles.

The following instructions for making a homemade mask are an improved design based on a Russian design. This mask is the best of several homemade types, and the following instructions for making and using it have been field-tested.

An Individually-fitted Fallout Mask

Materials Needed:

1. Three rectangular pieces of fluffy toweling (terry cloth preferred), each piece approximately 12X 15 inches (or use 10 men's handkerchiefs).
2. Elastic. (The best expedient elastic is from the waistband of a man's undershorts.)
3. Clear plastic (from a photo album, billfold, plastic storm window, etc.).
4. Sewing materials.

Measurements:

1. Tie a string vertically around your head and face, passing it 1/2 inch in front of each of your ears and making it quite tight.
2. Tie a second string horizontally around your head, crossing your forehead 11/4 inches above the top of your eye sockets. These two strings should cross each other at points X and X1, over your temples.
3. Measure the distance X-to-X1 across your forehead and the distance X-to-X1 going under your chin (around your lower jaw and next to your throat).

Construction:

1. Cut out 3 pieces of terry cloth, making the width of each piece equal to X-to-X1 (the curved distance across your forehead), and the height of each piece equal to the distance X-to-Y plus 1/2 inch -- that is, equal to half the distance X-to-X1 (measured under your chin) plus 1/4 inch.
2. Cut the low‹ǂ edge of each piece.

3. Stitch the 3 pieces of terry cloth together, one on top of the other, thus making the mask three layers thick. Stitch around all four edges of the cloth rectangle and down the centerline.
4. Mark and cut out the eye holes, as illustrated. Make the mask's dimensions smaller for children.
5. Cut one rectangle of clear plastic measuring s\;2 X 21/4 inches, and sew this plastic over the outside of the eye holes, stitching the plastic around its edges and down the centerline.
6. Fold the three pieces along their vertical centerline and stitch the lower side together, along the upper stitch line Y-to-Y1. Stitch /2 inch from the lower edge. Then sew a second row of stitches.
7. Sew on the elastic head bands, making them short enough to hold the mask tightly around your face. If the elastic is from the waistband of a man's undershorts, use a doubled elastic both over the top of your head and around the back of your head. Make these elastic pieces so short that you can just put all your fingers comfortably between the elastic and your head when the pieces are fully stretched. If using a weaker elastic, be sure to adjust the lengths to a tight fit, to prevent air leaks under the edges of the mask. Because of the thickness of material where the elastics are connected to the upper corners of the mask, it may be necessary to do this stitching by hand.
8. To keep fallout particles off your head and neck, sew a loose-fitting piece of bedsheet cloth (not illustrated) to the edges of the mask that fit around your face. This cloth should extend back over your head and down over your collar, over which it can be tied.

Use:

Put on the mask by first placing it over your chin, then pulling the back elastic down to fit around the back of your head.

8

Lighting and Signals

Numerous disasters have proved that many people can remain calm for several days in total darkness. But some occupants of a shelter full of fearful people probably would go to pieces if they could see nothing and could not get out. It is easy to imagine the impact of a few hysterical people on the other occupants of a pitch-dark shelter.

Under wartime conditions, even a faint light that shows only the shapes of nearby people and things can make the difference between an endurable situation and a black ordeal.

All of the family's flashlights and other electric lights had been used until the batteries were almost exhausted. They had no candles at home and failed to bring the cooking oil, glass jar, and cotton string included in the Evacuation Checklist. These materials would have enabled them to make an expedient lamp and to keep a small light burning continuously for weeks, if necessary.

At 2 AM on the third night, the inky blackness caused the mother, a stable woman who had never feared the dark, to experience her first claustrophobia. In a controlled but tense voice she suddenly awoke everyone by stating: "I have to get out of here. I can't orient myself." Fortunately for the shelter- occupancy experiment, when she reached the entry trench she overcame her fears and lay down to sleep on the floor near the entrance.

Conclusion: In a crisis, it is especially bad not to be able to see at all.

ELECTRIC LIGHTS

Even in communities outside areas of blast, fire, or fallout, electric lights dependent on the public power system probably would fail. Electromagnetic pulse effects produced by the nuclear explosions, plus the destruction of power stations and transmission lines, would knock out most public power.

No emergency lights are included in the supplies stocked in official shelters. The flashlights and candles that some people would bring to shelters probably would be insufficient to provide minimum light for more than a very few days.

A low-amperage light bulb used with a large dry cell battery or a car battery is an excellent source of low-level continuous light. One of the small 12-volt bulbs in the instrument panels of cars with 12-volt batteries will give enough light for 10 to 15 nights, without discharging a car battery so much that it cannot be used to start a car. Making an efficient battery-powered lighting system for your shelter is work best done before a crisis arises. During a crisis you should give higher priority to many other needs.

Things to remember about using small bulbs with big batteries:

- o Always use a bulb of the same voltage as the battery.
- o Use a small, high-resistance wire, such as bell wire, with a car battery.
- o Connect the battery after the rest of the improvised light circuit has been completed.
- o Use reflective material such as aluminum foil, mirrors, or white boards to concentrate a weak light where it is needed.
- o If preparations are made before a crisis, small 12-volt bulbs (0.1 to 0.25 amps) with sockets and wire can be bought at a radio parts store. Electric test clips for connecting thin wire to a car battery can be purchased at an auto parts store.

Candles and Commercial Lamps

Persons going to a shelter should take all their candles with them, along with plenty of matches in a waterproof container such as a Mason jar. Fully occupied shelters can become so humid that matches not kept in moisture-proof containers cannot be lighted after a single day. Lighted candles and other fires should be placed near the shelter opening through which air is leaving the shelter, to avoid buildup of slight amounts of carbon monoxide and other headache-causing gases. If the shelter is completely closed for a time for any reason, such as to keep out smoke from a burning house nearby, all candles and other fires in the shelter should be extinguished.

Gasoline and kerosene lamps should not be taken inside a shelter. They produce gases that can cause headaches or even death. If gasoline or kerosene lamps are knocked over, as by blast winds that would rush into shelters over extensive areas, the results would be disastrous.

Safe Expedient Lamps for Shelters

The simple expedient lamps described below are the results of Oak Ridge National Laboratory experiments which started with oil lamps of the kinds used by Eskimos and the ancient Greeks. Our objective was to develop safe, dependable, long- lasting shelter lights that can be made quickly, using only common household materials. Numerous field tests have proved that average Americans can build good lamps by following the instructions given below.

These expedient lamps have the following advantages:

- o They are safe. Even if a burning lamp is knocked over onto a dry paper, the flame is so small that it will be extinguished if the lamp fuel being burned is a cooking oil or fat commonly used in the kitchen, and if the lamp wick is not much larger than 1/16 inch in diameter.
- o Since the flame is inside ajar, it is not likely to set fire to a careless person's clothing or to be blown out by a breeze.
- o With the smallest practical wick and flame, a lamp burns only about 1 ounce of edible oil or fat in eight hours.
- o Even with a flame smaller than that of a birthday candle, there is enough light for reading. To read easily by such a

small flame, attach aluminum foil to three sides and the bottom of the lamp, and suspend it between you and your book, just high enough not to block your vision. (During the long, anxious days and nights spent waiting for fallout to decay, shelter occupants will appreciate having someone read aloud to them.)

- o A lamp with aluminum foil attached is an excellent trap for mosquitoes and other insects that can cause problems in an unscreened shelter. They are attracted to the glittering light and fall into the oil.
- o Two of these lamps can be made in less than an hour, once the materials have been assembled, so there is no reason to wait until a crisis arises to make them. Oil exposed to the air deteriorates, so it is best not to store lamps filled with oil or to keep oil-soaked wicks for months.

SHELTER SANITATION AND PREVENTIVE MEDICINE

Clean Water and Food

Disinfecting water by boiling (preferably for at least 10 minutes) or by treating it with chlorine or iodine. When water is first stored, it should be disinfected by the addition of 1 scant teaspoon of ordinary household bleach for each 10 gallons. To avoid contaminating water when removing small quantities from a container such as a waterproof bag, the simplest way is first to pour some into a pot or other medium-sized container, from which small amounts can be poured into individual cups. Dipping water with a cup runs more risk of contamination. The cleanest way to take small quantities of water out of a container is to siphon it with a flexible tube.

Sanitary storage of food in expedient shelters is often difficult. Although almost any paper or plastic covering will keep fallout particles from food, shelter dampness can cause paper containers to break. Ants, roaches, and weevils can cut through paper or plastic coverings to reach food inside.

Placing paper containers of food in plastic bags and suspending the bags from the ceiling of the shelter entryway gives good protection against bugs, and quite good protection against moisture for a few weeks. (Do not obstruct the air flow through an entryway if heat is a problem.) A small amount of insect repellent or grease smeared on the suspending string or wire will stop all crawlers. Metal and strong plastic containers with tight lids protect food best.

The hygienic preparation and serving of food in a shelter, especially in hot weather, require that all cooked food be eaten promptly. It is best to eat within half-an-hour after cooking. Canned foods should be consumed shortly after opening.

The cleaning and disinfecting of utensils, bowls, etc., should be done promptly, to prevent bacteria from multiplying and to lessen the chances of ants and other insects being attracted into the shelter. Sugar should be mixed with cereals in the cooking pot, to avoid spilling.

In Oak Ridge National Laboratory shelter tests, only a few infants and toddlers have been included among the occupants. Feeding infants and small children over a piece of plastic would be one good way to keep the inevitable spillage from complicating shelter life.

To avoid using dishes, most foods can be served on squares of plastic. Spoons and such plastic "dishes" can be licked clean after eating, then disinfected by boiling or by dipping them into chlorine bleach solution containing one tablespoon of Clorox-type bleach to a quart of water.

A shelter occupant without a spoon can eat very thick grain mush in a sanitary manner by placing it on a piece of plastic held in his hand, forming it into a ball, and taking bites. .Although Chinese peasants often eat wet-rice balls held in their bare hands, experiments have indicated -not unexpectedly that Americans do not like to eat this way.

Cooking without oil or fat makes disinfecting utensils much easier when water and fuel are being conserved. Cereals and sugar are easy to wash off with a little water, without soap.

Control of Insects

Insect sprays used in high-protection-factor shelters are likely to cause more problems than they eliminate. Poisonous insecticides should be used with caution. Insect repellents on the skin and clothing are generally helpful, but not likely to be in sufficient supply to last for weeks or months. Some insect problems and simple means of controlling them are described below.

Mosquitoes would multiply rapidly after an attack, because normal control measures would not be in effect. Using insect screen or mosquito netting to cover the ventilation openings of a shelter is the best way to keep out mosquitoes, flies, and all larger insects. The lack of insect screening-when it would be too late to obtain any-could result in more harassment, discomfort and possible disease than most people accustomed to modern living are likely to imagine. However, if the shelter has no air pump, it is impractical to use screens that obstruct the free movement of vital air except in cold weather.

The fly population would explode after a nuclear attack. Radiation doses several times larger than doses that would kill people do not sterilize insects, in extensive rural areas where almost all people could have adequate shelter to be safe from fallout, most domestic animals and wild creatures would be killed. Trillions of flies would breed in the dead bodies.

If you have prudently kept a can of modern fly bait in your survival supplies, a little sprinkled on top of the plastic covering can kill literally thousands of flies.

Shelter occupants should make every effort to prevent flies from reaching disease-spreading human wastes.

Ants, especially in the warmer parts of the country, could drive people out of expedient shelters. The best prevention is to try to find a shelter-building site that is not near an ant nest, if shelter occupants are careful in storing food and eating, ants are less likely to become a problem. Ticks and chiggers are usually found on grass and low bushes. To avoid carrying these pests into the shelter, do not bring grass or dead leaves into your shelter for bedding except in freezing weather. Cut leafy branches high above the ground: few pests live in tall vegetation.

Personal Possessions

Toothbrushes are not boiled or otherwise disinfected after being used, because we all develop considerable resistance to our own infective organisms. For the same reason, each individual should have his own personal drinking cup, bowl, and spoon. They should be cleaned as well as possible and kept covered when not in use.

Prevention of Skin Diseases

In crowded shelters, especially during hot weather, skin diseases are likely to be a more serious problem than is generally recognized. The importance of learning how to prevent skin diseases was made apparent by one of the very few shelter- occupancy tests to be conducted in the summer without air conditioning. This was a Navy test in which 99 men lived for 12 days in an underground shelter cooled only with outdoor summer air.15 The incidence of skin complaints was high, even though medical treatment was available on a daily basis. The total number of reports to sick call was 560; 34 of these 99 healthy young men contracted heat rash and 23 had other skin complaints such as fungus infections. However, these sailors lived in an inadequately ventilated shelter and did not cleanse their sweaty skins or use the other methods listed below for preventing skin troubles.

Even in shelters that are skillfully ventilated with adequate outdoor air, skin diseases will be a serious problem especially in hot weather unless special hygiene measures are followed. Humid heat and heat rash increase susceptibility to skin diseases. Most of the following measures for preventing skin diseases have been practiced by jungle natives for thousands of years.

- Wash off sweat and dead skin. (When it is hot and humid, dead skin is continuously rubbing and flaking off and starting to decay.) Many jungle natives rinse their bodies several times a day. Bathing several times a day with soap is harmful in humid heat: the rapid loss of normal skin oils is one of the causes of skin diseases.

Your skin can be kept fairly clean by rinsing off each day with just a cup of water, while rubbing gently with a very small cloth. A 6-inch square of bedsheet cloth serves well. So that you can dispose of the dirty water afterwards, wash yourself while standing on a piece of plastic with its edges held up slightly. (Place sticks or narrow boards under the edges.) Use about two-thirds of the precious water for the first rinse, starting from the face down and gently rubbing neck, armpits, stomach, groin, buttocks, and feet with a washcloth. Then use the remaining water to rinse off again, using bare fingers. If boiling water is available, sterilize washcloths every day by boiling them for a few minutes.

- Sleep as cool and bare as practical, to dry the maximum skin area.
- If practical, sit and sleep only where other members of your family do and avoid use of bedding by more than one family.
- Avoid infection from toilet seats by disinfecting with a strong chlorine solution and then rinsing, by covering with paper, or by not sitting down.
- Wash or disinfect clothing as often as practical, especially underwear and socks. Disinfecting clothing, not laundering it, is the most important health objective under difficult shelter conditions. Dipping clothing into boiling water disinfects it. Unless plenty of water is available for rinsing, do not disinfect clothing by putting it in a chlorine bleach solution.
- Wear shoes or sandals when walking about, to prevent fungus infections of the feet.

An Ounce of Prevention

Should fallout force Americans to stay crowded into basements and expedient shelters for days or weeks, they should protect themselves against the spread of infectious diseases by taking both accustomed and unaccustomed preventive measures. Thousands of our jungle infantrymen in World War II learned to practice many of the health- preserving techniques described in this chapter. If modern medical facilities were temporarily unavailable, the prevention of diseases would become much more important to all of us.

The following infection-preventing measures are simple, practical, and require some self-discipline. The author has observed their practice and has used them while exploring and soldiering in a number of jungle, desert, and mountain regions. I also have used these measures while field-testing nuclear war survival skills in several states.

Basic first aid also would be of increased importance during a major confrontation or war. Good first aid booklets and instructions are available in practically all communities, so most first aid information will not be repeated here.

Disposal of Human Wastes

To preserve health and morale in a shelter without a toilet or special chemicals for treatment of excrement and urine, human wastes should be removed before they produce much gas. A garbage can with a lid or a bucket covered with plastic will not hold the pressurized gas produced by rotting excrement. The following expedient means of disposal are listed in increasing order of effectiveness.

- Use a 5-gallon paint can, a bucket, or a large waterproof wastebasket to collect both urine and excrement. Use and keep it near the air-exhaust end of the shelter. Keep it tightly covered when not in use: a piece of plastic tied over the top keeps out insects and reduces odors. When such waste containers are full or begin to stink badly while covered, put them outside the shelter still covered to keep out flies.

For some people, especially the aged, bringing a toilet seat from home would be justified. Padding on the edge of the bucket also helps those who have to sit down. An improvised seat of plywood or board serves well. If only one container is available and is almost filled, periodically dump the wastes outside unless fallout is still being deposited. Before an anticipated attack, people who plan to stay in a shelter should dig a waste-disposal pit if they do not have sufficient waste containers for weeks of shelter occupancy. The pit should be located about 3 feet from the shelter in the down-wind direction. This usually will be the air exhaust end of an earth-covered shelter. The pit should be surrounded by a ring of mounded, packed earth about 6 inches high, to keep surface water from heavy rains from running into it.

Quickly putting or dumping wastes outside is not hazardous once fallout is no longer being deposited. For example, assume the shelter is in an area of heavy fallout and the dose rate outside is 400 R/hr enough to give a potentially fatal dose in about an hour to a person exposed in the open. If a person needs to be exposed for only 10 seconds to dump a bucket, in this 1/360th of an hour he will receive a dose of only about 1 R. Under war conditions, an additional 1-R dose is of little concern.

If the shelter design does not permit an occupant to dispose of wastes without running outside, he can tie cloth or plastic over his shoes before going out, and remove these coverings in the entry before going back inside the shelter room. This precaution will eliminate the chance of tracking "hot" fallout particles into the shelter, and the small chance of someone getting a tiny beta burn in this way.

- Have all occupants only urinate in the bucket, and defecate into a piece of plastic. Urine contains few harmful organisms and can be safely dumped outside.

Two thicknesses of the thin plastic used to cover freshly dry-cleaned clothes will serve to hold bowel movements of several persons. Gather the plastic around the excrement to form a bag-like container.

Tie the plastic closed near its upper edges with a string or narrow strip of cloth. Do not tie it so tightly as to be gas-tight. Each day's collection should be gently tossed outside. As the excrement rots, the gas will leak out of the tied end of the plastic covering. Flies will be attracted in swarms, but they will not be able to get into the plastic to contaminate their feet or to lay eggs. And because rotting excrement is so attractive to flies, shelter occupants will be bothered less by these dangerous pests.

If you have prudently kept a can of modern fly bait in your survival supplies, a little sprinkled on top of the plastic covering can kill literally thousands of flies. The most effective fly baits, such as Die Fly and Improved Golden Malrin, are sold in farm supply stores.

° Use a hose-vented, 5-gallon can or bucket lined with a heavy plastic bag: cover tightly with plastic when not in use.

The vent-hose runs through a hole near the top of the paint can shown and is taped to seal it to the can. Such a hole can be quite easily cut with a chisel or a sharpened screwdriver. The hose is long enough to extend outside the shelter. Its outer end should be secured about 6 inches above ground level, to prevent water from running into it during a heavy rain. When a toilet-can is tightly covered, foul gases can escape through the hose to the outdoors. With its opening tied shut, a large plastic trash bag containing as much as 30 pounds of wastes can be lifted out of a toilet-can and disposed of outside the shelter.

The 6-member Utah family described in preceding chapters used a home-like expedient toilet during their 77-hour shelter stay. The toilet was at one end of the shelter. A person sitting on this toilet could put his feet in the adjacent "stand-up hole" and be more comfortable. The blanket shown hanging on the left could be drawn in front of the toilet for privacy. Behind the girl's head was the emergency crawlway-ventilation trench. When the toilet was being used, the shelter-ventilating KAP pumped air under the blanket-curtain and out the ventilation trench, resulting in very little odor in the rest of the shelter.

Vomiting is certain to cause both morale and health problems, especially for unprepared shelter occupants fearing this first dramatic symptom of radiation sickness. Nervousness, combined with the effects of unaccustomed food and water, will cause even some healthy persons to vomit. In a crowded shelter, the sight and smell of vomit will make others throw up. Plastic bags, well distributed throughout a shelter, are the best means to catch vomit and keep it off the floor. Buckets, pots, or a newspaper folded into a cone also will serve.

Disposal of Dead Bodies

In large shelters which are occupied for many days, someone may die even when no occupants have been injured by blast, fire, or radiation. The sight or the sickly-sweet stink of a decaying human body is greatly disturbing. Some civil defense workers have theorized that the best way to take care of a corpse in a shelter until the fallout dose-rate outdoors is low enough to allow burial is to seal it in a large plastic bag. A simple test with a dead dog proved this idea impractical: gas pressure caused the bag to burst. One solution is to put the corpse outside as soon as the odor is evident. First, if possible, place it in a bag made of large plastic trash bags taped together and perforated with a few pinholes.

Respiratory Diseases

The spread of respiratory and other diseases transmitted by coughing and sneezing would be difficult to control in long-occupied shelters. Adequate ventilation would help in disease prevention. In small shelters, it would be better if persons who are sneezing or coughing could stay near the opening being used for air exhaust. In large shelters with many occupants, the risk of one or more of them having a disease that is easily spread obviously will be higher than in a small shelter.

SURVIVING WITHOUT DOCTORS

A Temporary Return to Self-help

Most doctors, hospital facilities, and medical supplies are located in cities. An all-out attack would destroy most of these modern blessings. Even if medical assistance were nearby, only a few of the survivors confined to shelters in areas of heavy fallout would be able to get needed medicines or the help of a doctor. For periods ranging from days to months, most unprepared survivors would be forced to live under medical conditions almost as primitive as those experienced by the majority of mankind for all but the past few decades of human history.

Benign Neglect

Life without modern medical help would be less painful and hazardous for those survivors who have some practical knowledge of what should be done or not done under primitive, unsanitary conditions. Information about first aid and hygienic precautions can be obtained from widely available Red Cross and civil defense booklets and courses. This knowledge, with a stock of basic first aid supplies, would reduce suffering and prevent many dangerous illnesses. However, first aid instructions do not include advice about what to do for serious injuries and sicknesses if no doctors or effective medicines are available.

Where There Is No Doctor, the excellent self- help handbook ;recommended by Volunteers in Technical Assistance, gives much information that goes far beyond the scope of first aid. But even this handbook repeatedly recommends getting professional medical help whenever possible for serious injuries and illnesses.

Fortunately, the human body has remarkable capabilities for healing itself, especially if the injured or sick person and his companions practice intelligent "benign neglect." Such purposeful non-interference with the body's recuperative processes was called "masterful inactivity" by Colonel C. Blanchard Henry, M.D., a widely recognized authority on mass casualty evacuation and treatment. Colonel Henry was one of the first medical officers to visit Hiroshima and Nagasaki after their destruction and was an experienced analyzer of civil defense preparations in several countries.

The following is a brief summary of Colonel Henry's medical advice for nuclear war survivors living under primitive conditions and unable to get the help of a doctor or effective medicines.

- Wounds: Apply only pressure dressings to stop bleeding unless an artery has been cut, as by a blast- hurled piece of glass. If blood is spurting from a wound, apply both a pressure dressing and a windlass-type tourniquet. Loosen the tourniquet pressure about every 15 minutes, to allow enough blood to reach the flesh beyond the tourniquet and keep it alive. There is a fair chance that clotting under the pressure dressing will stop blood loss before it becomes fatal.
- Infected wounds: Do not change dressings frequently. The formation of white pus shows that white corpuscles are mobilizing to combat the infection. In World War I, wounded soldiers in hospitals suffered agonies having their wounds cleaned and dressed frequently: many died as a result of such harmful care. In contrast, before antibiotics became available late in World War II, casts and dressings on infected wounds sometimes were not changed for weeks. (The author saw this treatment in China and India and smelled the stench resulting from such "benign neglect" of American soldiers' wounds--- neglect that helped save limbs and lives.)
- Pieces of glass deeply embedded in flesh: Do not probe with tweezers or a knife in an attempt to extract them. Most glass will come out when the wounds discharge pus.
- Burns: Do not apply grease, oil or any other medicine to the burned area. Cover the area securely with a clean, dry dressing or folded cloth. Do not change the dressing frequently. [For most burns, the bandage need not be removed until the tenth to fourteenth day. Give plenty of slightly salted water: about 1 teaspoon (4.5 gm) of salt per quart (or liter), preferably chilled, in amounts of 1 to 3 liters daily.
- Broken bones: Apply simple splints to keep the bones from moving. Do not worry about deformities: most can be corrected later by a doctor. Do not attempt traction setting of broken bones.

- Shock: Keep the victim warm. Place blankets or other insulation material under him. Do not cover him with so many blankets that he sweats and suffers harmful fluid losses. Give him plenty of slightly salted water [about a teaspoon of salt in a liter (or quart) of water].
- Heat prostration: Give adequate fluids, including slightly salty water.
- Simple childbirth: Keep hands off. Wait until the mother has given birth. Do not tie and cut the cord unless a potent disinfectant is available. Instead, use the primitive practice of wrapping the cord and the placenta around the infant until they dry. Avoid the risk of infecting the mother by removing the rest of the afterbirth: urge the mother to work to expel it.
- Toothache: Do not attempt to pull an aching tooth. Decaying teeth will abscess and fall out. This is a painful but seldom fatal process- --one which was endured by most of our remote ancestors who reached maturity.

Veterinarian Antibiotics

People who for decades have used antibiotics to combat their infections have not produced normal quantities of antibodies, and have subnormal resistance to many infections. People who have not been dependent on antibiotics have these antibodies. In the aftermath of a massive nuclear attack, most surviving Americans would be in rural areas: many would need antibiotics. A large part of their need could be met by the supplies of veterinarian antibiotics kept on livestock and chicken farms, at feed mills, and in small towns. Many animals are given more antibiotics in their short lives than most Americans receive in theirs. Hogs, for example, are given antibiotics and or other disease-controlling medicines in their feed each day. In many farming areas, veterinary antibiotics and other medicines are in larger supply than are those for people. Realistic preparations to survive an all-out attack should include utilizing these supplies.

Radiation Sickness

For the vast majority of Americans who would receive radiation doses from a massive attack, the help of doctors, antibiotics, blood transfusions, etc., would not be of life-or-death importance. Very few of those receiving acute doses (received within 24 hours) of less than 100 R would become sick, even briefly. All of those exposed to acute doses between 100 Rand 200 R should recover from radiation effects.6 However, under post-attack conditions of multiple stresses and privations, some who receive acute radiation doses of 100 R to 200 R may die of infectious diseases because of their reduced resistance. If total doses this size or even several times larger are received over a period of a few months in small doses of around 6 R per day, no incapacitating symptoms should result. The human body usually can repair almost all radiation damage if the daily doses are not too large.

The majority of those with acute doses of less than about 350 R will recover without medical treatment. Almost all of those receiving acute doses of over 600 R would die within a few weeks, even if they were to receive treatment in a typical hospital during peacetime. If all doctors and the equipment and drugs needed for heroic treatments magically were to survive an attack and persons suffering from radiation sickness could reach them relatively few additional lives could be saved.

The most effective way to reduce losses of health and life from radiation sickness is to prevent excessive exposure to radiation. Adequate shelter and essential life-support items are the best means of saving lives in a nuclear war. The following information on radiation sickness is given to help the reader understand the importance of building a good shelter and to help him distinguish between symptoms of common illnesses and first symptoms of radiation sickness.

The first symptoms of radiation sickness are nausea, vomiting, headache, dizziness, and a general feeling of illness. These symptoms begin several hours after exposure to acute doses of 100 R to 200

R. and within 30 minutes or less after receiving a fatal dose. A source of probable confusion is the fact that one or more of these symptoms is experienced by many people when they are first exposed to great danger, as in an air raid shelter during a conventional bombardment.

The occupants of a shelter might worry unnecessarily for weeks, mistaking their early emotional reactions for the initial phase of radiation sickness. This would be particularly true if they had no dependable instrument for measuring radiation, or if none of them knew how to use such an instrument.

The initial symptoms end within a day or two. Then follows the latent phase of radiation sickness, during which the patient experiences few, if any, symptoms. If the dose received was in the non-fatal range the latent phase may last as long as 2 weeks.

In the final phase, the victim of serious or fatal radiation sickness will have reduced resistance to infections and is likely to suffer diarrhea, loss of hair, and small hemorrhages of the skin, mouth, and; or intestinal tract. Diarrhea from common causes may be confused with the onset of radiation sickness, but hemorrhages and loss of much hair are clear indications of having received serious, but not necessarily fatal, radiation exposure. The final phase usually lasts for one to two months. Any available antibiotics should be reserved for this critical phase of the illness.

Doses of 1000 R to 5000 R result in bloody diarrhea, fever, and blood circulation abnormalities, with the initial symptoms beginning within less than 30 minutes after exposure and the final phase occurring less than a day thereafter. Death results within 2 to 14 days. The victim of a dose of over 5000 R dies a hard death within 48 hours, due to radiation damage to the central nervous system.

Recovery from most cases of radiation sickness will be more likely for patients who receive a well balanced diet, rest, freedom from stress, and clean surroundings. But most patients, even without these advantages, will survive -as proved by the survival of thousands of Hiroshima and Nagasaki citizens who suffered serious radiation sickness. Nursing radiation victims is not hazardous. Even persons dying from a dose of 5000 Rare not sources of dangerous radiation by wartime standards, and radiation sickness is not contagious.

Lifetime Risks from Radiation

The large radiation doses that many survivors of a nuclear attack would receive would result in serious long-term risks of death from cancer, but the lifetime risks from even large wartime radiation doses are not as bad as many people believe. Significantly, no official U.S. estimates have been made available to the public regarding excess cancer deaths to be expected if America is subjected to a nuclear attack. However, reliable statistics are available on the numbers of additional fatal cancers suffered by persons who received large whole-body radiation doses at Hiroshima and in other disasters, and who lived for months to decades before dying.

Dr. John N. Auxier -who for years was a leading health physicist at Oak Ridge National Laboratory, was one of the American scientists working in Japan with Japanese scientists studying the Hiroshima and Nagasaki survivors, and currently is working on radiation problems with International Technology Corporation-in 1986 summarized for me the risk of excess fatal cancers from large whole-body radiation doses: "If 1,000 people each receive a whole-body radiation dose of 100 rems [or 100 rads, or 100 R], about 10 additional fatal cancers will result." These 10 fatal cancers will be in addition to about 150 fatal cancers that normally will develop among these 1,000 people during their lifetimes. This risk is proportional to large doses; thus, if 1,000 people each receive a dose of 200 rems, about 20 additional lethal cancer cases would be expected.

"Rem" is an abbreviation for "roentgen equivalent (in) man." The rem takes into account the biological effects of different kinds of radiation. For external gamma-ray radiation from fallout, the numerical value of an exposure or dose given in roentgens is approximately the same as the numerical value given in rems or in rads. The rad is the unit of radiation energy absorption in any material and applies to all kinds of nuclear radiations. Therefore, for simplicity's sake, this book gives both instrument readings (exposures) and doses in roentgens (R).

The reader desiring good information on the long-term and worldwide effects of radiation is referred to two authoritative reports of the National Academy of Sciences, Washington, D.C. 20006: The Effects on Populations of Exposures to Low Levels of Ionizing Radiation (The BEIR Report made by the NAS Committee on the Biological Effects of Ionizing Radiation) (November 1972); and Long- Term Worldwide Effects of Multiple Nuclear- Weapons Detonations (1975).

From the standpoint of basic survival know-how, these and other complicated scientific studies show that to minimize lifetime risks from radiation, after a nuclear attack people should:

- Provide the best protection against radiation for pregnant women and young children, since fetuses and the very young are the most likely to be hurt by radiation.
- Realize that, with the exception of lung cancer, older people are no more susceptible to radiation injury than are those in the prime of life. Also, a 65-year-old probably will not live long enough to die of a cancer that takes 20 years or more to develop. Many older people, if they know realistic risk estimates, will choose to do essential outdoor work and take non- incapacitating radiation doses in order to spare younger members of their families the risk of getting cancer decades later.

PREVENTION OF THYROID DAMAGE FROM RADIOACTIVE IODINES

There is no medicine that will effectively prevent nuclear radiations from damaging the human body cells that they strike. However, a salt of the elements potassium and iodine, taken orally even in very small quantities 1/2 hour to 1 day before radioactive iodines are swallowed or inhaled, prevents about 99% of the damage to the thyroid gland that otherwise would result. The thyroid gland readily absorbs both non-radioactive and radioactive iodine, and normally it retains much of this element in either or both forms. When ordinary, non-radioactive iodine is made available in the blood for absorption by the thyroid gland before any radioactive iodine is made available, the gland will absorb and retain so much that it becomes saturated with non-radioactive iodine. When saturated, the thyroid can absorb only about 1% as much additional iodine, including radioactive forms that later may become available in the blood: then it is said to be blocked. (Excess iodine in the blood is rapidly eliminated by the action of the kidneys.)

An excess of ordinary iodine retained in the thyroid gland is harmless, but quite small amounts of radioactive iodine retained in the thyroid eventually will give such a large radiation dose to thyroid cells that abnormalities are likely to result. These would include loss of thyroid function, nodules in the thyroid, or thyroid cancer.

Sixty-four Marshall Islanders on Rongelap Atoll were accidentally exposed to radioactive fallout produced by a large H-bomb test explosion on Bikini Atoll, about 100 miles away. Twenty-two of them developed thyroid abnormalities beginning nine years later.6 In the two days before they were taken out of the fallout area, these completely uninformed natives, living essentially outdoors, had received estimated whole- body gamma-ray doses of about 175 R from the fallout all around them. They absorbed most of the radioactive iodine retained by their thyroid glands as a result of eating and drinking fallout-contaminated food and water during their two days of exposure. (Because of unusual environmental conditions at the time of fallout deposition, some of the retained radioactive iodine may have come from the air they breathed.)

An extremely small and inexpensive daily dose of the preferred non-radioactive potassium salt, potassium iodide (KI), if taken 1/ 2 hour to 1 day before exposure to radioactive iodine, will reduce later absorption of radioactive iodine by the thyroid to only about 1% of what the absorption would be without this preventive measure. Extensive experimentation and study have led to the Federal Drug

Administration's approval of 130-milligram (130- mg) tablets for this preventive (prophylactic) use only.36,37 A 130-mg dose provides the same daily amount of iodine as does each tablet that English authorities for years have placed in the hands of the police near nuclear power plants, for distribution to the surrounding population in the very unlikely event of a major nuclear accident. It is quite likely that a similar-sized dose is in the Russian "individual, standard first-aid packet." According to a comprehensive Soviet 1969 civil defense handbook,38 this first-aid packet contains "anti-radiation tablets and anti-vomiting tablets (potassium iodide and etaperain)."

° Prophylactic use of potassium iodide in peacetime nuclear accidents.

When the Three Mile Island nuclear reactor accident was worsening and it appeared that the reactor's containment structure might rupture and release dangerous amounts of radioactive iodines and other radioactive material into the atmosphere, the Government rushed preparation of small bottles of a saturated solution of potassium iodide. The reactor's containment structure did not rupture.

The 237,013 bottles of saturated KI solution that were delivered to Harrisburg, Pennsylvania-mostly too late to have been effective if the Three Mile Island accident had become an uncontained meltdown -were stored in secret in a warehouse, and were never used.

Since this famous 1979 accident, that injured no one, the Governors of the 50 states have been given the responsibility for protecting Americans against radioiodines by providing prophylactic potassium iodide. By May of 1986, only in Tennessee have Americans, other than some specialists, been given potassium iodide tablets; around one nuclear reactor some 7,500 residents have been given the officially approved KI tablets, to assure their having this protection if a nuclear accident occurs.

In April of 1982 the Bureau of Radiological Health and Bureau of Drugs, Food and Drug Administration, Department of Health and Human Services released "FINAL RECOMMENDATIONS,

Potassium Iodide As A Thyroid- Blocking Agent In A Radiation Emergency: Recommendations On Use". These lengthy recommendations are summarized in the FDA's "mandated patient product insert". (See a complete copy in the following section.) This insert is packed with every bottle of non-prescription KI tablets sold. However, the lengthy FDA recommendations contain many facts not mentioned in this required insert, including the following: "Based on the FDA adverse reaction reports and an estimated 48 x 106 [48 million] 300-mg doses of potassium iodide administered each year [in the United States], the NCRP [National Council on Radiation Protection and Measurements] estimated an adverse reaction rate of from 1 in a million to 1 in 10 million doses." (Note that this extremely low adverse reaction rate is for doses over twice as large as the 130-mg prophylactic dose.)

FDA PATIENT INFORMATION USE OF 130-MG SCORED TABLETS OF POTASSIUM IODIDE FOR THYROID BLOCKING

(Potassium Iodide Tablets, U.S.P.)

(Pronounced poe-TASS-e-um EYE-oh-dyed)

(Abbreviated KI)

TAKE POTASSIUM IODIDE ONLY WHEN PUBLIC HEALTH OFFICIALS TELL YOU. IN A RADIATION EMERGENCY, RADIOACTIVE IODINE COULD BE RELEASED INTO THE AIR. POTASSIUM IODIDE (A FORM OF IODINE) CAN HELP PROTECT YOU.

IF YOU ARE TOLD TO TAKE THIS MEDICINE, TAKE IT ONE TIME EVERY 24 HOURS. DO NOT TAKE IT MORE OFTEN. MORE WILL NOT HELP YOU AND MAY INCREASE THE RISK OF SIDE EFFECTS. DO NOT TAKE THIS DRUG IF YOU KNOW YOU ARE ALLERGIC TO IODINE (SEE SIDE EFFECTS BELOW).

Indications

THYROID BLOCKING IN A RADIATION EMERGENCY ONLY

Directions For Use

Use only as directed by State or local public health authorities in the event of a radiation emergency.

Dose

ADULTS AND CHILDREN ONE YEAR OF AGE OR

OLDER: One (1) tablet once a day. Crush for small children.

BABIES UNDER ONE YEAR OF AGE: One-half (1/2) tablet once a day. Crush first.

DOSAGE: Take for 10 days unless directed otherwise by State or local public health authorities.

Store at controlled room temperature between 150 and 300C (59 degrees to 86 degrees F). Keep bottle tightly closed and protect from light.

Warning

POTASSIUM IODIDE SHOULD NOT BE USED BY PEOPLE ALLERGIC TO IODIDE. Keep out of the reach of children. In case of overdose or allergic reaction, contact a physician or public health authority.

Description

Each iOSAT™ Tablet contains 130 mg. of potassium iodide.

How Potassium Iodide Works

Certain forms of iodine help your thyroid gland work right. Most people get the iodine they need from foods like iodized salt or fish. The thyroid can "store" or hold only a certain amount of iodine.

In a radiation emergency, radioactive iodine may be released in the air. This material may be breathed or swallowed. It may enter the thyroid gland and damage it. The damage would probably not show itself for years. Children are most likely to have thyroid damage.

If you take potassium iodide, it will fill up your thyroid gland. This reduces the chance that harmful radioactive iodine will enter the thyroid gland.

Who Should not Take Potassium Iodide

The only people who should not take potassium iodide are people who know they are allergic to iodide. You may take potassium iodide even if you are taking medicines for a thyroid problem (for example, a thyroid hormone or anti-thyroid drug). Pregnant and nursing women and babies and children may also take this drug.

How and When to Take Potassium Iodide

Potassium iodide should be taken as soon as possible after public health officials tell you. You should take one dose every 24 hours. More will not help you because the thyroid can "hold" only limited amounts of iodine. Larger doses will increase the risk of side effects. You will probably be told not to take the drug for more than 10 days.

Side Effects

Usually, side effects of potassium iodide happen when people take higher doses for a long time. You should be careful not to take more than the recommended dose or take it for longer than you are told. Side effects are unlikely because of the low dose and the short time you will be taking the drug.

Possible side effects include skin rashes, swelling of the salivary glands, and "iodism" (metallic taste, burning mouth and throat, sore teeth and gums, symptoms of a head cold, and sometimes stomach upset and diarrhea). A few people have an allergic reaction with more serious symptoms.

These could be fever and joint pains, or swelling of parts of the face and body and at times severe shortness of breath requiring immediate medical attention. Taking iodide may rarely cause overactivity of the thyroid gland, underactivity of the thyroid gland, or enlargement of the thyroid gland (goiter).

What to do if Side Effects Occur

If the side effects are severe or if you have an allergic reaction, stop taking potassium iodide. Then, if possible, call a doctor or public health authority for instructions.

How Supplied

Tablets (Potassium Iodide Tablets, U.S.P.): bottles of [number of tablets in a bottle] tablets. ( ). Each white, round, scored tablet contains 130 mg. potassium iodide.

Note that this official FDA required insert given above prudently stresses the name, the pronunciation, and the chemical formula (KI) of these Government-approved 130-mg potassium iodide tablets. Perhaps this emphasized information will keep some alarmed Americans (misinformed in a future crisis by the media that typically stated during the Chernobyl nuclear accident that "iodine tablets" were being given to people endangered by radioactive iodine from the burning reactor) from getting and taking iodine tablets, widely sold for water purification, or tincture of iodine.

Strangely, neither in official information available to the general public on the prophylactic use of KI nor in the above-mentioned FDA "Final Recommendations" is any mention made of the much greater need for KI in a nuclear war-even for Americans during an overseas nuclear war in which the United States would not be a belligerent.

Also note that this official insert contains no instructions for giving a crushed KI tablet to infants and small children. Nor is there any mention of the fact that the KI under the tablet's coating is a more painful-tasting drug than any that most people ever have taken. This omitted information is given in the next to last section of this chapter.

- Protection against radioactive iodine in fallout from a nuclear war fought outside the United States.

Most strategists believe that a nuclear war fought by nations other than the United States is a more likely catastrophe than a nuclear attack on America. Several of the Soviet and Chinese nuclear test explosions have resulted in very light fallout deposition and some contamination of milk by radioactive iodine in many of the 50 states. However, serious contamination of milk, fruits, and vegetables could result if war fallout from many overseas nuclear explosions were carried to an America at peace. These potential dangers and effective countermeasures are included in Chapter 18, Trans-Pacific Fallout.

If a nuclear war were to be fought in northern parts of Asia, or in Europe, or in the Middle East, a very small fraction of the fallout would come to earth on parts or all of the United States. This fallout would not result in an overwhelming catastrophe to Americans, although the long-term health hazards would be serious by peacetime standards and the economic losses would be great. The dangers from radioactive iodine in milk produced by cows that ate fallout contaminated feeds or drank fallout contaminated water would be minimized if Americans did not consume dairy products for several weeks after the arrival of war fallout. Safe milk and other baby foods would be the only essential foods that soon would be in very short supply.

The parents of babies and young children who had stored potassium iodide would be especially thankful they had made this very inexpensive preparation, that can give 99% effective protection to the thyroid. All members of families with a supply of potassium iodide could safely eat a normal diet long before those without it could do so.

The most dangerous type of radioactive iodine decays rapidly. At the end of each 8 day period it gives off only half as much radiation as at the start of that period. So at the end of 80 days it emits only about 111000 as much radiation per hour as at the beginning of these 80 days. Because of this rapid decay, a 100-day supply of potassium iodide should be sufficient if a nuclear war, either overseas or within the United States, were to last no more than a week or two.

The probability of most Americans being supplied with prophylactic potassium iodide during a major nuclear disaster appears low. Under present regulations the decision concerning whether to stockpile and dispense potassium iodide tablets rests solely with each state's governor.

° Need for thyroid protection after a nuclear attack on the United States.

After a nuclear attack, very few of the survivors would be able to obtain potassium iodide or to get advice about when to start taking it or stop taking it. In areas of heavy fallout, some survivors without potassium iodide would receive radiation doses large enough to destroy thyroid function before modern medical treatments would again become available. Even those injuries to the thyroid that result in its complete failure to function cause few deaths in normal times, but under post-attack conditions thyroid damage would be much more hazardous.

° Ways to obtain potassium iodide for prophylactic use.

* By prescription.

With a prescription from a doctor, a U.S.P. saturated solution of potassium iodide can be bought at many pharmacies today. (In a crisis, the present local supplies would be entirely inadequate.) The saturated solution contains a very small amount of a compound that prevents it from deteriorating significantly for a few years. It is best stored in a dark glass bottle with a solid, non-metallic cap that screws on liquid-tight.

A separate medicine dropper should be kept in the same place. An authoritative publication of the National Committee on Radiation Protection and Measurements states: "Supplies of potassium iodide can be stored in a variety of places, including homes,..."

In 1990 the price of a 2-ounce bottle of U.S.P. saturated solution of potassium iodide, which is sold by prescription only, ranges from about $7.00 to $11.00 in Colorado. A 2-ounce bottle contains about 500 drops. Four drops provide the daily dose of 130 mg for adults and for children older than one year. For babies less than one year old, the daily dose of a saturated solution is two drops (65 mg). Thus approximately 99% effective protection against the subsequent uptake of radioactive iodine by the thyroid can be gotten by taking saturated potassium iodide solution. If bought by prescription, today the recommended daily dose costs 6 to 9 cents.

* Without prescription.

In 1990 the leading company selling 130-mg potassium iodide tablets without prescription and by mail order in the United States is ANBEX, Inc., P.O. Box 861, Cooper Station, New York, N.Y. 10276. Two bottles, each containing fourteen 130-mg potassium iodide tablets, cost $10.00. Thus the cost per 24-hour dose is 36 cents. To the best of my knowledge, the company in the U.S. that in July of 1990 is selling 130-mg KI tablets without prescription at the lowest price is Preparedness Products, 3855 South 500 West, Bldg. G, Salt Lake City, Utah 84115. This company sells 14 tablets, in a brown, screw-cap glass bottle, for $3.50, postpaid, including shipping charges. For three or more bottles, the price is $2.50 per bottle.

After the disastrous Russian nuclear power reactor accident at Chernobyl in May of 1986, pharmacies in Sweden soon sold all of their 130- mg potassium iodide tablets and Poland limited its inadequate supplies of prophylactic iodide salts to the protection of children. In California, pharmacists reported abnormally large sales of iodine tablets, and also of tincture of iodine- apparently due to the buyers' having been misinformed by the media's reports that Europeans were taking "iodine" for protection.

Individuals can buy chemical reagent grade potassium iodide, that is purer than the pharmaceutical grade, from some chemical supply firms. No prescription or other authorization is necessary. In 1990 the least expensive source of which I am aware is NASCO, 901 Jamesville Avenue, Fort Atkinson, Wisconsin 53538.

The price for 100 grams (100,000 mg) in 1990 is $10.50, plus $2.00 to $4.00 for shipping costs. Thus the cost in 1990 for a 130-mg daily dose is less than 2 cents. NASCO sells 500 grams (500,000 mg- about one pound) for $35.50, plus $2.00 to $4.00 for shipping-making the cost per standard daily dose only one cent.

For years of storage, crystalline or granular potassium iodide is better than a saturated solution. Dry potassium iodide should be stored in a dark bottle with a gasketed, non-metallic cap that screws on tightly. Two-fluid-ounce bottles, filled with dry potassium iodide as described below, are good sizes for a family. Separate medicine droppers should be kept with stored bottles.

Thus at low cost you can buy and store enough potassium iodide for your family and large numbers of your friends and neighbors- as I did years ago.

° Practical expedient ways to prepare and take daily prophylactic doses of a saturated solution of potassium iodide.

To prepare a saturated solution of potassium iodide, fill a bottle about 60% full of crystalline or granular potassium iodide. (A 2-fluid-ounce bottle, made of dark glass and having a solid, non-metallic, screwcap top, is a good size for a family.

About 2 ounces of crystalline or granular potassium iodide is needed to fill a 2-fluid-ounce bottle about 60% full.) Next, pour safe, room-temperature water into the bottle until it is about 90% full. Then close the bottle tightly and shake it vigorously for at least 2 minutes. Some of the solid potassium iodide should remain permanently undissolved at the bottom of the bottle; this is proof that the solution is saturated.

Experiments with a variety of ordinary household medicine droppers determined that 1 drop of a saturated solution of potassium iodide contains from 28 to 36 mg of potassium iodide. The recommended expedient daily doses of a saturated solution (approximately 130 mg for adults and children older than one year, and 65 mg for babies younger than one year) are as follows:

* For adults and children older than one year, 4 drops of a saturated solution of potassium iodide each 24 hours.
* For babies younger than one year, 2 drops of a saturated solution of potassium iodide each 24 hours.

Potassium iodide has a painfully bad taste, so bad that a single crystal or 1 drop of the saturated solution in a small child's mouth would make him cry. (A small child would be screaming in pain before he could eat enough granular or crystalline KI to make him sick.

Some KI tablets are coated and tasteless.) Since many persons will not take a bad tasting medication, especially if no short-term health hazards are likely to result from not taking it, the following two methods of taking a saturated solution are recommended:

* Put 4 drops of the solution into a glass of milk or other beverage, stir, and drink quickly. Then drink some of the beverage with nothing added. If only water is available, use it in the same manner.
* If bread is available, place 4 drops of the solution on a small piece of it; dampen and mold it into a firm ball the size of a large pea, about 3A inch in diameter. There is almost no taste if this "pill" is swallowed quickly with water. (If the pill is coated with margarine, there is no taste.)

  As stated before, 4 drops of the saturated solution provide a dose approximately equal to 130 mg of potassium iodide.

° Preparing potassium iodide tablets to give to infants and small children.

The official FDA instructions for using KI tablets state that one half of a 130-mg tablet, "first crushed", should be given every 24 hours to "babies under one year of age", and that a whole tablet should be crushed "for small children."

Putting even a small fraction of a crushed or pulverized potassium iodide tablet on one's tongue is a startling experience, with a burning sensation. A slightly burnt sensation continues for hours. Therefore, a mother is advised to make this experiment where her children cannot see her.

To eliminate the painfully bad taste of a crushed or pulverized KI tablet, first pulverize it thoroughly. Next stir it for a minute into at least 2 ounces of milk, orange juice, or cold drink, to make sure that the KI (a salt) is completely dissolved. Then the taste is not objectionable. If only water is available, stir the pulverized tablet into more than 2 ounces of water.

KI is a corrosive salt, more injurious than aspirin to tissue with which it is in direct contact. Some doctors advise taking KI tablets after meals, except when so doing would delay taking the initial dose during an emergency. All recognize that taking a dilute solution of KI is easier on the stomach than taking the same dose in tablet form. This may be a consequential consideration when taking KI for weeks during a prolonged nuclear war emergency.

Warnings

* Elemental (free) iodine is poisonous, except in the very small amounts in water disinfected with iodine tablets or a few drops of tincture of iodine. Furthermore, elemental iodine supplied by iodine tablets and released by tincture of iodine dropped into water is not effective as a blocking agent to prevent thyroid damage. If you do not have any potassium iodide, DO NOT TAKE IODINE TABLETS OR TINCTURE OF IODINE.
* DO NOT MAKE A FUTILE, HARMFUL ATTEMPT TO EAT ENOUGH IODIZED SALT TO RESULT IN THYROID BLOCKING. Iodized salt contains potassium iodide, but in such a low concentration that it is impossible to eat enough iodized salt to be helpful as a blocking agent.

Other Ways to Prevent Thyroid Damage

Besides the prophylactic use of potassium iodide, the following are ways to prevent or reduce thyroid damage under peacetime or wartime conditions:

* Do not drink or otherwise use fresh milk produced by cows that have consumed feed or water consequentially contaminated with fall- out or other radioactive material resulting from a peacetime accident or from nuclear explosions in a war.

* As a general rule, do not eat fresh vegetables until advised it is safe to do so. If under wartime conditions no official advice is obtainable, avoid eating fresh leafy vegetables that were growing or exposed at the time of fallout deposition; thoroughly wash all vegetables and fruits.
* If a dangerously radioactive air mass is being blown toward your area and is relatively small (as from some possible nuclear power facility accidents), and if there is time, an ordered evacuation of your area may make it unnecessary even to take potassium iodide.
* For protection against inhaled radioactive iodine, the FDA Final Recommendations (which are mentioned in the preceding section) state that the following measures "should be considered": "..sheltering [merely staying indoors can significantly reduce inhaled doses], evacuation, respiratory protection, and/or the use of stable iodide."

Research has been carried out in an effort to develop a thyroid protection procedure based on the ordinary iodine solutions which are used as disinfectants. Since iodine solutions such as tincture of iodine and povidone-iodine are dangerous poisons if taken orally, these experiments have utilized absorption through the skin after topical application on bare skin.

All reported experimental topical applications on human skin have given less thyroid protection than does proper oral administration of potassium iodide. Moreover, undesirable side effects of skin application can be serious. For these reasons researchers to date have not recommended a procedure for the use of ordinary iodine solutions for thyroid protection.

Potassium iodide, when obtained in the crystalline reagent form and used as recommended above on pages 114 and 115, is safe, inexpensive, and easy to administer. Prudent individuals should obtain and keep ready for use an adequate supply of potassium iodide well in advance of a crisis.

EXPEDIENT SHELTER FURNISHINGS

Importance of Adequate Furnishings

Throughout history, people have endured being crowded together while living and sleeping on hard surfaces. In times of war and privation, people have lived in such conditions for much longer periods than would be necessary for shelter occupancy due to fallout.42Realistic basement-shelter-occupancy tests conducted by research contractors for the U.S. Office of Civil Defense (now the Federal Emergency Management Agency) have shown that modern Americans can live and sleep for two weeks on a concrete floor. In some of these tests, only 8 square feet of floor space was provided for each person; only pieces of corrugated cardboard 3/16-inch thick lessened the hardship of sleeping and sitting on concrete.

Nevertheless, shelters should be adequately furnished whenever possible, for these reasons:

- More people can occupy a properly furnished shelter for weeks, if necessary if adequate additional ventilation is supplied for the additional occupants.
- Cleanliness, health, and morale are better if well designed furnishings are used. More serious complications than discomfort are likely to result if occupants have to huddle together on a bare floor especially if the floor is damp earth.
- Persons occupying a shelter made relatively comfortable by its furnishings are more likely to stay in the shelter long enough to avoid dangerous exposure to fallout radiation.

Chairs, Benches, and Bunks

The father of the previously described Utah family of six knew that the members of his family would be most uncomfortable and probably would have sore backs if they spent the requi ˙.d 72 hours of continuous shelter occupancy huddled on the floor. (Their shelter room was only 3-1/2 feet wide and 16-1/2 feet long.) So this family took with them from home four folding chairs and two pieces of plywood (each 21 inches wide by 6 feet long) tied as part of the load on top of the family car. Four small wooden boxes served as food containers during the drive to the shelter-building site. In the shelter, the boxes were used to support the ends of two narrow plywood bunks.

The family's system of sleeping and sitting in shifts worked reasonably well. There were discomforts: the adults found the two plywood bunks too narrow, and the plywood was so hard that all the family members used their sleeping bags for padding rather than for needed warmth on chilly nights. The father and oldest son, whose turn to sleep was during normal waking hours, had trouble sleeping in such a small shelter while the lively 4-year-old son was awake.

Covering earth walls with plastic or bed sheets makes for a cleaner shelter, with less earth falling in the faces of people who sleep on the floor. Bedsheets on the walls make a shelter brighter, but are flammable and a potential fire hazard. The plastic film prevented the earth walls from drying and crumbling as a result of the hot, dry desert air pumped through the shelter during the day.

A well-designed expedient shelter should be as small as practical, with all space used very efficiently. The builders should make the heights and widths of benches and bunks as specified in the detailed shelter drawings, such as those for the Small-Pole Shelter.

Serious difficulties can result from failure to use specific dimensions that may appear unimportant. For example, in field tests at Fort Bragg, N.C., 48 airborne infantrymen, working only with hand tools, cut pine trees and built two 24-man Small-Pole Shelters in less than 24 hours.

The men did not think it necessary to use the specific dimensions when they made the furnishings. As a result, they built the benches too high and the overhead bunks too far below the ceilings. This error forced the men to sit for hours in hunched positions. Even these able-bodied young men would have developed very sore backs and would have wanted very much to leave their shelters if they had been forced to sit in a bent-over position for days.

This opening led to a small, chimney- like, air-exhaust duct made of boards, with its cross- sectional area as specified in Russian civil defense handbooks for natural ventilation of small expedient shelters. With such a small air-exhaust opening- only 4 square inches (10 square centimeters) per person a fully occupied shelter of this size would soon become dangerously overheated in warm or hot weather, even though a good low-pressure expedient shelter-ventilating pump (a KAF or a Directional Fan) were to be used. A much larger air-exhaust opening is needed.

Bedsheet-hammock and Chair

On the last night of the Utah family's shelter stay it was clear that the six members would win the cash bonus offered them for their 72-hour occupancy of the shelter starting immediately after they completed building it. Therefore, the author showed them that night how to make boat-shaped hammocks out of bedsheets. (Any strong cloth of the right size can be used.) They were shown how to hang these short, yet stable, hammocks securely from poles of the shelterroof. With three members sleeping in hammocks, two on the plywood bunks, and one on the floor, all six could sleep at the same time.

In a shelter this size without bunks, hanging four short hammocks at slight angles to the length of the trench would permit four occupants to sleep comfortably. An additional two persons could sleep on the floor. In the Utah family's shelter, the floor was made comfortable by covering the damp earth with pieces of polyethylene cut from trash bags, then placing strips of shag rug over the plastic.

In shelters with ceilings at least 6 feet high, one hammock can be hung above another. In a SmallPole Shelter that is 6 feet wide, a greater number of people can sleep or sit comfortably at the same time if Bedsheet-Hammocks and Bedsheet-Chairs are used rather than benches or a combination of benches and overhead bunks.

In an evacuation during a real crisis, carrying comfortable folding chairs and the materials to make wooden bunks would not be advisable. If the family car were loaded instead with an equivalent weight of additional food and clothing, the members' prospects of surviving would be improved.

But in an actual crisis evacuation, a family planning to occupy a shelter with a strong roof should take along a bedsheet for each member. The other lightweight Items described in the instructions for making a Bedsheet-Hammock and a Bedsheet-Chair also should be carried. By following the instructions at the end of this chapter, a comfortable hammock can be made and quickly converted to a comfortable suspended chair when not needed for sleeping.

Hammocks hung high off the floor and above other sleepers must be strong, securely suspended, and cupped so that it is impossible to fall out accidentally. This is why the instructions emphasize using a double thickness of bedsheet and folding the cloth so as to make the hammock boat-like, with high sides.

In a cold shelter, keeping warm in a hammock is somewhat difficult. Easily compressible materials, such as those used in a sleeping bag, are squeezed so thin under a person's body that they lose most of their insulating value. Pads of newspapers about an inch thick, protected by cloth coverings, will reduce heat losses. The best insulation is a quilt, fastened to the underside of a hammock by attaching it with rows of stitches every few inches and at right angles to each other.

It occupies less than half the floor space used by the two hammocks shown in the preceding illustration. If a reclining seat is desired, the two support-points on the ceiling to which the chair-arm cords are attached can be located farther out from the wall.

Enough padding material should be placed in the bowl-shaped seat of a Bed sheet-Chair to make it rather flat. Extra, clothing or a folded blanket can be used. The three cords suspending the chair should be adjusted for length so that the sitter's feet can rest on the floor and the edge of the chair seat does not press on the undersides of his thighs. (Such pressure cuts off circulation. During the London Blitz of World War 11, many of the people who sat night after night in shelters on folding chairs with canvas seats developed serious leg conditions. Authorities later prohibited bringing such chairs into shelters.)

CAUTION: To prevent skin infections and other diseases from spreading, a person's hammock or chair should not be used by others. This precaution is particularly important if the shelter is hot and its occupants are sweaty.

How to Make a Bedsheet-hammock and Convert it to a Suspended Bedsheet-chair

1. PURPOSE: To enable more people to occupy a shelter more comfortably.

2. ADVANTAGES:

* The hammock can be made in a few minutes, once you have the materials and the knowhow.
* The only materials required are a strong double-bed sheet (or an equally large piece of any strong fabric), a few feet of rope (or a piece of strong fabric from which expedient "rope" can be made quickly), a few large nails, and some wire.
* It is difficult to fall out of the hammock because its sides are each made about 8 inches shorter than its lengthwise mid-section, 50 as to produce a boat-like shape.
* It provides room for head and shoulders close to either end; thus it is practical to hang this hammock between supports that are as close together as 6 feet.

Before beginning work, someone should read aloud all of the instructions for making the hammock. This will help to avoid mistakes.

Making a Bedsheet-hammock

A. How to fold and tie the bed sheet:

1. Select a strong double-bed sheet (one containing polyester is best) and use a ruler or tape measure to avoid guessing at measurements.

2. Fold the bedsheet lengthwise down its center line, so that pairs of corners are together.
3. With the sheet folded, mark the center of each of the two folded ends; then hold one end up.
4. Starting at one corner of one end of the folded bedsheet, make accordion-like pleats. Make each pleat about 2 inches wide; make the left corner of each pleat about 1 inch lower than the left corner of the preceding pleat, when the sheet is being held as illustrated. Use your left hand to hold the completed pleats in place, while making new pleats with your right hand.
5. When one-half of the upper end of the sheet has been folded into pleats almost to the CENTER MARK, adjust the pleats so that the CENTER MARK is about 4 inches below the STARTING CORNER.
6. Continue making 2-inch pleats on past the CENTER MARK, but make the right corner of each pleat about 1 inch higher than the right corner of the preceding pleat. When the pleat-folding is completed, the STARTING CORNER and the other corner should be at the same height (4 inches) above the CENTER MARK.
7. Tie the hammock-supporting rope tightly around the end of the sheet about 3 inches below the edge with the CENTER MARK. (If a rope strong enough to support at least the weight of two men is not available, make an expedient "rope" by tearing a 16-inch- wide strip from a sheet or other strong cloth and then rolling this strip crosswise to its length to make a tight roll several feet long. Then tie string or small strips of cloth about 1 inch wide around it, spaced 4 to 6 inches apart, to keep the rolled-up cloth from unrolling.)
8. Bend the pleat-folded end of sheet downward around the hammock rope, so that the knot of the hammock rope is uppermost.
9. To keep the sheet from being pulled through the encircling hammock rope, bind the doubled-over end of the sheet with

cord (or with narrow strips of cloth) about 1 inch below the rope. Tie the binding cord at least four times around, knotting it each time around.

10. Repeat the procedure (4 through 9) with the other end of the double-folded sheet, thus producing a boat-shaped hammock with its two sides each about 8 inches shorter than its lengthwise center section.

How to hang the hammock:

1. To suspend a hammock from a strong wooden roof such as the poles of a Pole Covered Trench Shelter, drive two strong nails (at least 3-1/2 inches long) into the wood at approximately 450 angles, crossing and touching each other. Bind the two nails together with wire. To prevent a hammock rope from being rubbed directly against fixed metal, make a loose loop of strong wire (best if doubled) through the crossed nails; tie the hammock rope to this free-moving wire loop.
2. To suspend the hammock from a wooden wall, use the same type of crossed-nails supports, with the nails driven in one above the other.
3. For comfort and safety, hang the hammock with the head end 18 inches higher than the center and with the foot end 24 inches higher than the center.
4. To make sure that the hammock is strong enough, two persons should place their open hands on its centerline and put all of their weight on the hammock.
5. To suspend hammocks and hammock-chairs from a pole roof that is not being built under fear of immediate attack, use loops of strong wire around the poles at the planned support points. (The correct placement of wire loops takes considerable time and delays completion of the shelter.) To reduce stresses and possible breakage, the loops should be loose, as illustrated.

Making a Suspended Bedsheet-chair

A Bedsheet-Hammock may be quickly converted into a comfortable Suspended Bed sheet-Chair so that a shelter occupant can sit comfortably, yet occupy less floor space during the daytime. Follow these steps:

1. Select one end of the hammock to be the top of the back of the chair.
2. From this end, measure 52 inches (4 ft 4 in.) along each side-edge of the hammock (see sketch), and mark these two spots.
3. About 2-1/2 inches in from these two marks (toward the centerline of the hammock), make two more marks.
4. To make an attachment point for a chair "arm", hold a pebble (or a lump of earth) under one of these last marks, pull the double-thickness cloth tight around the pebble, and tie it in place. (See illustration.) Repeat on the other side-edge of the hammock.
5. Tie the end of one rope (or "rope" made of 10- inch-wide strip of strong cloth) to one attachment point, and the end of another rope to the other attachment point.
6. Suspend the top of the back of the chair to a suspension point on the ceiling at least 4 inches out from the wall, and adjust the length of this suspending rope so that the chair arms will be about the same height from the floor as the arms of an easy chair (see sketch).
7. Suspend the arms of the chair from two suspension points 20 inches apart and 20 inches farther out from the wall than the suspension point of the back of the chair. (Study the illustration.)
8. Fold the unused end of the hammock up and back into the "seat" of the chair; fill the hollow of the seat with coats, a blanket, or anything else soft, to make it comfortable.
9. Adjust the lengths of all three suspending ropes so that the 'chair seat is the right height for the person sitting in it.

When both feet are flat on the floor, the front edge of the seat should not press against the undersides of the thighs.

10. To simplify repeated conversion of the hammock to a chair, mark the spot on each of the 3 suspending ropes where each is tied to its suspension point on the ceiling; also mark the spot on each suspending rope for a chair arm where each is tied to its suspension point on a chair arm. If enough light rope or strong cord is available, the easiest and quickest way to connect and disconnect the arm supports is to suspend each arm with a double strand of rope, looped around an attachment point as illustrated by the sketch of the attachment point.

9

Use of Fallout Radiation Meters

The Critical Need

A survivor in a shelter that does not have a dependable meter to measure fallout radiation or that has one but lacks someone who knows how to use it will face a prolonged nightmare of uncertainties. Human beings cannot feel, smell, taste, hear, or see fallout radiation. A heavy attack would put most radio stations off the air, due to the effects of electromagnetic pulse, blast, fire, or fallout from explosions. Because fallout intensities often vary greatly over short distances, those stations still broadcasting would rarely be able to give reliable information concerning the constantly changing radiation dangers around a survivor's shelter.

Which parts of the shelter give the best protection? How large is the radiation dose being received by each person? When is it safe to leave the shelter for a few minutes? When can one leave for an hour's walk to get desperately needed water? As the fallout continues to decay, how long can one safely work each day outside the shelter? When can the shelter be left for good? Only an accurate, dependable fallout meter will enable survivors to answer these life-or-death questions.

Gamma radiation is by far the most dangerous radiation given off by fallout particles. Gamma rays are like X rays, only more penetrating and harmful. The roentgen (R) is the unit most commonly used to measure exposures to gamma rays, or to X rays, and most

American civil defense instruments give readings in roentgens (R) or roentgens per hour (R/hr).

Therefore, for simplicity's sake, in this book almost all radiation doses are given in roentgens (R), and radiation dose rates are given in roentgens per hour (R/hr). This simplification is justified because, for external whole-body gamma radiation from fallout, the numerical value of an exposure or dose given in roentgens is approximately the same as the numerical value given in rems or rads.

The dose (the quantity) of radiation that a person receives, along with the length of time during which the dose is received, determine what injuries, if any, will be suffered as a result of the dose. Of people who, in a few days, each receive a dose of 350 roentgens under nuclear war conditions, about half will die. Doses are measured with small instruments called dosimeters, either by directly reading the dose between the time at which a dosimeter is charged to read zero and the time of a subsequent reading, or by calculating by subtraction the dose between two readings. However, to avoid receiving a lethal or sickening dose, the most useful instrument is a dose rate meter. The National Academy of Sciences' Advisory Committee on Civil Defense in 1953 concluded: "The final effectiveness of shelter depends upon the occupants of any shelter having simple, rugged, and reliable dose rate meters to measure the fallout dose rate outside the shelter."

With a reliable dose rate meter you can quite quickly determine how great the radiation dangers are in different places, and then promptly act to reduce your exposure to these unseen, unfelt dangers. For example, if you go outside an excellent fallout shelter and learn by reading your dose rate meter that you are being exposed to 30 R/hr, you know that if you stay there for one hour you will receive a dose of 30 R. But if you go back inside your excellent shelter after 2 minutes, then while outside you will have received a dose of only 1 R. (2 minutes 2/60 of an hour = 1/30 hr; and receiving a dose at the rate of 30 R/hr for 1/30 hr results in a dose of 30 R/hr x 1/30 hr = 1 R.) Under nuclear war conditions, receiving an occasional dose of 1 R (1,000 milliroentgens) would be of little concern.

WARNINGS FOR BUYERS OF FALLOUT METERS

You are "on your own" when buying a dose rate meter or dosimeter because:

- No U.S. Government agency or other Government facility advises the public regarding sources of the best available radiation-measuring instruments for use in time of war, or warns concerned individuals that certain instruments are either incapable of measuring adequately high dose rates or doses for wartime use, or are dangerously inaccurate. For example, a dose rate meter that in 1982 sold nationwide was tested in that year at Oak Ridge National Laboratory to determine its accuracy for measuring gamma radiation. This instrument was reasonably accurate at low dose rates, but at the high dose rates of life or death importance in a nuclear war its readings were dangerously low: When it should have read 150 R/hr, it read 13.9 R/hr. Another dose rate meter of this same model, tested in California by Dr. Bruce Clayton, read only 16 R/hr when it should have read 400 R/hr. Obviously, if this model were used and trusted by a person doing rescue work for hours outdoors in heavy fallout, while believing that he was receiving a non-incapacitating dose he actually would be getting a fatal dose!
- Instruments that measure only milliroentgen-range dose rates are sold for war use by some companies. Since most Americans have no idea what size of radiation doses would incapacitate or kill them, and do not even know that a milliroentgen is 1/1000 of a roentgen, some people buy instruments that are capable of measuring maximum dose rates of only one roentgen or less per hour. For example, an American company advertised and sold for $370.00 in 1986 its dose rate meter that has a maximum range of "0 1000 mR/hr." It is the only dose rate meter in that company's

listing of "Radiation Detection Products for the General Public", described as...., applicable for use in case of nuclear war." The highest dose rate that it can measure, one roentgen per hour, is far too low to be of much use in a nuclear war.

Used and surplus dose rate meters and dosimeters are likely to be inaccurate or otherwise unreliable. Very few buyers have access to a radiation source powerful enough to check instruments for accuracy over their full ranges of measurements. My education regarding bargain fallout meters began in 1961, after I bought two dosimeters of a model then being produced by a leading manufacturing company and purchased in quantity by the Office of Civil Defense. Within a week after receiving these instruments, one of them could not be charged. The other was found to be inaccurate. Later I learned that the manufacturing company sold to the public its instruments that did not pass Government quality tests.

Most Federal and State organizations do not criticize faulty civil defense products, apparently because they are not charged with this responsibility and want to avoid angering manufacturers and sellers who may go to their Congressmen or Legislators to seek redress for lost sales.

In this book I am not giving the names of any of the companies that sell or have sold potentially life-endangering survival items. To do so would reduce the chances of this book being distributed or advocated by Government agencies.

WAR RESERVES OF FALLOUT METERS

One of Americans' most important assets for surviving a nuclear war is the Federal Emergency Management Agency's (FEMA's) supply of fallout meters.

These instruments include approximately 600,000 dose rate meters and about 3,300,000 dosimeters, all suitable for wartime use. In 1986 almost all of these old instruments-that can be found-reportedly still are in good working condition.

Because of continuing inadequate funding for civil defense, in recent years most of FEMA's instruments have been serviced, calibrated, and, if necessary, repaired only once every four years. In a few localities these instruments are no longer being serviced.

Most of these critically important instruments are kept in cities, in buildings likely to be destroyed by blast or fire in the event of a massive Soviet attack.

If there were a sufficiently long, officially recognized period of warning before an attack, it might be possible during such a worsening crisis to move a large fraction of these fallout meters outside the areas of probable blast or fire damage, and to place them in officially designated fallout shelters.

However, this unlikely development would not provide private family shelters with instruments. Most families need their own fallout meters. This need is greatest for families living in localities not likely to be damaged by blast or fire, and for those planning to evacuate to such less hazardous localities during a worsening crisis.

Bibliography

Bellamy, C.: *Knights in White Armour: The New Art of War and Peace*, London, Random House, 1997.

Chandra, R.: *Judicial System in India, Lucknow*, Print House (India), 1992.

Davies .A.: *Telecommunications and Politics. The Secentralised Alternative*, London, Pinter, 1994.

Friedman, G.: *The Future of War: Power, Technology and American World Dominance in the 21st Century*, N.Y., Random House, 1996.

Heimanson, Rudolph: *Dictionary of Political Science and Law of War*, N.Y.: Oceana Publications, 1967.

Huntington, S.P.: *The Soldier and the State Rescue*, N.Y., Vintage Books, 1964.

Jones, W.H.: *The Government and Politics of India*, London, Hutchinson, 1971.

Kelly, John B.: *Britain and the Persian Gulf 1795-1880*, Oxford, Clarendon Press, 1968.

Mary, W.: *Asian Power and Politics: the Cultural Dimensions of Authority*, Cambridge, Belknap Press, 1985.

Nair, A. M.: *An Indian Freedom Fighter in Japan*, Bombay, Orient Longman, 1983.

Posen, B.R.: *The Sources of Military Doctrine*, Ithaca, 1984, Cornell Univ. Press.

Rosen, P.: *Societies and Military Power: India and its Armies*, Ithaca, Cornell University Press, 1996.

Simon, D. : *Public Administration and Military Wars*, New York, Knopf, 1950.

Index